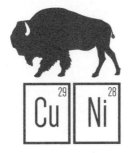

CuNi

number 33 / fall 2021

EDITOR
Wayne Miller

CO-EDITOR
Joanna Luloff

POETRY EDITORS
Brian Barker
Nicky Beer

FICTION EDITORS
Teague Bohlen
Alexander Lumans
Christopher Merkner

NONFICTION CONSULTING EDITOR
Nicole Piasecki

SENIOR EDITORS
Ashley Bockholdt
Caitlin Collins
Greg Ferbrache
Ahja Fox
Jack Gialanella
LeShaye Hernandez
Ven Hickenbottom
Joe Lyons
Holly McCloskey
Kira Morris
Lyn Poats
Emilie Ross
Angela Sapir
Karley Sun
Kristen Valladares

ASSOCIATE EDITORS
Lucas Duddles
Abbey Lawrence
Brenda Pfeifer

INTERN
Alejandro Lucero

CONTRIBUTING EDITORS
Robert Archambeau
Mark Brazaitis
Geoffrey Brock
A. Papatya Bucak
Victoria Chang
Martha Collins
Robin Ekiss
Tarfia Faizullah
V. V. Ganeshananthan
Kevin Haworth
Joy Katz
David Keplinger
Jesse Lee Kercheval
Jason Koo
Thomas Legendre
Randall Mann
Adrian Matejka
Pedro Ponce
Kevin Prufer
Frederick Reiken
James Richardson
Emily Ruskovich
Eliot Khalil Wilson

ART CONSULTANTS
Kealey Boyd
Maria Elena Buszek

OFFICE MANAGERS
Francine Olivas-Zarate
Jenny Dunnington
Emilio Marquez

Copper Nickel is the national literary journal housed at the University of Colorado Denver. Published in March and October, it features poetry, fiction, essays, and translation folios by established and emerging writers. Fiction is edited by Teague Bohlen, Joanna Luloff, Alexander Lumans, and Christopher Merkner; nonfiction is edited by Joanna Luloff and Wayne Miller; poetry is edited by Brian Barker, Nicky Beer, and Wayne Miller. We welcome submissions from all writers and currently pay $30 per printed page. Submissions are assumed to be original and unpublished. To submit, visit coppernickel.submittable.com. Subscriptions are also available—and at discounted rates for students—at coppernickel.submittable.com. Copper Nickel is distributed nationally through Publishers Group West (PGW) and Media Solutions, LLC, and digitally catalogued by EBSCO. We are deeply grateful for the support of the Department of English and the College of Liberal Arts & Sciences at the University of Colorado Denver. For more information, visit **copper-nickel.org**.

CONTENTS

FICTION

NONFICTION

POETRY

111 / A "FIELD" SYMPOSIUM ON CIARAN CARSON

With essays by Sandra Alcosser, Don Bogen,
Marianne Boruch, Troy Jollimore, Paul Perry, Stephen Sexton,
Connie Voisine, and Tess Taylor

TRANSLATION FOLIOS

On the Cover / Panteha Abareshi, *Hollow*
India ink, acrylic ink, watercolor and gouache on hot-press paper, 14 x 17 inches,
2019

(for more on Abareshi's work, visit:
https://www.panteha.com)

Editors' Note

AFTER OUR SPRING hiatus, we're back!

It's been quite a year—full of uncertainty, isolation, violence, rampant conspiracy theories, and more U.S. deaths from Covid than total U.S. deaths in World Wars I and II combined. We also saw the swell of the Black Lives Matter movement, the Chauvin verdict, the dissemination of safe and effective vaccines, and other potential glimmers of optimism. And now, terribly: the Delta variant. We hope you've been surviving—and sometimes maybe even thriving—in the midst of all of it.

In anticipation of our hiatus, last fall's issue was a double-length issue.

But it turns out it was impossible to take time off from publishing while continuing to receive exciting work from all over the world for a full year and not over-stuff this next issue. In addition to so many poems, stories and essays we admired, issue 33 includes a 40-page symposium on Irish writer Ciaran Carson, who died in the fall of 2019. We're thrilled to be able to reprint a small sample of Carson's work and to offer commentary through the appreciative lenses of a number of excellent writers. We're also thrilled to have five wonderful translation folios in the issue—including "true weird tales" by 18th-century Chinese writer Ji Yun and a moving tribute essay by post-World War II Japanese writer Endō Shūsaku.

We're very grateful to our staff, who have continued to read and evaluate *Copper Nickel* submissions through an impossible year, and we're particularly grateful to our senior and associate editors who met twice-a-week via Zoom to discuss and evaluate unsolicited submissions. Finally, we want to say a hearty thank you to intern Alejandro Lucero, who took on added duties while Wayne was on sabbatical, and whose work was consistently dependable and excellent.

One other note: For the past two years Alexander Lumans and Christopher Merkner have been serving as fiction "consulting editors." They teach at CU Denver with the rest of the faculty members on staff, but are tasked with heavier teaching loads, which is why we didn't want to ask them to perform a full slate of editorial work. And yet, for these past two years they have been doing exactly that—and proving invaluable—alongside all their teaching and writing. It seemed only fair to promote them to full fiction editors (which is actually just their titles catching up with reality).

Thank you for continuing to read *Copper Nickel*. We hope you find the issue ahead of you as exciting and engaging as we do! And we hope with all our hearts that this next year manages to look up for all of us.

—Wayne Miller & Joanna Luloff

ADAM TAVEL

National Poetry Month

Alan, he kept calling me, Alan my medicine
is broke. He shook his empty flask
upside down, dour as a vicar. The rain

hammered my Silhouette as I shifted
into gear. No worries, I said, there's one
on every corner in this town. Selfishly

I hoped to hear about his prize, his ancient
love affairs—anything but eleven
bird poems on rumpled loose leaf,

mumbled on stage. The worst part of living
near the beach, he said, must be eventually
all your shirts smell like sunscreen.

Quaking, his left hand futzed with the dial
and found some Mahler. We drove and lost
the strings in static. An OPEN sign

flickered bloodshot. I tossed my wallet
in his lap. Behind the wave
of blades I watched him slosh into the light.

Practice Room

Inside this padded door the only sounds
are ours—a little cough, the drag of soles
across some dingy shag, how fingertips
awake to warm the keys with minor chords
that drain the gray from clouds. Our weather pours
into this closet air and dies against the walls.
There is no teacher here or metronome
to clack us back in time. What shadows pass
pass dimly in the hall, in muffled light,
omissible as mimes who flee the crowd's
fatigued applause. Whose charts now shall we play?
The tortured brilliances some centuries
have made lie in a heap. Our songs or theirs,
the world won't hear us talking to our hands.

LEIA DARWISH

from The Yellow Front Grocery Store

All day the roofers and carpenters
make a racket upstairs.
None of them wear masks.
She doesn't want to wear a mask.
Life has become so quiet
she can hear every process
in her body and every thought.
There was a time when she'd mix
Percocet and cocaine together
in one line; now raw garlic
makes her heart race.
Distraction is a survival technique
she's lost. At 4 pm, she finally mounts
the cordless Dyson to the closet wall.
She calls a friend to flirt
but they end up on opposite sides
of the PPE debate.
She takes her temperature.
She puts on a velvet sports bra
in case the carpenters happen
to see her through the window
and paces, trying to feed off the energy
above her, trying to feel useful
and necessary like a person
who puts a roof over another person's head.

from The Yellow Front Grocery Store

She stands at the window
watching the wind affect things.
The crape myrtle shakes like jello.
She fits herself closer
so the single-pane glass
feels cold against her breasts.
She tries to think of something to do
with the black walnut limbs piled
against the fence.
Shouldn't the maple
be yellow by this time of year?
What is it like at the river right now?
The neighbor's house music
builds to a crescendo, giving purpose
to the thrashing trees outside.
She looks out at her Prius,
parked there so long it will need a jump
when she finally decides to leave.
Isn't there a bag of chips in the car?
She loved the river in autumn.
That rock on Reedy Creek.
She should stop eating dried papayas
but she can't. She can't leave.
She pumps her elbows back rapidly
with tight fists to get the blood moving
and soothe her tense back.
I want to see you she says to no one.
She tests the aloe branch in her kitchen
as if it's a muscle,
giving it a tight, tentative squeeze.

Matryoshka

I had a dream
     where you brought me every single shoe I've ever dreamed
          of. Metallic & jewel-toned. You
             said it was all for me.

I had a dream
     where the only thing I could think of was
          why would you spend all of your income on
             shoes, metallic & jewel-toned? I started
               to regret your maternal love.

I had a dream
     where I woke up, but it didn't matter
          because the past was all metallic & jewel-toned, &
             you had brought me every single shoe I had ever dreamed of.
             And I had been your doll.

And when I woke up,
     I was wearing your coat,
          and that's two grand.

ALAN MICHAEL PARKER

People in Light and Shadow

PEOPLE ON THE TELEVISION KILLED people on the television. In her upstairs television room, not the downstairs television room that was really for the kids, Little Joanie saw a flash out the window, and she went to the window, and slid the two locks open, then slid the window up.

But she had forgotten her wine, so she went back to get her glass and then Little Joanie returned to the window. The night was thick in the air, and maybe she should worry about bugs, since there was no screen—so she went back again, turned off both lights, and once more went to the window.

People on the television threw things at other people on the television. Blue shadows jumped around the upstairs television room. It's funny how a shadow can be bigger than its thing.

People on the television ran from other people on the television, and there was a lot of shouting and chanting. The commentators tried to get someone on the street to comment, but it was happening too fast. People on the television wore uniforms, and then there were the homemade uniforms.

Little Joanie was Little Joanie in her family, and even in her own head, because growing up, her aunt was Big Joanie. Her ex used to call her LJ, which was okay when she loved him. She had been trying different names for a week, now that he was her ex—how strange to be divorced over the computer, and to see her ex's red face, and his eyes get smaller. She had wanted to pinch his whole face closed, on the screen.

So far: Joan, Joan Marie, Joan-Marie, or even go all the way with only her middle name, Marie. Make it legal too.

There were lights and maybe a fire downtown, the top floors of the taller buildings a couple of blocks from here visible from her window during the day, or at night when people worked late, office lights. A siren came closer, and another siren headed the other direction, but the sounds kind of bounced, that effect.

People on the television were only on the television, click.

She liked this new guy, Tom, even though he couldn't stay the night yet because of the kids. Once she found him naked in the kitchen except for his cowboy hat, grubbing in the fridge for something to eat after sex. He had a look on his face, like he had been caught stealing or worse, but also a little proud of himself, maybe how he looked in his hat. She gave him a slice of leftover pizza and a glass of white wine with an ice cube. She put a dish towel in his lap, in case of the kids.

Someone was running down her block, away from downtown. Into the sidewalk light from the streetlight, into darkness, under a tree, and then there was another streetlight. Moving from being seen, and then not, then seen again. That was how she felt about Raymond, her ex, and Tom, the new guy—the light, the dark, the shadows. Her feelings moving.

She liked the sound of Marie. "Marie," she said out the window.

In Defense of Solitude

If I were a truck and I made my last delivery, I would like how complete I am.

If I were a road that ended at the sunrise where the new houses ran out of money, in the spangly dew, I would have a place to rest, unbothered.

If I were the separate thing that is a tree, and still belong.

If I were myself, back then, but with what I know now. Come to the table, my mother would say. Put down your crayons, stop smashing together your little army men, stop staring into those words. Each of us belongs, my mother would say. We're all immigrants in this country, my mother would say. Of course, not the Indians. Go ask your grandmother.

If I were a roller coaster I would have fun, *weeeee.*

If I were a fountain I would feel pretty, *ahhhh.*

Why are you so quiet, my mother would say. Why are you always so awfully moody. Why are you so goddamn moody.

If I were the book I would close the book, and inside the book, in me, I would be safe.

If I were the music I would sneak through the drapes into people's lives.

You're sitting there like your father, my mother would say.

Translation Folio

MARIANGELA GUALTIERI

Translator's Introduction

Olivia Sears

The daily assault of horrors from the world, from mankind, rings in my ears like the same old refrain of doom. Enough, I say to myself. I thank anyone who brings me a luminous word. I know how hard it is to do without falling into an Arcadia of rhetoric and honey. But it seems to me we can no longer do without this naming of good. It can no longer be postponed.

—*Mariangela Gualtieri*

Italian poet Mariangela Gualtieri, known for her compelling and innovative poetry, wrote these words in 2005, a decade and a half before we faced the worldwide horrors of 2020—not least the trifecta of global pandemic, accelerating climate crisis, and creeping autocracy the world over. She also posed this question: what should we, as spectators and authors of "this human disaster," tell those who are born today? Her work over the decades can perhaps be read as an effort to answer that question. During the worst of 2020, when it was difficult to imagine the future, I personally found tremendous solace in her work, as did so many of her readers. (Her most recent book went into its third printing in the first month of sales.)

Gualtieri often proclaims joy to be "the highest form of prayer," and most of the poems translated here appeared in her collection *Bestia di gioia* (beast of joy). The title could be viewed as an attempt to unify the physical and the spiritual, but Gualtieri's poems don't abide by the terms of a Cartesian body-mind dualism or a beast-spirit opposition; rather, all of us are beasts, and all of us spirits, enmeshed. For Gualtieri, the poetic word itself is rooted in the physical, in the body, almost inseparable from the voice, and she has devoted her career to presenting her work holistically. As a leading performer of poetry for the stage, Gualtieri creates what she calls a *rito sonoro* (sound ritual), combining live music, song, and dance to amplify and complicate the poetic word. The avant-garde theatrical work of her Teatro Valdoca (where she is dramaturge as well as cofounder) focuses on the word, but the performer's body moving on stage and the voice pronouncing the words are also integral to her vision.

In addition to the presence of bodies and sound, Gualtieri's work exhibits a fascination with their absence. One group of poems, entitled *Un niente più grande* (a greater nothing), explores the vital, creative power of the *vuoto*, the void. Here space-time has substance (that can be torn), silence accumulates, and lacunae can open up anywhere. Like the void, silence plays a significant role in all aspects of Gualtieri's poetry—organization, content, and performance. Rather than just evoking isolation or disconnection, though, silence for Gualtieri seems to be also a precondition of kinship and empathy because it allows us—or forces us—to listen. And she wants us all to do more listening, to the world and to our fellow beasts, to engage in a communal meditation on the state of being *us*, an all-inclusive us. The final poem published here urges us to find our way back to *pietà* and all it entails—to the compassion, mercy, pity, piety, sympathy, remorse, respect, and devotion that are all evoked by this single word in Italian.

The energy of Gualtieri's words propels her work, but her rhythms never gallop. Unusual syntax and unexpected segues make the reader pause, inviting reflection and allowing us to explore different avenues of thought. At the start of a poem, I often feel as if the poet is entering an intriguing mystery, carrying her lantern in the dark, and has invited us to follow, slowly, as she narrates in whispers what she sees. She asks her readers to proceed with careful attention and curiosity rather than fear or judgment. Seemingly simple poems often unfold in enigmatic ways as she repurposes linguistic materials, employing adjectives as nouns, turning verbs into things. Poetic devices like repetition, chiasmus, and juxtaposition often appear in her poems, but these structures seem to arise organically, almost spontaneously. Gualtieri has written that the conflict for her around the poetic word is always "between song and thought, between dementia and intelligence, between welcoming the word or dominating it, between serving it or using it." Her words are sparse, measured, and often chosen intuitively.

In the "naming of good" that Gualtieri advocates, her poetry doesn't deny or ignore darkness and pain—she often speaks of "this broken world"—but rather than sinking under the weight of dread she seeks out wonder. "Too easy," she writes, "to remain so long on the shadow side of the species. Now the highest and most risky undertaking is to speak of joy, to pronounce the word love." She invites everyone in, to reflect on existence, to listen to the earth, to see one another. Among her many aspirations as a poet, Gualtieri says, is to offer beauty, joy, and a voice of comfort in the dark. Amen.

MARIANGELA GUALTIERI : Six Poems

I pondered the animal—certain
it was a messenger still disguised
in fur and feather. My head in such
a spin, skittish in the vicinity
of porcupine or badger. Their sudden
silence, their hiding, it wounded me.
How I longed to move beyond names! laws!
realms! taxonomies! all the chromosomes!
forms! substances!
As their hearts neared mine
I was petrified.

Irregular the air around the dead man—
snags and tears in the web
that anchors here to now.

Supremely urgent the silence
that's coming. So very urgent
this silence heaped in piles
ready to collapse onto all that's waiting.

I was transported
to the highest peaks but did not sing their praises. Instead
I traced other routes. And those peaks
remained unsung and alone. They who had waited so long,
for ages.

I don't know why I must dive
into an undersea silence
in distant vacant houses
where the flight of a small being
echoes with a frightful mantra
and my husked heart
bare flayed rabbit on marble
pike that swims upstream
my heart bare winter tree
bare stark old slab
inspects itself in its red rooms,
its vast heart chamber, a bit
nineteenth-century, childish,
it sparks wonder,
like watching the world primarily
up close to the circulatory
secret of things.

Now the mind will quiet itself
and this is its highest side.

Let's not cry,
or else let's cry and cry
so at least our blackish heart
brimming with snakes and decay
might come back better.
Let's cry just a little
every now and then
that we are runts of compassion
that we no longer have virtuous acts
no longer have our songs and banners of mercy
but only little plumes.

translated from the Italian by Olivia Sears

BRUCE BEASLEY

Mission Statement

The Mission Statement's final draft consists
entirely of the only

two words to which all parties could agree:
WE MUST.

Must what? would not be addressed
by the Best Practices.

Nor could the purpose, location, or wherewithal of the Task
ever be assimilated
more satisfyingly into words. So hectic so
urgent, its whereabouts
in time changing every few moments:
hand trucks stacked with duct-taped crates
addressed NO SCRUTABLE ADDRESS:

the undertaking too
unmappable, hyperscheduled and vast
for any diminishing abstract articulation.

Fumble at the time
clock with no apparent
apparatus for punching out.
Simply, compactly, *WE MUST.*

•

I'm here to DATE you, declared the round-faced
bespectacled teacher to her class
at a transient Base of Operations.

She unpacked her equipment: strontium-8 kits,
carbon-14 tests for each

of our old and chosen bones.

•

There's so much still to be said

for the excruciating
bewilderment of unextractable beauty—
at the mobile Nerve Center
of the Bedroom Exhibit's mating display
a snub-nosed monkey's prehensile tail

reveals it can in no way coil
around the peacock's dust-clumped, dragged-
off-behind-the-bed
turquoise plumes.

•

How is it that
you who read this should be—

with dreams at least the mass and spoil of mine—
nonetheless only half-afraid?

We must pursue the Task as laid
so ambiguously before us.

You must come to terms with this
that's laid
so obliquitous and ungraspable before you.

We must, at this pre-
ultimate
Start of Business, this
Museum of Our Childhoods, pass

counterclockwise
from room to room stark
naked that each artifact

(my long-lost diary spewing its breath-stopping spores,
your wheel-crushed Stop sign re-

recoiled red and red again around
the axle it snapped in two) might be
exposed
with as little as possible unnecessary
interference to our obligatory touch.

DANIELLE DeTIBERUS

Self Portrait as Artist Painting a Self Portrait

—After Artemisia Gentileschi

I'm sorry, Artemisia. The truth of your life
Is murky. You either died in 1653 or in '56 when

The plague hit. Bodies in the streets all spring.
You drew the curtains, locked the doors, waited

For a summer that never came. The air inside
That house soon smelled same as the filth

Outside. You always hated Naples—*because
Of the fighting* and *because of the hard living*.

What sad luck to die there, then. Unfinished
Canvas on its easel, ring of fleabites itching

Round your neck. This is me imagining me
Talking to you—about imagining what happened

All those years ago. Because I cannot remember
What happened to me, can't bear to paint my own

Face onto my story just yet. Little pink-cheeked
Girl. Starbursts of busted capillaries on the apple

Of each, & was it from too much laughing or crying.
Never mind that now, Artemisia, because this is

About you. Watch me—all swagger & persona—
Paste you right over my face. A palimpsest

Of rosy cheeks. Same frown lines, same big tits.
That'll do. & now I try to move you through time

Like a doll I'll bend this way & that. Make you into
Both me & you. Does that make me more like you?

When Susannah winces away from leering men.
When Judith works her sword through. When

Lucretia grabs a handful of breast & readies
For the knife. All these bodies used & used again.

Artemisia, I have to borrow you. Blend your story
With mine so no one can tell what's true. I'm the one

Calling out for help, my thighs vised apart
By his knee. Delicate Roman handkerchief

Stuffed in my mouth. Me arcing Holofernes' blood
With my brush. A breeze through the studio lifts

A loose hair to the wind. My hair soft as my brush.
No man will ever grab me again the way I am making

Judith grab him by his scruff. & her violence will last
Longer than any lifetime. This is not a woman's

Revenge. *Bastardi del cazzo*. Fucking fools. This is how
She survives. I sketch her in my dreams, charcoal

In one hand, fistfuls of hair in the other—until
I am all claw. *I'll show you what a woman can*

Do. She makes a mirror of herself each month
In blood. I paint her in yellow, in blue, in red.

I furrow her brow same as mine, give her chin
A slight slope. I know nothing of her particulars—

What she ate, who she kissed, how she slept. Only
Fragments that I snatch for my own. She almost

Didn't know what she could do until I gave her
A sword. I put the sword in her hands because

My hands were empty & I needed a war. Look,
they will say for centuries, Look, she's just like me.

MICHAEL MARK

[The center of the universe keeps moving]

The center of the universe keeps moving
on me. Lunchtime, it was in the salad place
on 4th, the woman with plastic gloves, thumb-
smashing cloves in the silver bowl with the
sweet ginger and turmeric dressing. Then in
the plump folds of our zoo's newborn hippo.
In the nostril of a cloud. I showed a suited stranger,
late to a party, whose pointer finger kept drifting.
Over, I guided, *Over!* In matters of the center,
exactitude has its place. *There!* Between us,
in the air, in his words. I gave him my glasses,
but the stranger wobbled off, the center of the
universe rowing in his shadow, uninvited.

ASHLEY KEYSER

Kelpie

If a hippocampus is a seahorse, what's memory
to a kelpie? Unridden, unbidden, unbroken,
he rides the breaking tide with crusted hooves.
Kelp twines in the mane of the kelpie. His hide,
soft and musty as moss to the touch. Don't touch,
or you will not be able to lift your hand again.
A boy caught by a finger at the kelpie's starry brow
hacked it from his knuckle and free with a knife
before the creature galloped back down the deep.

Deeper than memory, which is prone to tricks
and lets the flighty workaday mind muffle it,
his pasture clacks with coins, dissolving bones,
old wars' ordnance, nurdles and Garfield phones,
their eyes half-closed in exasperation or missing,
while species flare and gutter to effluvia before
they've been given names. If you could eat them
you would eat the little plastics of your own world.
The kelpie will leave you be if you say his true name.

He came to me as a beautiful young man
and lay his head in my lap to sleep. I ran a comb
through his hair and the teeth revealed his nature,
full of pearls, bits of flotsam, blue-hearted shells.
If I knew the secret of his name, I'd forgotten,
so I kissed him for any taste that wasn't human.

Eating the Siren

The ocean goes bluer as it warms and dies.
Phytoplankton carry off their green

to the poles, the forests gnawed away by urchins—
"roaches of the sea." But every creature on land

used to have a twin below, covered in scales.
Mermaids, of course, and more: a writhing haul

of mer-wolves, mer-rams branching horns,
a mer-elephant, which dwarfed the elephant

and gasped on the rocks when the tide pulled back.
Lions, too. The mermaids gave them suck.

Carved along church pews, they proffer teats,
while only Orthodox sirens have kept their wings

and vengeful looks like angels full of death.
Familiar hierarchies bound them, sea-bishops

ministering to schools of monkfish in habits.
East Indian mermaids lolloped in the sand.

They weighed some three hundred pounds,
slung with human breasts, which weren't enough

for the sailors to dream about, their nights torn
by some hunger too much to glut with a briny kiss.

Cooked merfolk, they reported, tasted like veal.
The *sirenia*, on the other hand, tasted like beef,

Steller's ample sea-cow, like she and the siren
were slightly botched copies from terrestrial molds.

Unless the reverse were true, and they the prior,
more potent halves, the salt-glittery originals.

Lamps lit by their fat, those sea-cows are gone,
and the mermaid's tarnished girlish mirror

reflects dimly the moon she once held, her comb
demoted from a harp like a burning seraph's.

She might sing again, now that lions emerge
grimacing from permafrost with their fur still on,

the ice disgorging worms and Siberian unicorns.
Are they delicious? Pack dogs champed happily

on a wooly mammoth defrosting across a beach
at the beginning of the nineteenth century

in his waterlogged flesh and forty pounds of hair.
As fabulous beasts return, surely someone will find

a lucrative use for them. They must have flushed
with pride, the men who bagged the mammoth,

but they would truly rejoice if they could know
the Northwest Passage is at last melting open,

that route they coveted to spices, silk, its blue
a blue from beyond the sea, ultramarine,

for the robes of angels painted in our image.

SEAN HILL

Early September, Fairbanks, Alaska

All the changing leaves
me wanting to stop.
I need to balance.
Here we're in the cusp.
Time more a feeling
than a moment, less
measure than act such
as a gasp,—a quick
rising of the chest,
intake of breath as
now the leaves all change
right now just here on
this trail gilded by
time—more than a feeling,
reminds me of Las
Vegas—the Golden
Nugget's dazzling
façade inviting
me to try my luck
when I maundered down
The Strip or when I'm
home visiting and
my brother and I
go for a friendly
game of pool and his
English and his leaves
leave me little to
do but lose. These leaves
the one-ball's color
which he wouldn't let
me hit nor any
of the others. Such

wanting then as now
halting me with these
leaves as they whisper
and meander down
to the ground. They've changed
and I'm less aghast
than astonished here
in the thunderclap
of this sudden fall.
I need to balance
right here on this gilt
path under these leaves.
All the changing leaves
all the leaves changing.

RACHEL RICHARDSON

Approximate Distance

Say her name: the reeds
move. Nina in the undergrowth. Nina
in the coffee's steam. The dead simply
don't have bodies anymore, someone
said to me. It doesn't mean they're gone.

The word horse unhorses
every other word, C. D. Wright wrote.
I think she wrote that.

Approximate Distance

Held in books, in flesh, in the thread that binds
us to those who we know are also
putting a child to bed, changing a tire,
slicing a potato.

There you are, across
the abyss. Your generalized
body now, unhorsed:
the fog that catches, sometimes,
here, between the rolling hills.

DAN BEACHY-QUICK

Canto XXXVIII (after Buson & Issa)

—for Mai Wagner

Memory's green inch—
sunlight's white snow
    bright on August pine

        needle. Memory's green
    inch—half-moon
        in morning sky, the pine

tree on the near hill,
its tip taller than the tip
    of the distant mountain—

        by a green inch. Memory's
    sky blue through branches
        of the pine, the ocean

smells of resin when wind
blows the ocean
    through the pines. Or no,

        I'm wrong, it is not
    snow, it is the morning
        dew in afternoon light, so bright

of the August sun—memory's
green wish. The man writing poems
    points the way with a poem.

        The man who asked the way
    has disappeared. The deer bounding
        away stops to see what

scared it. Some sound. Spare
no arrows, sparrows—
    sing. I want a wound.

    All my life written down
with a pine needle—
    memory's green inch:

I've never been closer
to that sound than across
    a river.

ARIEL KATZ

A Sort of Inescapable Sense of Impending Calamity

WHEN ANNE FIRST HEARD ABOUT the bus accident, it didn't even occur to her that Philip might have been in it. She was fourteen at the time, making dinner with her mother. As the evening news reported the details of the collision, they paused for the requisite moment, performed a polite amount of grief—Anne furrowed her brow, her mother clucked her tongue and sighed. Then they lowered the volume and continued their conversation. Anne had been explaining a drawn-out drama within her group of friends: Lauren's parents were letting her bring one friend to the lake for the weekend, and Lauren had agonized between Anne and Elizabeth. Finally, Lauren had quietly picked Anne. Now, with a voice full of stagey regret and half-concealed pride, Anne was relating to her mother the whispered locker conversations and snippy comments at lunch that had followed Lauren's selection. Meanwhile, the television camera panned briefly over the wreckage of the city bus, half-flipped over the guardrail, and the bakery truck, cab burned out, bright boxes of donuts and pound cakes on the sidewalk. Later, when Anne would retell the story of the night of her father's death, the feeling she remembered most clearly but never mentioned was the satisfaction of chattering over the newscaster, the glow of having been chosen as the favorite by her friend.

Like most adolescents, Anne had been taught to deliver condolences, but didn't know how to inform others of her own loss. She hadn't anticipated that breaking the news of personal tragedy would become a pattern in her life; she had falsely assumed it would be over after a few weeks, once the obituary had circulated in the paper and the principal had made the announcement at school. Instead, the process of telling stretched on. At first, Anne used her father's death as a weapon: when Elizabeth kept asking to read Anne's draft of a paper on *The Crucible* "just as an example," Anne stood up and said, "My father just *died*," and stormed out. It was supposed to signal that she would no longer be complicit in youthful things like casual plagiarism. It was an outburst to which no one could respond.

Other times, she played at catching adults in their empty, sunny phrases. Some well-meaning substitute teacher would ask, "So, what do your parents do?" and Anne would say without intonation, "my mom sells lamps, and my dad is dead." She relished in the fall of faces.

After a year or two, she tired of embarrassing others with the revelation of Philip's death. She learned to enjoy the ease of polite conversation, and preferred not to interrupt its flow. Sometimes, she wouldn't correct her interlocutor when they assumed her parents were both living. Mostly, she learned to use words like "deceased," or "passed" and could arrange her face to look strong and serene, so that the listener wouldn't have to provide effusions of grief. They could say "I'm sorry" and the conversation would move on. In the early years, when speaking with a friend's mother, Anne had left that irrelevant, insufficient condolence hanging, forcing the woman to mumble mis-matched platitudes ("he's in a better time" and "good places happen for a reason"). By twenty, she learned simply to absolve listeners who said "I'm sorry," or "How awful" with a wistful smile: "it was a long time ago." She began to imagine herself as an older woman in an earlier decade: balanced, even-tempered. She carried family photos in her wallet, wore rings on her left hand before marriage, and painted her nails and lips the same dim pink. She married at twenty-three and moved to a small town in North Carolina, where she had never been. By the time she turned twenty-four, those who knew her called her "a fixture."

THE COUPLE WHO had just been to Anne and Lyle's house for dinner were overwhelming. The wife, Elana, was in graduate school with Lyle, and had immediately engaged him in a highly technical conversation about linguistic relativity. Bored, Anne took up the work of asking Elana's husband where he was from and what he did. It was easy for them both; they had each polished their questions and responses long ago. After dinner Anne washed the dishes while Lyle slumped in his chair, massaging his temple.

"Elana's a little much?" Anne said over the water.

"It's not that."

Anne turned off the tap and leaned against the sink, arms crossed. "What's up?"

"My sister called me earlier and said she's been kicked out of college."

"Oh," Anne crinkled her eyebrows and sat across from Lyle.

"And—you're not going to love this—she wants to come stay here for a while."

Anne had met Lise at the wedding. Her toast had lasted twenty-two minutes, during which she'd sung two songs from a Sondheim musical, directed three younger cousins as they acted out a bit from a sitcom, and asked Anne about her preferred method of birth control.

"Oh." Anne focused on the olive-green phone above Lyle's head. He teased her for relying on a landline, just as he needled her about her matronly Subtle Satin lipstick. He gave her a look he often used: narrowing his eyes as if to see through a sheet of wavy glass.

"Well? What do you think?"

"She's your sister."

He sighed. "We'll limit it to a week, how's that?"

"Fine," she said, and went back to the dishes.

The night they were married, after the ceremony, Anne had sat down, nauseous and dizzy, away from the lighted tent, the dancing people. Lyle found her; he brought her water, cake, and asked her nothing. She felt waterlogged as he led her back to the circular tables. They danced; they were silent, and she was grateful, though what she wanted most were his questions.

"PROPRIETY." ELANA WAS saying, her voice echoing off the walls. It was the day after the dinner party; Elana had come to pick up her casserole dish. "That's my thesis, in layperson's terms. There are structures and patterns of speech that signal a conversation as decorous rather than, say, intimate, intellectual, or crude. Pleases, thank yous, formal titles, small talk. What happens to communication when there's a breakdown of propriety? By and large, it means a sort of opening up of discourse, and spaces for minority groups to self-express and question existing linguistic structures of oppression. My question, though—" here, she touched Anne's arm as though sharing a secret, "my question, is what if the breakdown of propriety actually makes certain topics inaccessible? And by propriety, I mean small talk, niceties, ex cetera, ex cetera—"

"Et cetera, I believe," Anne said. She glanced out the window, where snow was starting to fall lightly, like glitter.

"And I argue, I argue that these niceties serve a dual purpose as points of entry and points of deflection—"

The olive-colored phone rang. This, Anne thought, was the reason to keep a landline—to interrupt these sorts of conversations.

"Look," Lyle said when she picked up. "You're going to have to get Lise from the airport tonight. I'm stranded. They're putting us up in Greensboro."

Lyle was at a conference two hours away. The plan had been for him to come home, eat dinner, and pick up Lise afterwards.

"Is her flight still coming in?"

"A little delayed, but not cancelled. They're saying midnight."

Once she was off the phone, Anne went into the kitchen and gave Elana her dish—hideous, ceramic, decorated with childlike paintings of the sun and moon that she had "done herself."

"It was a great meringue. You and Paul have to come back over sometime."

"Oh, yes, yes, and we'll have to have you over." After a brief pause: "You must be proud of Lyle. He was telling me the other night about the paper he's giving today."

Anne nodded. She rarely asked Lyle about his research, and he rarely asked her about her work at the small tourism office downtown.

Elana began to gush about Lyle's work using syrupy words like "brilliant" and "fascinating." Fatigued, Anne put a hand on the small of Elana's back, guided her toward the door. "Elana, I hate to rush you out, but it looks like I should stock up on groceries before we're snowed in."

In the parking lot of the supermarket, people were stuffing their trunks with crates of bottled water and boxes of nonperishable milk. Inside, the aisles were full of shoppers and the shelves were emptied. Students from the college barreled down the lanes, picking out beer and cereal, loudly discussing what time to start their parties. Neighbors blocked the canned goods shelf, discussing where to get shovels and chains. Disoriented professors asked attendants for chicken, tomatoes, water, but again and again they were told there wasn't any more.

She'd seen it before: the town didn't know how to deal with snow. In winter, every forecast became a proclamation of doom. Schools closed, states of emergency were declared, people frantically bought crates of bottled water. Anne remembered winter mornings as a child in Boston, waking to the sound of plows, pulling back the curtain to see men sprinkling salt on the sidewalk, going into the kitchen to find her parents reading their papers, preparing for a normal day. All as it should be. Business as usual.

THE BUS HAD crashed on a cloudless day in spring. It was the line that went from the river to the center of the city. Anne's father worked in the center of the city, and drove home at six p.m. He almost never took the bus, and certainly never at that time, in that direction. In the weeks after his death, Anne and her mother kept waiting for some revelation, a terrible blow: there was a mistress, a fraudulent business; he had lost his job, he was looking to move out. But nothing came to light, and year after year, nothing did.

Inspired by television tropes, Anne donned the aggressive mourning garb of the sullen teenager, wearing all black, lining her eyes in black, painting her lips black. Her mother wore very little black. It seemed impossible to Anne that her mother could continue to wear her everyday clothes. But there she was in her turquoise pullover, scrubbing a Tupperware in her khaki slacks and Kiss the Cook apron, driving to the store in her gray pumps. In these clothes she graciously thanked neighbors when they added a tenth lasagna to the family fridge. She designed the headstone, flipping through the catalog as she and Anne watched Seinfeld reruns. She made up the spare bedroom for out-of-town guests, apologized for the disorder of the house. And she did cry, sparingly, pressing her face with a tissue. Anne admired her mother: this, she supposed, was strength. But underneath the admiration was a discomfort that grew every time she saw her mother deftly handle an arrangement or accept a condolence. She began to watch her for signs of strain, loose threads. But she only saw this: her bedroom light was on late into the night, and she no longer blow-dried her hair in the mornings.

As the funeral drew nearer, Anne's sense of anticipation grew. This would be it: where else to keen, to unravel? The cemetery was on a hill across from a strip mall where Anne would get her first job, selling raincoats. The mourners stood in a line by the grave. Philip had been cremated; Anne's mother had chosen to bury the urn. Anne watched her mother through the hymns and anonymous elegies led by the pastor. Her mother cried in the same way she did at home, dabbing her face. Anne's anticipation became internal begging. Tear your hair. Sink to the earth, pound it with your fists. Rend your clothing. Throw yourself on the casket. Why hadn't they dispersed the ashes? Why had he been burned if not to be dispersed? Crumbs, she thought, he's crumbs, and almost laughed.

Lauren and Elizabeth came to the funeral. They bought new dresses for the occasion, and the next weekend they quietly went to the lake without Anne.

"Oh, it's you," Lise said when Anne picked her up just past midnight. "Where's Lyle?"

The drive to the airport hadn't been treacherous: the snow was not yet sticking to the highway. Still, she'd seen two minor accidents: a teenager who'd skidded off the road, a couple who'd rear-ended a pickup truck. Minivans drove at forty miles an hour with their hazard lights on.

Anne explained Lyle's situation. Lise was wearing a short dress with no tights and no coat.

"They're predicting an ice storm." Anne said. Lise smelled like bourbon and had small yellowing bruises on her knuckles.

"Great. Out of the frying pan and into another frying pan."

"Into the fire, I think you mean."

"No, I mean frying pan. I mean, like, this is the exact same shit as in Chicago. Into the fire would at least be a change."

"Well, sorry we couldn't be more exciting," Anne said, not entirely masking her irritation.

"It's fine. I deserve it. It's what I get for choosing a goody-goody bitch of a roommate who can't think for two seconds about the impact of her actions. I deserve to be exiled to the middle of nowhere to do God knows what and feel sorry for myself."

Anne had known girls like Lise in college, whose preferred form of discourse was the provocative, expletive-filled monologue, the purpose of which was not to engage the listener but to get the listener to react.

"It's not all that godforsaken out here. Lise, I meant to ask, any allergies? The store was pretty cleared out, but I got peanut butter, bananas, some steak—sound good?"

She glanced away from the road when Lise didn't respond, and found Lise looking directly at her. It was a look of betrayal, a pleading, angry look. And then it was gone.

"I eat everything. Literally, everything. I've gained, like, fifty pounds this semester."

For the rest of the drive home, Lise slumped over her phone, snorting or shaking her head every so often. The venom of her initial comments was gone, and whenever Anne asked her anything she looked vacant and gave glossy answers. The road near Anne's house seemed darker than usual, and she felt the brakes grumble over the ice forming on the road. The more vacant the answers, the more questions Anne asked, and she became nervous. She'd thought she understood Lise from Lyle's accounts of her. Lise had been born in the same affluent Chicago suburb as her brother. In high school she had been a driven track runner and cellist. She didn't sleep much, acted in the school plays, edited the paper, and was known for carrying a translucent green water bottle perpetually filled with coffee. As far as Anne knew, Lise's childhood, like Lyle's, had been unblemished. So when she'd met her at the wedding and suffered through her aggressive toast, Anne grouped her with similar girls she'd known, who took on poor haircuts and racy speech as an aesthetic experiment, then graduated to ponytails and jobs in marketing. Now, seeing Lise slumped in the front seat, Anne felt that she had underestimated in her some pain.

Anne and Lyle's driveway was long and curving, and at the end was a metal gate. As usual, Anne stopped before the gate. Behind it, the house was dark, though she'd left a light on in the hallway—the power must have gone out. Anne shrugged out of her coat, passed it to Lise, and asked her to open the gate.

Lise looked at Anne darkly, but stepped out into the snow. She walked past the beams of Anne's headlights and instead of hearing the clank of the fence sliding back, Anne heard a yelp. Already on edge, she ran through scenarios in her head: there wasn't an outage, there was a murderer who had cut the power, who was now terrorizing her sister-in-law; or, Lise had slipped in the snow and broken her arm. Usually, Anne didn't let herself imagine such scenarios. It was something she'd done the year after Philip's death, when she and her mother couldn't find their car in the mall parking lot, or she hit her head in a soccer game. She would immediately find in these situations the greatest possible danger, and relate the possibilities to her mother in a laughing, half-joking voice, until her mother said, enough, Anne, nobody *stole* our car, you are not going to slip into a *coma* tonight. Anne felt foolish and went silent. Still, once she and her mother came home to the bathroom door locked from the inside, light within. Though they both figured one of them had just forgotten it in the morning, they went around the house yelling about their "uncle the police officer" who was "coming over for lamb chops." They pressed their ears to the door, not breathing, listening for movement. Finally, Anne's mother picked the lock with a hairpin while Anne held a butcher's knife, both of them talking in strange voices, pretending the thing was ridiculous, masking their fear. The door came open, and inside it was bright and empty.

So Anne was fearful as she walked to the gate. Lise came into view first, hands on hips, shaking her head. Then the tail and legs of the deer, kicking and struggling between the slats of the fence.

"WHAT IS THIS," Lise was saying. "What is this? Does this happen often?"

If Anne had been alone, she might have parked her car, slipped around the fence, and dealt with the animal in the morning. But because Lise was there, she knew she would have to do the responsible thing, whatever that was.

The deer was twisting from side to side; the fur on each flank was rubbed away. The skin was red and beginning to bleed. Its antler was torn, and it smelled like the pig farms Anne would pass when driving on small highways to visit her mother. Although she wanted to feel pity, Anne instead felt disgust, and anger at Lyle for being in Greensboro. She continued to stare at the deer and Lise continued to stare at her.

Across the street Elana and Paul's house was lit up. At dinner, Anne and Paul had discussed the uneven power grids in the neighborhood. In the fall there had been a hurricane, and Anne had lost power while Paul hadn't. At dinner, he'd made a gesture of polite disappointment and said, if only we'd known each other then, y'all could have crashed at our place! Anne had joked that if this next one was as bad as they said it would be, she'd have to take him up on that!

Later, Anne would wonder why she hadn't used the landline to call Animal Control. When she tried to remember the moment of decision, it slipped away from her, mixing with the memory of the snow and the panic at Lise's flatness in the car. She had already accepted that this was a disaster, and that normalcy needed to be restored as quickly as possible.

IT WAS STRANGE that Elana answered the door immediately, as if she'd been waiting there. She was fully dressed, down to the pair of cowboy boots she'd worn to pick up the sun-and-moon dish at Anne's house. She was holding a slouching earthenware mug filled with coffee. She welcomed them in as if she always received visitors at this hour.

"Anne! Lovely to see you, lovely to see you—and who's this?" The table was spread with papers, and she set plates on top of them and insisted on serving cake.

"Good to see you too. This is Lyle's sister. Lise, this is Elana. Elana, Lise."

"You holding up in the storm? Power out? I heard you're on a different grid? Lyle's not back?"

Anne explained about the conference, but didn't mention the deer immediately, though all she could think of was it writhing in the snow, blood on the fence and the ice.

"Yes, yes, they're very interested in his work. Professor Andrews has taken a liking to him. I don't suppose that will be his only offer, though. And I guess you'd like to move somewhere more like Ann Arbor or Manhattan, rather than Greensboro? That would be a downgrade, Chapel Hill to Greensboro. Ha!"

Anne forced a smile and cut her cake, which lay on top of a grainy printout of an article called With the Mostest: The Semantics of Entertaining in Britain and America. Lise followed Anne's eyes.

"I like the placemats," she said, gesturing to the paper.

Elana reddened and, as if just remembering the articles spread across the table, lifted the plates and swept them into a stack.

"Apologies, it's for my research."

"What's your research?"

"Propriety, in layperson's terms," Elana said.

Anne was surprised at Elana's brevity. "Is Paul awake?"

"No. He sleeps at nine. Bakery hours, you know. Though probably they'll be closed tomorrow."

Anne wanted to ask the question without sounding weak, without begging for Elana's help. The snow, Lyle's absence, Lise's obscure pain, the struggling deer—if she described the situation too completely, Anne thought she might begin to giggle or weep. So she chose her words carefully, the way her mother did when dealing with a difficult customer or unpredictable family friend.

"We've come over with a bit of an agenda. We got home and there's a deer stuck in the fence."

Elana looked confused, and then began to laugh a big, bellowing laugh.

"Oh, God," she said. She pulled on her jacket and, noticing Anne was without one, threw her a puffy red coat. "Let's go take a look."

When they reached the fence, Elana put her hands on her hips and let out another short laugh and said in a faux, exaggerated mountains-of-North-Carolina accent, "Well, ain't that something."

The night seemed wild. In the snowy dark the house and trees were stripped of their context. The stars were close and eerie, the landscape vast.

"I grew up on a sort of farm, you know." Elana said. "That's the last time I saw something like this, except it was much worse. There was a pregnant cow, and she'd gotten loose overnight, and the barbed fence—" she waved a hand. "I won't go into it."

"Where was the farm?" Anne asked.

"Near Saxapahaw. My parents were hippies, didn't know anything about farming. Met in Asheville—you been up there yet?"

"No."

"Lot of pot and dreadlocks. Cute mountain town. Did you know," Elana said, looking directly at Anne, "did you know, I used to have an accent?"

"No."

"I trained myself out of it, in high school, too, when it's hardest. That's why I first got interested in linguistics."

Anne began to respond, but realized that Lise had slipped through the fence to where the deer's head was.

"It looks bad," she called. "It's got a big scratch across its nose."

"That was my first research project, about suppressing accents."

Anne wished she were alone, to be able to think about what to do.

"So you grew up on a farm. What do you do with this?"

Elana was staring distractedly at the deer. "My parents were in town last week, did Paul tell you at dinner?"

"No."

"I took them to Franklin Street, they really liked that, my father kept putting his hands on his hips and using the word 'cosmopolitan.'" Elana grimaced as she said this, then laughed.

Anne thought of her own mother, walking the labyrinth of lamps at Luminous Homes.

"Have your parents seen Chapel Hill?"

The year after Philip's death Anne's mother talked a lot about Luminous Homes, retelling the elaborate stories she invented to sell lamps, tales of Venetian palaces and frontier cottages, designers gone mad, notebooks recovered from Virginian swamps. At the end she would laugh: *People don't like to buy lamps* just *because they need a light in their living room.*

"They haven't seen Chapel Hill."

"Still working, your parents?"

"Yes."

"What do they—"

"Sorry, what should we do with the deer?" Lise said in the tone of a parent speaking to distracted children.

You'll never know why. It was a warning, when this thought darted across Anne's mind, deerlike, always at night. *You'll never know.*

She was suddenly terrified of the head of the deer, which faced away from her. She imagined its eyes dead, eaten by flies. What if it died there in the night, became a carcass in the fence? From the shadows its family watched, its dangerous clan, ready to spring. She was breathing quickly.

"I'm *cold.*" Lise said. "What do we do?"

From the deer there came a sheep-like sound, deeper than Anne would have expected.

Elana was looking at Anne. "Are you all right?"

Throat constricted, Anne nodded.

"Give me your coat," Elana said to Anne.

Elana threw the coat over the head of the deer, and after a minute it stopped kicking. "Okay, Anne, you take the legs."

Anne felt a fear so sharp and sudden that she began to shiver. If she walked into the grocery store now, no one would think she was a fixture. They would see her as she was: a scared girl in a new town, coatless.

And she was on the back porch of her childhood home, where her mother had found a newly dead raccoon. It was starting to rain, and they had to dispose of the body before it became soft and began to smell. Anne's mother had a shovel and a trash bag and Anne hadn't been able to conceal her disgust. This was the period in which she still wore her heavy black makeup, and she had felt this same unmasking as her mother said, impatiently, "Come on, you just have to hold the bag. I'll do the shoveling." She hadn't been able to hold the bag still.

That same weekend, her mother had gone away for a night with girlfriends who had insisted she needed massages and manicures and wine. It was the first time Anne was allowed to stay alone in the house overnight, and she'd invited Lauren and Elizabeth to sleep over. They watched a movie and ate sour candy and practiced their skill with liquid eyeliner. Later, after everyone was asleep, Anne wandered the house, unable to settle down. She ended up at her mother's desk and opened the drawer. Inside was a folder labeled "research," and Anne opened it because she was feeling restless and powerful.

At first she couldn't make sense of it. It was mostly flyers, news stories, and bus schedules. Once Anne noticed the date on one of them, she realized what this was. February 6th—Contra Dancing Lessons with Katie Arnold! February 6th—Wine Tasting at Pine Street Brewery! February 6th—The Miles Series on Sex and Sexuality. February 6th—Singles Meet and Greet at Limelight. February 6th—Meet the Author of *Fifteen Tips for Your Business* at Blackbird Books.

Anne imagined her mother at the desk logically going through the possibilities, weighing their likelihood. She expected this revelation to comfort her—months after Philip's death her mother still had not shown any signs of the disorientation she felt. But leafing through the folder Anne only felt more disappointed. This was just more of her mother's relentless organization—she hadn't noted any theories, hadn't underlined key passages.

Then, under the clippings, Anne saw the Post-It notes. They were in Philip's handwriting. *Eggs, pancake batter, orchid,* said one. *Remember, you get Anne today! xo.* One looked like notes from a conference call, and in the margins were pen drawings of insects. *Hon—will be a bit late for dinner, getting coffee with Al. I'll bring cannolis! P.S. let's see* Pier Nine *tomorrow? JAIME—drop Annie at office after school? Want to show new whiteboard. Plus you can go to book club.* The final one looked as if it had been taped to a gift and torn off and kept. *To Jaime and Annie—use for rainy Saturday mornings.*

Anne tried to visualize her friends downstairs, asleep in their pastel bags. She tried to think of a prank to play on them, something to write on their faces. No use. She cried as she hadn't cried since the funeral. She knelt on the floor and buried her face in the cushion of the chair. Each note suggested the fullness, intricacy, and mystery of the day from which it came. They reminded her that he had written reminders on the backs of his hands, that he'd folded napkins into flowers but never remembered to hang his coats, that he'd helped her off the high kitchen chairs as a child. The contexts that the notes suggested were the most difficult and most painful to remember—a normalcy that had become distant the moment it had ceased. She realized, with shame, that she had made his death a problem of language—how to tell it?—and hadn't confronted the horrible implications: he was as much as I am, and in a moment he ceased to be.

Now: THE DEER, the snow.

"Won't it kick?" Anne asked, aware of her frantic voice.

"No, that's the point of putting on the jacket as a blinder," said Elana.

"I'll do it," Lise said, sliding back through the fence. But Anne grabbed the animal by the hooves before her sister-in-law could. For a moment, holding the deer's ankles, she was triumphant. They were slim, and reminded her of holding Lyle's wrists when they'd first met: surprisingly light and slender for a man his height. She glanced at Lise, who seemed disappointed, and Elana, who looked relieved. The moon was out, whitening the still-falling snow. The neighborhood was quiet. Later, she would remember very few of these feelings—the stillness, the calm, the invincibility. After all, it was less than a minute that she held the legs before they kicked her.

ALL ANNE WANTED was her own kitchen, a little tea, and sleep. But here she was again at Elana's table, refusing all food except the frozen pineapples Elana gave her to put on her injured shoulder.

Elana was spewing the bright, nervous talk that emerges when one is in the room with a hurt person.

"And so Paul, well, he starts to take the pie out of the oven. And my little nieces have spent the whole day in the sun at one of those Pick-Your-Own strawberry fields. Paul starts to take it out of the oven, and looks at the kids with this big "here it comes!" smile, and all of a sudden it flips face-down onto the floor!"

Lise had said little since they'd come back inside. She accepted all the food that Anne refused, and now sat before a flock of little china plates, toast and cookies and truffles and oranges.

"Lise, what brings you to Chapel Hill? February, not the ideal time to visit."

Anne saw in Lise's face the impulse both to confront and to lie. "I'm taking some time off."

"I did the same thing, after my first year of school. I went home and worked on the farm for a few weeks, I was feeling discouraged, and had romanticized all my childhood chores. Of course, three months collecting eggs and harvesting tomatoes will get one back to the library quickly."

A flicker of interest in Lise. "Were you glad you left school for awhile?"

Again, Elana laughed her bark-like laugh, and then said with a coldness Anne couldn't have predicted, "Oh, no. No, no."

They sat in silence. Finally, Anne put her hands on the table in a gesture of departure, said she was going to call animal control and go home. Elana, as if coming out of a trance, insisted they stay the night and deal with the deer in the morning. Lise excused herself to the guest room; Anne stayed. She'd noticed that Elana's fingers were trembling slightly.

"My parents had the entire Britannica," she said. "They would read me entries before bed. When I was Lise's age, when I left school for a few months, I thought it would be a haven. But the longer I stayed, the longer I realized I wasn't going to go back to the farm after school. And I realized once they died, it would all disappear—and it would be my fault. I would sell it to developers. I haven't had to do it yet, but I'm sure I will."

Anne stayed very still, as if she were dealing with a bear.

"Growing up, they were the most sophisticated people I knew—my dad with his facts about trains, my mom who read Taoist fables before bed. And now they come here and they're so . . . provincial. And I know I'm going to eventually destroy what they've worked on their whole lives. And here I am, high and mighty, the daughter who's spending an eighth year working on a dissertation no one will publish."

Everything in the kitchen seemed sharper, the disorder more apparent: grounds scattered around the coffee pot, a paper bag near the garbage filled with shattered glass, unwashed dishes attracting flies in the sink. Elana, who had always struck

Anne as hummingbirdish, quick-witted, mobile, suddenly seemed witchlike, brown curls sticking out uncombed from her head, black circles under her eyes, nails broken, teeth stained.

"I'm sorry, Anne. I didn't mean to—I've just been up for hours, I'm not thinking about what I'm saying."

"That's all right," Anne said. Elana continued to look at her expectantly.

"And then I see people like Lyle . . . he's only been here three years, and already . . . sorry, Anne, sorry. Are you sure you wouldn't like any tea?"

"No, thank you."

"And we have this house, and our vegetable garden, you know, and the other day I woke up and realized, all of this is contingent on how I do. We're here because of me, and if I fail we leave. I'm the string you pull to unravel the cloth."

Anne nodded, averted her eyes.

"Do you ever feel that? A sort of . . ." she half-laughed, belatedly trying to take some of the tension out of the conversation, "a sort of inescapable sense of impending calamity?"

She looked at Anne now with a desperate need for confirmation. And Anne, for the first time in years, genuinely wanted to agree, to comfort. Yes, this was what she felt when she saw the deer in the fence, when the snow began to fall, when she heard Lise's cry in the dark, something was wrong, the order was going to be upset, but she didn't know what was going to be broken.

The sense was so strong that she feared if she said "yes," if she began to commiserate, she would be somehow knocked off course, made to step out of herself. So she said, "Not really. I'm sorry you feel that way."

She watched Elana fold away her vulnerability. With half-suppressed yawns she thanked Elana for the food and shelter. She went to bed without any routine.

Lying in the dark an image kept coming back to her, of her mother shaking hands at the reception after the funeral. It was so colorless and cliché she wondered if it hadn't come from an episode of a soap opera. Mourner after mourner, shaking hands, and even giving polite smiles. Ridiculous, Anne had thought as a teenager. Now the rote predictability of the ritual comforted her.

She drifted in and out of sleep; the pain in her shoulder grew. Not wanting to wake Lise, she waited until her breathing was steady and then rose, headed for the kitchen, to get more ice. But when she crossed to the door, she saw Lise was awake and tearful.

"Everything okay?"

A short laugh. "Obviously not. Don't you even *care* why I was kicked out of school?"

Anne had never been good at this sort of talk when she'd been fourteen, or eighteen—she could never supply enough genuine, effusive sympathy for whatever problem her girlfriends faced. (*Oh, you got a D in math this semester? Wow, that really . . . it's really . . . it sucks. I'm sorry. You broke up with Carl? He was a jerk . . . he didn't deserve you . . . Of course I care, of course I care.*)

"Yes, I care," said Anne. "What happened?"

"It's a long story."

She felt nervous—as a teenager she'd constantly been aware of adults misjudging her, reading the black makeup as comfortable suburban rebellion, her quietness as stupidity, her meanness as hormonal. Now, as she recognized that she had classified Lise in similar ways, she felt obligated to stay and listen. As an offering, she said, "My arm's killing me; I'm not going to sleep anyway. Why don't you tell me about it."

The snow outside had intensified, and wind was rattling the kitschy sunflower flag outside the guest room. Lise spoke loudly, to impose evenness on her tear-strung voice.

"I passed out in class one day. It was September, still super hot out. There was no air conditioning, I hadn't had any water that whole day, and it was this dumb required science class, and there were bugs in jars, and I just sort of slipped out of my chair. So they rush me to student health—more specifically, my supposed friend, Kate, rushes me to student health. And I wake up on the way there, and I'm like, take me back to class, please. But Kate's all set on taking me to the emergency room, God knows why, she's a nervous mess most of the time, always leaving notes around the apartment telling me to clean up, I don't know why she can't just ask me in person."

Lise had dropped her surly, black-leather persona. She spoke now like the college girls Anne remembered, unaware of the specificity and intricacy of the world in which their problems played out.

". . . so I talk for a while with this nurse, and she says everything seems normal, but I'm going to have to come in again next week to be weighed. So I miss that appointment, and suddenly they're freaking out that I've missed it, so I go for a few weeks in a row. Finally this doctor tells me in this scary voice that if I can't get my weight up in the next few weeks, I can't stay at school." Lise shrugged. "I guess it's not really that long a story. I didn't weigh enough, and they kicked me out."

Anne didn't say anything, just nodded and made a sympathetic humming noise. She wondered what Lise had told Lyle, and their parents. Details were missing, but she couldn't pinpoint which. Then, before she could think of something mature and comforting to say, she said:

"Unbelievable, about your friend Kate."

Lise began to cry in a heaving, childlike way, pulling the covers around her chin. Anne wanted to cry, too, though of course she didn't. She smoothed Lise's hair, which was coarse and oily, but Lise turned violently away.

"That bitch," she said. "I was doing completely fine in my classes. She's like, 'I'm worried about you,' when really, she didn't give a damn when all the other shit was happening last year, with me and Robert."

"Robert?"

"My ex. He ended up having some trouble with alcohol, and took time off to go into a program. Anyway, before he was in the program, I was drinking sort of a lot too, nothing crazy, just enough to make me a fatass. So sue me if I was just trying to lose a little weight. That's why they freaked out, because probably when they'd first got my weight I'd been like 300 pounds."

"So what are you going to do now?" Anne asked. Anne thought of Lyle and Lise's parents, snowed in at their home in the Chicago suburbs, discussing plans for the addition on their house, unaware of their daughter, shivering and oily in another state.

"Who knows," Lise said, burrowing her face into the mattress. Anne waited for more, some grand plan. Lise seemed to be the kind of girl who would buy a bus ticket for California and scrabble at an acting career, or find friends in New York to put her up while she waitressed and wrote poetry. But she didn't say anything else, and before Anne could think of anything—comfort, encouragement, admonishment—Lise had fallen asleep.

Her own failure hung around her—she could feel pain in this room, and in the next room, where the light was still on and Elana was shuffling her papers. No matter how much she thought of ways to assuage their grief she couldn't come up with any words or gestures. And the deer in the fence, and no one had called Animal Control, and even if they'd called no one would come. She knew if she went into the kitchen she would be unable to talk to Elana because something was pressing at her chest and making her breathe quickly. She sat on the edge of the bed, pain mounting in her shoulder, trying to forget the deer, its bloodied sides. Why didn't it go around the side, leap the hedge? What was so desirable that it squeezed itself through the unwelcoming bars?

Years ago, when Anne's mother had returned from her weekend trip, Anne had talked obsessively about the sleepover, though she hadn't enjoyed it. They'd played charades, they'd played cards, they'd gone stargazing on the lawn. They hadn't done any of these things; they'd hardly known what to do, since Elizabeth and Lauren had a whole new series of inside jokes from their time at the lake house. Anne wanted to distract her mother from realizing that her "research" folder was out-of-order. But of course she did realize—and again Anne hoped for a confrontation, a breakdown. After reading her mother's folder, she also hoped for some shadow of an explanation, a lead on the cold case. Instead, her mother said tiredly:

"It's just a silly project. We're never going to know, really."

"Maybe if you asked the other passengers on the bus, you could know where he got on? And then look for things in that area?"

"Anne," her mother said sleepily, "there's no use in that. I don't know who they were. It's not worth it."

"I bet they keep records of the drivers. I don't think the driver was killed. Maybe the driver would remember him."

A sharpness now to her mother's voice. "The driver was killed. The fire caught in the front of the bus, and Daddy was in the front."

"There aren't many stops on that line. It's only a matter of time before your research—"

"Anne. Enough."

A few weeks later, when Anne dared to check her mother's research folders, they were gone. The bus schedules, flyers, newspaper clippings. Panicked, she searched her mother's bedroom, dresser drawers, closets, under the bed, the couch cushions. Gone—even the Post-It notes.

EARLY IN THE morning, Anne went into the kitchen to ask for painkillers and coffee. Elana was asleep at the table, but woke immediately when she heard Anne reaching for a mug.

"You won't believe it," she said. "But the deer's gone."

Anne's heart quickened; she was disappointed. She had wanted to resolve this. Without responding to Elana, she opened the front door and looked across the street at her fence.

Branches and sidewalks were ice-coated, and the street was quiet in the way that only snow quiets. The darkened house under its snowcap seemed alien, as did the black fence, clean and stern. The only suggestion of emergency was the car, parked at an angle, its headlights shining weakly at the spot where the deer had been.

"Oh no," Elana said from behind Anne, "looks like you left the lights on. I don't know how I didn't notice that."

Anne went without a coat to the car. Once the headlights were off, she inspected the fence, expecting to see blood, traces of skin. There was nothing except some thick brown hair, which she brushed into the snow. On the ground, a few dark droplets, but nothing here suggested the violence of the kick, the terror of the animal wedged between the bars. It had all evaporated: Lise's defiance, Elana's frontier confidence, the strangeness of the storm.

Later, when Lyle was home, when the lights were back, when the snow had stopped, and Lise had unpacked into their spare room, Anne went walking. Lise had told Lyle the story of the deer immediately after he returned: in her voice the story was dry, comical, horrifying. It had a beginning, it had suspense, it was resolved.

As Anne walked, she thought of the story, and became more and more agitated. She imagined calling her mother, telling her about the deer. But she could think of no words, no frame for the image: only, it appeared, it struggled, and it was gone.

Translation Folio

VERÓNICA GONZÁLEZ ARREDONDO

Translator's Introduction

Allison deFreese

GREEN FIRES OF THE SPIRITS (*Verde fuego de espirítus*), the book in which Verónica González Arredondo's "[Water in the Sky]" originally appears, is a unique collection of verse that is not easy to classify. It is "at once one book and many," as Verónica González Arredondo announces in her brief introduction to the text.

The six cycles of poems in the book—all referencing weather or water—forge a new, and altogether original, score. In these pages, Verónica González Arredondo debuts an unmistakably beautiful and haunting style all her own. Though the writing in *Green Fires* can at times be light, magical and entrancing, this is a world where teeth hide in the flowers and there are jaws at the bottom of the staircase; where a cherry tree may produce both cheerful red fruit and ash as gray as the fog that transports us back to WWII, the Holocaust or Hiroshima; and where an airy dream of dragonflies may end abruptly when the dreamer opens a bedroom door and finds herself perched at the edge of a precipice. These pieces are a house of horrors staged in a dollhouse and yet, as Véronique Elfakir suggests in her French-language review of another of Verónica's books (Élise Person's translation of *Ese cuerpo no soy/Je ne suis pas ce corps*), the resilience in these poems is unmistakable. VGA's verse is: "a force that cannot be extinguished. In the shadow of this void [she] unravels words that become a song of lost life, uncovering among the remains stories of abbreviated endings that sound an alarm we refuse to hear today" (*Terre à ciel: poésie d'aujourd'hui*).

For more than three years, I had searched for a translation project from Latin America exploring the themes related to social justice that Verónica González Arredondo explores in her poems: immigration, human rights, and the disappearances of girls and women. Considering the relevance of Verónica González Arredondo's writing today, I feel fortunate and honored to have the opportunity to translate her poetry, especially given her leadership as a human rights advocate of the world stage and the fact that her work is the forerunner of wider poetic and social movements; from #metoo to #SiMeMatan/#IfTheyKillMe—a hashtag addressing femicide and violence against women. As she guides us through both the underworlds and the heavens while providing a voice for those who are often silenced, Verónica González Arredondo's subtle and lyrical activism brings a message timelier and more urgent than ever in 2021.

[Water in the Sky] from *Green Fires of the Spirits*

In the room
we keep looking at each other's entrails
we are totally absorbed

You ask about the chrysanthemum garden
about the turquoise lake
about my birth

All I did was caress you
in a landscape of hummingbirds,
and then I fled

We embrace
with our entrails showing

Intoxicated by the heat of a single body
and dampened by a warm mist—

the gray hand that conceals us,
caressing us like a tree filled with cherries
and ash

There are two girls in the garden
      one whose face is ashen
      the other's   smudged with soot

They are two swans:
one black and the other white,
sharing an orchid as their backscratcher

What game are they playing?

They make the world visible
      with their invisible world

I remember the night of black lilies
it was raining

You took the windows off the wall
to fall back asleep

And while you were sleeping
the room filled with feathers

Are wasps really ants?

I heard them in the wee hours
smashing their heads against the glass

At daybreak, only their remains
lay scattered in the bedroom

In that room
we forgot to look out the window
where we might find ourselves
inside the abyss
of the cherry tree in bloom
in the owl's eyes
in the sleepless hail
in the corners of the tree

A whirlwind
left us without a room
        without a window
        without a gray tree

I am the one looking at you from eyes set like gemstones

I am the fog

From ash the flowers of Edo grow
saffron-colored with spots of violet
as if the earth had a memory

They are silently screaming
                              : house
                              : body

Cut to the ground during the night of the fire
the flowers of Edo
consume everything

translated from the Spanish by Allison deFreese

CHARLES O. HARTMAN

The Donkey in the Air

While I stood as usual,
as usual they added stones
to the back of the cart
presumably, presumably

behind the axle, so,
not suddenly but at some tipping point,
the market square began to fall away.
Look at that bell tower.

Who would have guessed.
Meanwhile the chest, supposed to hang
from the firm arch of the spine,
ached in harness. The clapper lolled.

If I've been sure of anything
it's footing. Now I find
less traction than a swimming dog.
Could try what the birds do. No.

You're gaping. I would too.
I have a couple of ideas
which unfortunately involve hands.
You capped fool with the camera:

why not scurry to unload stones,
return me to the useful earth?
No, this is too much fun. Snap on,
develop, print, make a postcard

to amuse your tourists
from Pakistan to Naples,
till it slips into the fist
of a Greek who will do a trick

to transpose my hung,
ridiculously elevated body
into a picture of his own
village to shame the locals.

Then one of you can turn it into words,
also good for bandying about—
always glad to be of whatever service,
in the quarry of your decades.

At last, since nobody wants
to deal with me dead, somebody starts
to lift off counterweights.
No plummet,

just hind legs, a little kicking,
watch the tail, then fore,
back in the belonging dust.
That's settled.

MARTHA SILANO

Like Picasso's *Weeping Woman*

my face is both straight-on and sideways.
Like the walls of the house next door,
the days accrue, accrue, accrue,

until it's time for the terror lilies to bloom,
until every speck of interstellar dust
has fallen between the breasts

of Sister Domenica, Patron Saint
of Plagues. Like the tiniest
asteroid moon, one mile across,

we're pulled by gravity
whether we like it or not.
You ask me what I pray for;

I tell you I don't. That it's more
like wishing on a fisherman's brow,
nodding to the cheery-fucking-upping

robins. Straight-on and sideways:
is that a band? The ache is nameless,
its color stomach-in-knots pink,

blue like the diagram explaining
how the virus hatchets our happy
like a solar system of woe.

Each day brings a new carcass
for a turkey vulture to munch,
a red line resembling the one

that ran up my father's arm
when he got that infected bite.
Like a dentist office receptionist's

dreams, like an old-man's tooth,
there's a fissure in the fuselage,
a viral Hiroshima in every blessed

bowl. In gym class, Miss Joyce
called out the steps: *Apart, together*
together. Together, together, apart.

JACKSON HOLBERT

Lithium

I was cutting my brother's hair when my father
crashed his Ford F-150 into the living room.
He was blazing drunk and tried
to get out through the driver's side door
but it was too bent so he shimmied over the gearshift
and got out through the passenger side and
immediately started kissing my mother deeply.
My brother and I were embarrassed
so we got in the car and turned on the radio.

Lithium

My doctor gave me lithium yesterday. Thanks, doctor! Today I woke up shaking, and very scared. I'm scared of a lot of things, but I'm mainly scared of having a seizure because that would mean I couldn't drive, and that would be bad because driving is my job. I drive a garbage truck on weekdays, and some weeks I even drive on weekends. If I have a seizure they won't let me drive for half a year, which means I'd get fired, which means I wouldn't be a garbage man anymore, and I am a garbage man. It's what I do. I'm the garbage man. The other issue is that I'm on a lot of other medicines—some legal and some illegal. And some of them are weird plants from southeast Asia so none of the medical websites say anything about them, so I have to go to those weird forums that look like they are from 1998 and where people post things like "Meth-psychosis stories . . . you know you have one . . ." and "can you fax acid?" I do like the forums. They make me feel like I'm a part of a community. One of those weird communities you hear about in songs, where a bunch of druggies all live in the same house and shake together on the couch and fight over bread and hot dogs and dirty lettuce. I lived in one of those houses when I was in college. It always calmed me down, living there, because I knew at any time there were enough drugs in that house to kill me.

LISA LOW

Cut

In the mirror I watch the scissors,
the stylist's Crush-colored pixie. I love her

whiteness, her broken-in vintage
jeans, the salon's whiteness. I'm not

stringing together a poorly-constructed
sentence like at a Chinese salon,

not feeling bad I don't know more.
My mother explaining me, my whiteness.

The stylist tilts my head sideways. I hold
still like a good listener or student

or daughter. I watch my hair fall away,
her checkerboard shirt, the fallen black

pieces. I miss all the Asian hair models
in magazines. She says, Look straight

ahead. I look ahead but in the mirror I'm tilted
downwards. Is this my default look? I picture

myself walking alone in public, my head
dropped down like I'm folding inwards, as if

bowing. Am I always trying to be so small?
Have you seen *Bird Box* on Netflix? she asks.

I don't know why I don't say I hate horror
movies. She says, Let's take your cape off

so you don't look like a floating head. But I
don't mind. The cape itches me but I love

where my arms have disappeared.

CASSANDRA J. BRUNER

Dewclaw Child, Hibernating in the Basement Darkroom

Down here
                              I learn the way absence latches
            onto descending motes
                              of mold. Learn
      to time the exaltation of my joints
                              re-aligning to the beat
            of the soil, pocketing open—

      Anymore, I keep myself cellared, a rationer
of bruised nectarines & lavender sprigs.
                              Some mornings,
      I craft dioramas from anemic tufts
                              of insulation—
            depicting me, for want
                              of live adders, gone rapturous & tangoing
            with snakehusks. Or the county fair as scene
                              for the resurrection
      of the dead, bloomed up in flash floods &
                              warbling every name for
            YHWH & Lucifer.
                              Or a hometown without
      need of hideaways—

My vision stares back & always fails
                              to see its lack. Believe me
            I never wanted
                              this end-times cadence. This sentence

naming the bone but never its

                                       sponge, pores, cavities. All those
            villages built   around emptiness—

How many nights did we—the left behind—rise

                                aboveground & roam
                 the unattended earth, searching
      for signs of the departed,
                     their imprint cinching
our sternums shut?
             I'd photograph the clues—clawmarked
                 orchards, bucketfuls of forked tongues,
    snaggleteeth caught in bumpers—& distribute
                        the prints
      at our next outing like manifestos.
By the time I realized these were
                 traces without pattern, without
     answer, I'd bleached my hands in fixer &
                   nearly remade
   my claws into molds of silver gelatin.
                My heart, a moonburnt filmroll,
     shuttered ceaselessly in my throat—

                  It shutters still
as I whisper belated apologies to the birchroot
    reaching through
            the eastern wall. As if
  my words could funnel
       through ventricles & shared
           claybeds, sounding a countywide
    broadcast when the hostas blossom & peal—

             Forgive me,
I never meant to give up, but restlessness washboards me
           senseless. It begs me

to sleep so I might wake to sundials

in reverse. To a memory re-tinted,
with each cocoon of frost reducing

to foam.

RENÉE KAY

the oxford guide to owning a body

i heard that once a god told the stars to wake / & they never slept again / i tell myself to leave the house / but trace the edges of the bed / splintering pine into my fingerprints / if history repeats itself / i am bound / to end up the architect / of my own massacre / my blood trying to split from itself / & i too am often trying to leave my body / the first time / i was six / & floating / above myself in the faded green / of a hotel bed / thinking / death looked peaceful /

so yes / maybe i should never have been trusted with one / but i am repenting / reading the guidebook / my notes in the margins / all questions curving up

the body can be operated at will

(whose)

the body remembers

(does it forgive)

the body is the history of the bodies
it's made of

(how many people have died to give my blood a home)

some days i try to enchant myself / most sacred rituals involve a love of numbers / if i tattoo infinity on my arm / the skin will still rot / it doesn't matter if i'm inside it / i mean i can spoil / the great beyond / it is just that space right past the edge / of your fingertips

MORGAN HAMILL

Osteogenesis Imperfecta Type XVII & Others

I can't put my finger on the sensation of breaking. Perhaps shock
as my toes scrape concrete in my neighbor's backyard.

Perhaps the slow rasp of palms on pavement
as I lower myself inch-by-inch into frigid water.

Above the watermark, my skin is at first hot, sticky from sun—
as I slip beneath, tight. Frozen.

My mother, who brought me to this pool, says cold's first brunt
is good pain.

I don't think I know what that means: good pain. I spend so much
time here that the ends of my hair bleach and break.

Perhaps she means my shortness of breath in the frigid blue water,
the top of my soaked head radiating heat before touch.

No. I don't think

I know what she means.
I know only the drift of leaf

litter and the ache of my toes
touching bottom.

JULIAN ZABALBEASCOA

Distant Laughter

WHEN I CAME UPON THE Spanish Nationalist soldier, he was sitting on a log and seemed at peace. Surprisingly, I didn't hate him for this. In fact, since deciding to go through with it, I'd been buoyed by a euphoria I hoped would remain beyond this day, which I intended to be my last.

The Nationalist was smoking a cigarette or thumbing some pebbles or reciting poetry to the shrubs—I couldn't tell, as his back was to me, and I had time to decide where to place my crosshairs, choosing to shoot the log directly beneath him. If I missed, the bullet would rip into his ass, but I didn't miss, and he jumped, his arms flailing as he fell forward to run. My thinking had been that after passing on this lightness to someone, thereby guaranteeing its preservation, I'd stick my rifle butt on the ground and lean over it, pressing the barrel to the spot between my throat and bottom of my chin. The headaches had become unbearable, the incessant high-pitched frequency in my ears I couldn't escape, the burden and tension of survival. We are each issued a role in this life, and there was only one relief from mine. But I couldn't do it with that Nationalist falling every ten meters, making negligible distance between us.

Unfortunately, the others—my brothers in arms—roused by my rifle shot, rushed to me and took aim. Watching the Nationalist's desperate and frantic efforts, I understood it was not only this euphoria he strove to carry forward, but that I had given him his life back and he was now attempting the same for me. If I get away, his pitiable try at flight told me, you can't put the barrel under your chin. "Come on," I was surprised to hear myself saying. And: "Faster." Our bullets started for him but, as I said, he couldn't go a few meters without tripping, which was likely what kept saving him. Several times he'd tumble in tandem with a rifle shot, and I'd think, with neither sadness nor relief, so that's it, the two of us have been caught, at which point he'd crawl forward, each limb out of concert with the other, stumble to get himself upright and soon skid onto his face once more. Maybe a piece of the log had penetrated his leg. Nothing else could explain his difficulty in staying on his feet.

I suppose it would have been easier for one of us to run after him and dig a knife into his back, but who was to guess he'd continue falling as often as he did? I began thinking the others were missing on purpose so as to prolong this comedy, up to the horizon if possible, and if that was the case, he and I had more in common than I could have imagined—somebody, something, found humor in delaying our end.

Isidro, another of my fellow soldiers, bumped me as he went to a knee. He pressed the rifle butt snug to his shoulder, and I saw that this one was it, the line was direct, a tight thread knotted straight from his rifle to the Nationalist. I held my breath. I waited. But Isidro paused and cocked his head slightly to study me in his periphery. He was working the whole thing out—that was my life, too, in the round eyesight of his stock's end.

There was still time for him to ease his finger against the trigger, nothing had happened to that line, but he lowered his rifle and looked at me directly and nodded, his lips screwing to the left side of his face, an expression that said: *vale*, let's see, sure maybe he was a murderer of children, but who knows, he might be the one to save us all, let's see. I nodded, too, then I laughed, realizing how foolish I'd been, how I'd been seeing the world through a pinhole these past weeks.

The sky was a muddy sort of steel, the color of water off our hands whenever we found the rare fountain. A few more shots went after the Nationalist, but the bullets wouldn't have been able to do much from that distance. It was like scaring off a coyote. So he got away. And what can I say? I could have drunk the sky. Isidro was still nodding, his lips turned down, his thoughts finding my ears: let's see, he kept saying. Let's see.

And I wish it had lasted—this *let's see*, the not knowing how the war would go, the chance it might—finally!—turn in our favor. However, hours later, the Nationalists surprised us, starting their offensive. Christ, how their planes split the sky while they shelled us. The only faces I can recall within that deafening intensity were the faces of those the shrapnel tore apart, the resigned look each held in their eyes the moment before it happened. A look that told me they'd always known fate had determined this would be their end, that none of this came as a surprise, regardless of how they tensed when shrapnel met flesh.

It, fate, explained why I was among the few taken prisoner. A ridiculous confidence possessed me—I was the sort not allowed to die. "Don't worry," I whispered to Isidro, "we won't be executed but instead put to work, chained to each other, toiling on some project meant to bring forward the Nationalists' still-born vision."

I was playing my role, and this made the next few days of sleeplessness and starvation a bearable experience. I knew how the rest would go and there was some comfort in that. A diminishing supply, as it so happened.

Soon, the headaches returned and the world was once more reduced to that jaw-clenching high frequency. I wanted out. Thankfully, orders came for our captors to move camp. A three-day march to the Ebro where the oddsmakers predicted our side's final defeat. We prisoners wouldn't be joining them. Unlike the four others, this came as a relief to me. "I was wrong," I told Isidro, perhaps too giddily. "There is no prearranged story. We are in nobody's hands."

But then, of course, it all went sideways.

We were chugging down a road to the pit that had been dug for the five of us. We sat in the lorry's back, encircled by seven Nationalist soldiers who were to serve as the firing squad, along with the one up front in the driver's seat who was easing off the gas for the sodden bend ahead, when the earth suddenly ripped open in a deafening crack. A golden light flooded the world and flew me away, into a blackness that was upside down, or, at the very least, not right side up.

Slowly, my vision returned, and I groaned as I pushed myself off the ground. I was in a field where a few trees stuck up solemnly like quiet statues in a garden— an attempt at a forest. Maybe somewhere ahead I'd find a grey- and wild-bearded man with pristine wings who'd begin a recitation of my sins. But someone else was next to me, another of the prisoners, Isidro. He was on his hands and knees, throwing up, and behind us I saw the lorry on its back feeding a fire, the heat of which I couldn't feel. I couldn't feel anything, not even as I stood and searched for the others.

Isidro spun me around by the shoulder, and I remembered that we'd been sitting side-by-side in the lorry, catapulted in that moment the others were pulped. I probably looked as scorched and singed as he did. You and I are not allowed to die, I tried to tell him, but some part of my mouth wouldn't obey. His eyes were covered by a film of blood. They were the size of cannonballs, and they told me: run. Or maybe he was shouting it. I don't know. A pair of hands had been slapped over my ears ever since awakening. I swatted at them but only came away with blood, then tilted my head and smiled. The high frequency whistle was gone. Isidro pulled me forward. We should have been hobbling, but I doubt I've ever run so quickly. There was no reason to. None of those unidentifiable parts back there were chasing us.

We sprinted among the trees, the branches painlessly slapping my face, and gradually I began to hear something, not the ceaseless ringing that had long plagued me but distant laughter, a muffled laughter I couldn't outrun. I understood with terror it was the laughter of a graceless, unpitying god. A laughter letting me know there was no way out.

It was, it turns out, Isidro hollering with a crazed smile the remaining branches couldn't tear from him. Ahead I saw the full light of day. Where are we going, I yelled, or tried to. He didn't answer but kept howling at the great clearing that opened before us.

Translation Folio

JI YUN

Translators' Introduction

John Yu Branscum & Yi Izzy Yu

IMAGINE IF A PUBLIC FIGURE with the cultural heft of a Benjamin Franklin had not only overseen such national departments as those of War and Public Works, had not only been one of the most celebrated scholars and poets of their time, but had also—after experiencing several otherworldly events—taken it upon themselves to investigate eighteenth-century X-files and write about them with a story-telling flair that reads like a combination of H. P. Lovecraft and Zhuangzi.

In China, there was such a figure. His name was Ji Yun (纪昀).

Beginning in 1789, when he was sixty-five years old, Ji Yun published five volumes of weird tales. In one stroke, they revolutionized Chinese horror and creative nonfiction, revitalized Chinese occult philosophy, and offered the reader a vision of China never before depicted: one poised between old ways and new, where repeating rifles shared the world with Tibetan black-magic shamans, Jesuit astronomers rubbed elbows with alleged fox spirits, and a vibrant sex trade of the reanimated dead was rumored to be conducted in the dark of night.

Astoundingly, Ji Yun claimed several of these stories were autobiographical accounts or records of his friends' and family's first-hand encounters with the numinous and the anomalous.

To be sure, some of the stories—while terrifying or gruesome—seem plausible: a famine-struck town that sells butchered women like livestock, a pear-stealing cat out for revenge, a poet's dangerous, rat-exploding aphrodisiac. Others though directly challenge our understanding of reality: precognitive dreams, mystical transformations, sentient fogs that linger after the execution of rebels, abductions by flying orbs, and a research center where everything is so mystically connected that an opened gate can cause a parent's death.

There are also accounts of the terrifying "sha" (the strange entity into which the soul transforms after death), the "jiangshi" (the Chinese vampire), yeti, the occult secrets of the red sect of Tibetan Buddhism, and nightmarish tales of soul swapping.

Ji Yun's claim that such stories are true is of course baffling for many contemporary readers, as is his decision to include them in collections that contain other narratives he explicitly identifies as fables. To understand his reasoning, it's important to understand the strange tale genre he wrote in: "zhiguai xiaoshuo" (志怪小说), typically shortened to "zhiguai."

Zhiguai first rose to popularity during the Han dynasty (206 BCE to 220 CE). At this time, they took two primary forms. The first was strange personal or historical accounts too odd or heretical for the emperor's official library archives. These were catalogued as "shadow histories." The second form was personal accounts AND fables or parables used by Taoists and Buddhists to illustrate metaphysical concepts. These were catalogued as philosophy.

The word "zhiguai" functionally translates to "true weird tales." But this description glosses over zhiguai collections' typical inclusion of diverse materials—a diversity that became over time even more wide-ranging than just "fables" and "personal accounts." The narratives found in collections range from eyewitness and hearsay testimony about paranormal encounters, debunking of the same, urban legends, and bizarre sex tales to discussions of scientific phenomena and physical and mental prodigies, fables or parables intended to convey allegorical rather than literal truths, lyrical essays on philosophical and legal matters, and narratives that sit between these genres and consequently challenge our literary classifications.

Despite this diversity, nearly all zhiguai share commonalities. They are short-shorts that blend spare, evocative narratives with brief meditations on the strange. Furthermore, they are not meant to be stand-alone pieces but to convey their truth inductively and cumulatively through functioning as one small part of a larger collection. Thus, they're meant to work like multiple eyewitness reports. While perhaps individually flawed due to misremembering, deceit, or exaggeration, nevertheless collectively they are thought to still offer a testament to deep truths and metaphysical principles. Thus, ultimately what unites zhiguai is their aesthetic use as occult technology, their incitement in readers of a sense of sublime weirdness that alerts them to previously unseen and frequently unsettling dimensions of reality.

In his 1791 introduction to the zhiguai collection *Qiudeng Conghua*, the scholar Hu Gaowang puts it this way: "Zhiguai are to be respected because they possess the power to awaken readers to the deep principles of reality. They do this by fixing their attention on that which they previously looked away from, while filling their hearts with fear and awe."

This is not to say that all zhiguai writers adhered to such lofty goals. In fact, by Ji Yun's time, many authors simply used the genre's weirdness to entertain and consequently fictionalized at will. A harsh critic of this development, Ji Yun actively worked against it. While he embraced fables that functioned like philosophical parables, he turned his attention largely to writing about true accounts based on eyewitness or secondhand testimony, expressed skepticism when called for, and was as invested in depicting social and concrete details from the real world and the psychology of fraud as he was in sharing accounts of the strange.

Ji Yun's tales are easily the equal of other legendary collections, such as *Arabian Nights*, *Strange Stories from a Chinese Studio*, *Kwaidan*, or *Grimms' Fairy Tales*—in terms of artistry and influence. They include ground-breaking pieces that establish the mythology of the "jiangshi" (Chinese vampire) and the "huli jing" (fox spirit), predecessors to contemporary alien parasite and alien abduction tales, and accounts of astral travel and body swapping that presage modern narratives about journeys through computer simulations and downloadable minds. Thus they prove themselves to be foundational works of Chinese horror, fantasy, and science fiction—even as they stretch how these genres are understood.

Astoundingly, their contribution to creative nonfiction is just as striking. Ji Yun's liminal corpus contains masterful examples of flash, lyrical, meditative, and montage forms, as well as forays into crime writing. It showcases the Chinese tradition of occult writing too, particularly of the weird creative nonfiction variety and sheds light on Chinese theories about dreams and the spirit world, other dimensions of reality, spiritual development, and the mysterious workings of "ganying" (the mystical resonance between things).

In the end though, Ji Yun's voice is the most enthralling thing about his tales. It is not a loud, showy voice. Its power is found in its restraint and subtlety, in its suggestiveness and the quiet application of a Confucian's skeptical rigor to traditionally Taoist and Buddhist metaphysical concerns. And too there is in it a concern with the plight of the defenseless, with human grief and struggle, so that his ghosts reveal themselves to be very much human and his humans turn out to be as mysterious and haunted as ghosts.

What Things Become

MY LATE GRANDMOTHER, LADY CAO, told a story about another Cao—Cao Hua-chun, the infamous Ming Dynasty royal eunuch.

For his burial, the eunuch's family dressed him lavishly, including a jade belt cinched around his waist. A few years after his funeral, a cream-colored snake with a slightly darker and unusual segmented pattern was frequently seen lurking around his tomb—as if it had a nest nearby.

Eventually, the eunuch's tomb and gravesite were severely damaged by a flood that laid waste to that part of the country, and he needed to be reburied. When his shattered coffin was picked from him and the dirt brushed away, except for natural decay the eunuch was found to be the same as when he was entombed. His jewelry, wine and grain jars, and funerary replicas were still with him. But one thing was missing—the jade belt. Those who had seen the snake realized then that its pattern was exactly like that of the missing belt.

One can't help but wonder if a snake's soul found a way to make the jade belt into a body through some mystical process of transmutation or if the jade found a way to become a snake. Whatever the case, things constantly change into other things, and this is a matter that invokes both awe and sadness.

Red in Darkness

SOME TREES ARE NOT TREES. This is clearly indicated by an incident that occurred at a school in Tingzhou, Fujian. A row of trees lay in front of the examination hall. The two tallest were ancient cedars that dated back to the Tang Dynasty. Their broad and thick branches stretched so far out over the hall that they could be seen from every window.

I was serving as the school's superintendent at the time of the incident. Right after I was hired, I was told about the old cedars. Being of a very advanced age, they were said to have developed souls. One of the administrative staff even suggested that I bow to them, as if they were important officials, so as not to cause any offense. However, I didn't do this. I wasn't sure the trees were anything more than trees. And even if they did harbor souls, I didn't feel like they would care if I bowed or not—especially since there was no established protocol when it came to such situations. It seemed to me that it was best to just let them be.

One night though I was walking across the examination hall deck in the moonlight when I felt something watching me. I looked up to see two women dressed in red robes floating in the mist swirling around the tree tops. Both bowed solemnly to me and then started to fade away. I immediately shouted for my assistant to hurry and bear witness to the phantoms. He made it out just in time to glimpse the figures before they vanished completely.

The next day, I made the bow that I had neglected when I first arrived. To make up for my earlier neglect, I also had the following poem written on the examination hall gate:

Certain things appear only when the darkness is deep.
Some of these things nod respectfully.
Some of these things wear red.
In this, am I not speaking of you?

Carriage

THE SPRING IS FULL OF storms. Sometimes, it will rain for a week in the capital city, and many of the roads leading to the city turn into mud. The road that runs from Huangcun Village to Fengyi Gate is one of those routinely affected by the spring rains. It was on this road one darkening afternoon that Li Xiu of Gu'an County spotted a flash of white face and dark hair ahead of him while shouting at his carriage horses to pick up their pace.

The stranger turned to the sound of the carriage. Xiu saw that he was quite young—about fifteen or sixteen-years-old—as beautiful as a woman and blessed with soft, glowing skin. Imagining he saw desire for a warm ride in the boy's expression, Xiu—never the sort to deny himself pleasure—pulled at his horses' reins and invited the boy into the carriage.

The boy shyly accepted Xiu's offer and sat beside him in the carriage. At first, Xiu's efforts to woo the youth were limited to significant glances. But when they stopped at a tiny village for food, Xiu strategically treated the boy to some snacks. While the boy eagerly wolfed down the food, Xiu flagrantly remarked on the boy's good looks. The boy played dumb though, limiting his responses to more blushes and demure smiles.

Then a thing happened when they were back in the carriage and again on their way. Suddenly, the boy looked different, as if someone had made a copy of him—exact except for a few crucial details—and swapped this copy out for the genuine article without Xiu noticing until that moment. Now that he did notice, the difference was palpable. The lips were less rosy and the cheeks less fat. The look in the boy's eyes was blunter and less shy.

Initially, Xiu managed to convince himself that the boy's changed appearance was a visual effect generated by the fading light of evening—which generally tended to make everything look a little older. But soon the differences became so obvious they were undeniable. By the time they had travelled ten li more, the "boy's" upper lip and chin were covered with hairs, and his hands and arms had turned lean, knotted, and muscled.

Boy no longer, the stranger had somehow become a man in his twenties. Unnerved, Xiu abandoned his romantic intentions. By the time they reached the city, and the carriage was rattling by the West Gate of Nanyuan, the boy had become a middle-aged man: wrinkled forehead, receding hairline, rough skin, a beard massive and black.

And then at last they reached the inn where Xiu intended to stay and the carriage rattled to a stop. By this point, the stranger looked nothing like he had at the start of the trip. What had been fresh and young, blossoming and tempting, was now toothless, shriveled, and gray.

The gray thing took Xiu's limp hand between its own and pressed. As it did, Xiu felt panicked and disordered as if he himself was a vulnerable young boy and the stranger an old letch—so that for a terrible moment Xiu felt the horror of what he himself was.

"Thank you for your attention this whole trip," continued the stranger. "I appreciated the hinted offers and was quite flattered. But, alas, I've slept with time too long to be interested in sleeping with man anymore. Such desires have been washed away along with much else."

The old man then barked out a laugh and disappeared into the night.

Xiu related this encounter to his younger cousin who worked in our family's kitchen for a while. I was so struck by it that I researched the experience to see if I could match the behavior of the demon he encountered to any other accounts. I found no match to anything in history. His species remains mysterious.

Beneath a Green Coat

THIS IS A STORY ABOUT an event that transpired at the country estate of my grand-father—as told to me by my mother.

One summer, something began to dance violently in front of the family compound late at night, bewildering all who lived there. While it was clear the "something" was dancing, it was not clear what the something was. It danced in the shadows. And whenever anyone ran toward it for a closer look, it ran off.

Finally, one evening when the moonlight was streaming down, the household got a good look at the thing from the windows of the main house. However, that glimpse did little to unravel its mystery. From a headless turtle-shaped torso that glinted silver beneath a green brocade coat, four spindly limbs emerged. These approximated arms and legs but culminated in lumps rather than fingers and toes. No one had ever seen such a thing before.

Several days later, Ziheng Gong—my mother's uncle—assigned several of his tallest and stoutest servants, armed with knives, clubs, and ropes, to crouch outside of the front gate in the bushes and await the creature's arrival.

Soon, the creature made its nightly appearance and started in on its dance. Immediately, the group of men leapt. It took off at a surprising speed though, flashed through the compound front gate, and up to the top of an outside staircase where it hid in the shadows.

A lamp was shone on the shadows to confront the creature. But there was no creature there. Instead, the lamp's light shone down on something leaning against the back wall near the staircase, something wrapped in green silk. The fabric was unwrapped. Beneath it was a tiny silver boat with four wheels.

The boat was identified as a large toy one from years before when the family's fortunes were greater, and they could afford as many expensive toys as the children wanted. The dancing fiend's green coat was the silk cloth the boat was wrapped in, and its limbs must have bubbled up from the wheels. There was no part of the boat that could serve as a head though. That was why it lacked one.

An old servant woman later said, "That toy disappeared while I was still a young girl. I remember because all the servants my age were beaten for the crime of stealing the toys of our master's children. I thought it had just been lost, but I guess someone stole it and hid it in this room. And here it stayed, lost and forgotten, until after a long time it became the creature we all saw. Perhaps anything that's forgotten by those that once cherished it can become demonic."

Shortly after this, the toy was melted into more than thirty taels of silver.

•

SOME people find such transformations hard to accept. But Confucius—as recorded in Gan Bao's *Anecdotes on the Sacred and the Supernatural*—taught that animals and such things as grass and trees can change into human-like creatures once they reach a certain age. Why shouldn't they? After all, everything is made of the same five elements, and it is quite common for substances to take on new natures with age, such as rice aging into wine. And once you think of a monster as a collection of changed and aged elements, why be scared? Such creatures are probably no more dangerous than those things from which they sprouted.

Yellow Leaf

EARLY AUTUMN IN JIAHE COUNTY is beautiful. The air is both warm and cool, the trees blaze with vibrant colors, and there is a lake in the area that is a very lovely place to visit. These charms brought Wang Kunxia, a Taoist priest of my acquaintance, to hike there one morning and stray from the popular path to explore the far side of the lake.

A few hours into Kunxia's walk, the woods suddenly gave way to a bamboo grove and then to the remnants of an orchard and an abandoned mansion. Excited, he exhausted himself exploring his discovery and decided to take a nap in the mansion's overgrown garden.

Except Kunxia didn't quite fall asleep. When one sleeps in the usual way, one's spirit is no longer bound to fixed forms or the laws of time and space. Then, imagination and reality, and dreams and spiritual experiences, freely mingle. Sleeping and waking are thus distinct ways of being. But sometimes a person will get stuck between realms. This is what happened to Kunxia. He was limited by the laws of the physical world and still tethered to his physical body. Yet, at the same time, he could perceive the spirit world. So it is that his spirit looked up from his resting physical form to see a ghost—dressed in old-fashioned, powder-blue robes—bowing with his hands intertwined in front of Kunxia.

When the ghost saw that Kunxia saw him, he smiled and bowed. "Welcome," he said. "It has been years since I had a visitor, and decades since anyone has actually slept here. I am delighted to find you. Which is to say please don't fear me."

Kunxia relaxed at the man's words, although they identified him as a ghost, and he asked him where he was from.

"My family name is Zhang," the ghost said. "Originally I come from Leiyang, but I moved here during the Yuan dynasty. When I died, I decided to stay rather than returning home because this land and I are well suited to one another. We've been a good match for a long time—long enough for the lake to grow larger then smaller again, and for the garden to have over a dozen different owners, then none, and finally to be forgotten by all."

"Isn't it rare for someone to remain a ghost for so long?" asked Kunxia. "I thought most spirits move on to be reborn."

The ghost nodded. "True. Many spirits feel out of sorts if they remain this near the earthly plane without occupying matter themselves. This is not my sentiment though. Whether dead or alive, one remains oneself. A living person can see mountains, rivers, forests, the moon, and other sights. So too can a ghost. A living person can lay on a hillside at night to be clarified by the immensity of the stars and then write a poem. So too a ghost. Therefore, in no way is a ghost inferior. Indeed, there are many secluded places in the mortal realm too isolated or dangerous, too deep or too high, for a human to venture. In these, ghosts, however, can wander and witness in the silence of the night and the dawn.

"The only things we ghosts lack is the ability to touch what we see or to keep a souvenir from our adventures. This inability disturbs those who cling to life because they can't imagine no longer being able to embrace a lover or a child, or to drink wine or eat fruit. Such a person upon entering the nether world feels unbearably lonely and impotent—like a high official sent back to his home village after losing office.

"But there are people who have always lived in the countryside. There are people who have never held rank. There are people in the world who have remained unattached to family or friends for their whole life, people who sit silently while others chat and drink. They need no company. They are content to dig their own wells and plow their own land. They find nothing to feel sad about."

"Even if you feel that way though, the cycle of death and rebirth are part of the deep design. How did you escape it?" asked Kunxia.

"By realizing the greatest secret. Everything is a choice. Whether you're talking about a ghost avoiding rebirth or a person declining a position, all of it is a choice. Once you understand this, you are free."

After the ghost finished speaking, both he and Kunxia were quiet for a time, each lost in their own thoughts. Then Kunxia said, "One who is as fond of sightseeing as you must have composed a lot of poems."

"I chant a line or two when in the mood," said the ghost. "But I seldom complete a poem. I find myself forgetting them almost as soon as I begin to compose them. Consequently, there are only four or five poems that I've written that I can remember."

Kunxia's eyes flickered with interest, and so the ghost recited:

The fading sunlight leaves the mountain empty.
Chant this while all goes dark and vast again:
There is no inside;
There is no outside.

When the ghost finished its stanza, Kunxia cried out in admiration and implored him to recite more. Flattered, the ghost agreed. But it just managed to utter the phrase "yellow leaf" when a loud noise from the side of the lake awakened Kunxia. Sitting up, he looked at the lake and saw some fishermen yelling greetings to one another as they pulled creatures from the water.

translated from the Chinese by John Yu Branscum and Yi Izzy Yu

DUSTIN PARSONS

The Handsome, Benevolent Brother of Vlad the Impaler: An Apology

For this apology you need to know that Huffy bicycles manufactured during a certain time period in the 80s attached the handlebars to the frame with a single front headset compression nut, chunky and hexagonal, collaring the handlebar tube like a choker.

For this apology you will also need to know that Vlad the Impaler, the brutal 15th century Wallachian ruler upon whom Dracula was based, had a younger brother.

It also helps to know that my brother, two years younger than me, had whispy long dirty blond hair that the wind picked up and pushed forward at times as he rode on the back of my bicycle home from school.

This apology isn't possible unless you know the two boys who took my bicycle from me were significantly older, maybe in high school. They wore blue jeans and I seem to remember they both wore brown t-shirts.

This apology was written while reading about Radu cel Frumos, AKA Radu the Fair, AKA Radu the Handsome, the brother of Vlad the Impaler. This apology was written while also musing on the ways that two brothers might find very different paths in life.

Apologies are impossible without a respect for the past.

This apology is influenced by a fact I uncovered: that Radu and Vlad were offered as collateral to the Ottoman Empire by their father, Vlad II, so he could have Ottoman support in his return to the Wallachian lands after being ousted in 1442. The boys were raised and educated there together. Radu made a number of friends amongst the Ottomans. The boy who would grow up to be Vlad the Impaler did not.

Apologies, sincere apologies, also require acceptance that you've done something wrong.

Our apology's drama unfolds behind a Methodist church, in that paved alley in a small town in Kansas, where now I understand there was, hidden away from the general traffic of town and the prying eyes of adults, a choke point for bully ambushes. The brown-shirted boys were polite as they could be at first, asking if they could ride my bicycle. I didn't think I had the right to refuse, and gave over my brown bicycle. Against the light brown of the limestone of the church, my vision turns to earth. They rode, in turns, the bicycle down the alley. They weaved around, and they rode in tandem, one on the small bolts that protruded from the axle of the rear tire.

The apology only tangentially requires that you know I have two sons who fight bitterly at times, but love each other very much, and more directly requires you know that though I love my own brother, who was on the bicycle with me as we left school for home, we rarely talk and have little or nothing in common. This is not to say I don't appreciate his life, or he mine, but that we are two men in middle age now who could at least share a beer and small talk, pictures of our kids, like men at a bar waiting on their dinner bills.

To this apology's surprise, Radu led 40,000 Ottoman cavalry into Wallachia to dethrone Vlad after it became clear his brother's rule was cruel and brutal. While Radu chased Vlad through their home country, Vlad burned and scavenged everything in his path so the Ottoman soldiers couldn't use any of the supplies to continue their pursuit. Vlad earned his name "the Impaler" because of the forest of men, women, and children he staked to the ground, called "The Forest of the Dead." Radu halted, mouth agape, and turned his forces back when they encountered the atrocity.

But this apology returns to the boys and the bike. You no doubt remember the compression nut that holds the handlebars on, and you may have deduced by now that this nut was not there because I'd taken my bicycle apart and put it together so many times the threads were stripped, allowing the handlebars to come loose of the frame with a simple yank upward. When they tried to pull the front tire off the ground to pop a wheelie, the handlebars flashed upward like a divining rod, and the boys were deposited onto the pavement, giving one a slick wet gash near his ear. You might think this apology is for them.

The older boys, thinking they had ruined the bicycle, threw down the U-shaped piece of metal, got up and ran away. It felt, at the time, like a victory, and even now I think they got what they deserved. My brother and I laughed when they ran off, and my brother grabbed the handlebars so I could slip them back into the stem of the bicycle's frame and go home.

But this apology is not for them. This apology is for my brother. As happy as we were when the boys fell, I know he stood that day and watched as those boys took the bicycle from me. He stood behind me as I watched them ride it for what seemed like hours, but was obviously only a few minutes. My own brother didn't know what to do, and neither did I. I don't apologize for not knowing. But I wasn't a comfort to my brother in that moment, and in fact I took my anger and shame out on him with silence.

This apology wants to put an arm around that small boy back then. This apology would have let him know I was as scared as he must have been when they took the bike.

I am sad when I read about Radu and Vlad's battles, but like any rational person, I take solace in the idea that my own battles with my brother are nothing in comparison. I want to believe that Vlad and his brother looked out for one another when they were held hostage in their childhood. That is the narrative I choose to believe. There is a lot about brothers I still don't know. But what I do know for sure about brothers is learned from my two young sons. One evening not too long ago I went in to check on my sons after they went to sleep. Their room is arranged in a perfect symmetry: one twin bed and desk on one side of the room, another twin bed and desk on the other. It is hot in a Mississippi summer night, and on that night there was a scuffle after an evening at the neighborhood pool—I can't remember who started their fight or who ended in tears. Silence at last came from their room after forced goodnights, and I expected to find them facing away from one another, each in his own bed. Yet they were together, in my eldest's twin bed, arranged back to back, sleeping that sleep produced by a hard day of play, their tender noodle legs resembling handlebars come loose from dreams.

EMILIE MENZEL

Ellis

Ellis has been coveting a stone in her neighbor's front yard for some months now, but here at the dawn of October, the ice cream truck is still singing rounds outside her bedroom window, the sparrow still feeding, and the stone still untouched. Tomorrow will make three months since she began her coveting. "We're unlikely to find a better one," advises her brother, and he is right; such specimen are rare.

Each evening, Ellis and her shadow walk along the gutter of Eckerd's Lane to the warm asphalt cul-de-sac to observe the stone in neighborhood evening. It is a grey stone amongst an arrangement of mostly white stones. Bold nose, bold shoulder, thin scar skirting its back—it is easy to spot from the end of the neighbor's driveway. Each evening the fluorescence sits kindly in the trees, each night the fluorescence sits kindly, and Ellis checks on the thin scar stone. "It must be quite lonely," pressures her brother. "You should capture it soon," pressures her brother.

But Ellis has been trained as an observer, not as enacter. How to perform a list of tools and nets required for extraction? She is exceptionally cautious about approaching the stone with an incorrect arrangement of skin. Should she approach incorrectly, the stone might grow startled and turn in character. A stone may sleep steady at the edge of the azaleas, but approached by rough boots or scrape of a trowel—the mode of acquisition is essential.

The last weekend of October, Sunday morning sunning day, Ellis ties her boots to her feet, selects a silver fishing net from the garage, and walks the gutter of Eckerd's Lane to the cul-de-sac. To sleep the lawn, to sleep the lawn gently. She steps onto the lawn.

And the old wolf saw his reflection in the local swimming pool, a small path through the woods to reach the water. The trees stood kindly in their fluorescence, their fluorescence sitting kindly in the trees.

PETER KRUMBACH

Caravan

I admire you, toddler caught in my headlights at 2:27 AM,
crawling north on all fours in the fast lane of Interstate 5.
I know you want me to think I'm dreaming you, so quaint
in your naïveté and sequined diaper. I guarantee,
toddler, you'll be a judge. Every toe and dimple
part of the justice, and as I follow you in first gear—
making sure some eighteen-wheeler on meth
doesn't swipe you off the road—I pray for you,
for your invisible sheep, ducks, and the world's tunnel
you gaze into with your huge doubloon eyes. Your body
will catch up to your head, toddler, don't worry.
Keep crawling, I see no blood. You float, frictionless,
an inch above ground. By dawn you'll disappear again,
hide somewhere midair, known only to swallows and gnats.
I'd love to buy you socks, gloves and kneepads, toddler,
or a tiny rolling bed. But you favor unhindered crawl,
the breeze kneading your dough. Do you have a breast
or two to feed you? At some point you'll need a haircut.
Do you mind if I stop my car, give you a sponge bath?
You can keep moving while I scrub your back. You look
like a cub, toddler. No, you look like the future coming on,
passing signs and billboards, ignored by guards
and minutemen. Here's my exit, toddler.
Can I let you re-enter the unlit night?

JOHN McCARTHY

When You're Young You Always Take Too Much

As if life had drawn some predictable divide between
the driver and passenger sides, two boys and two girls
each occupy half of the car. The four of them fill
the cabin with that naïve sense of youth that believes
it can usher everything lost or dead back into existence
if they drive around long enough in the freezing light
of January. They take turns one-upping each other,
sharing stories about family who have died
on their own or for causes they didn't believe in.
The ending always involves needles or bullets
and a graphic depiction of the body's humiliation.
Their faces contort and give way to a grim silence
before telling a dark joke, laughter breaking out
with the undeserved assuredness that they will always
be able to grow their hair long in the name of
some indescribable anarchy. Even now, as they park,
crack the windows, and pull the glass pipe to their lips,
exhaling a cone of smoke into the frost-bitten air
where it disappears upward like the music they love
and sing to each other at night because they lack
full personalities—and where the snow covers
a field that, in the spring, will turn into oilseed.
They take turns passing the bowl as the sun falls through
the naked trees like someone startled by the piercing
of skin. For a few minutes, everyone loses themselves,
staring at the muted fields that look like a future
that hasn't become anything yet. It's this thought
that brings them hurtling back to a self-consciousness
and fear that causes one of the boys to panic.
He says *I need to go home now,* and the other three look
at him as if his statement was the most important story
ever told. The other three force a laugh, trying

to save the mood that is now silently out of control.
It's left unsaid, but they all want to go. The other three
are glad they didn't have to be the ones to say it.

JEANNE OBBARD

Seed*

I wanted to be one of those girls
who always has a win to report,
but the truth is, I'm more gifted at envy.

And anyway haven't you grown tired
of my helpfulness by now,
the sweeping sameness of it,
a halo looking for a hook?

When I came here I was convinced
everyone hated me.
Now I know. It's me
who harbors the hate,

singular trespass in an oyster's soft innards.
Every petty fury accrues to me
while people keep assuming
my meekness has no sequelae.

Do I dissipate
into the milk of my extreme
forbearance? Do I luminesce with ire?

I heard *Elizabeth Regina* ensured every pearl
on the Spanish Main made its way
back to her fingers, her neck;
Oh Gloriana! no shame in her hunger!

---

* Note: pearls were often referred to in the 16th century as both "margaritas" and "seeds."

I have made myself small, small. And I was told
there would be prizes.
Now I am ravenous
from my long abnegation,

open-mouthed as the dragon sea.

How to know if you are experimental filmmaker Maya Deren

If you fall up the stairs
into a wind,
If you fall asleep with a dahlia
but wake up with a knife,
If you constantly take a key
from your perfect mouth,

you might be Maya Deren.

Who am I to posit
if you are or aren't?
Aren't we all a little Maya Deren,
all we strange and deranged

women stepping precisely, cutting precisely our own
throats with loaves and love and blooms.

If you come home to find yourself
at the table with yourself,
three Mayas trading
knowing looks, shuffling keys like cards, pulling keys
like a tarot.

If you stride, beautiful colossus,
through city through shore through fields—
If you are unafraid
of the edges, the partings.

If you know no death is more a death
than to stay sleeping.

NATALIE TOMBASCO

Ferry Song, Half-Sung

i.

Staten Island Ferry, you found your place,
the in-between—Dante's wet dream—
as creamsicle badda-bing, as neon-lit stream,
or as goldfish in the bowl; your orange
has all the passengers rooting for you
like Seabiscuit of the harbor & somehow I'm running,
always running, through announcements,
"Downtown 1-Train to South Ferry,"
through the beatbox of yellow cabs,
through stairwells of warped saxophone,
hopping the turnstile in a tread of Timberlands,
stomping the life out from alliums
in Battery Park, & I'm staring up
the bronze snout of *Charging Bull*,
running through Daniel Pantaleo motherfuckers
& Dad's voice saying, "don't give authority any lip,"
dipping by the guys selling tourists a ticket
to Ellis Island, but they can tell
by my don't-talk-to-me face & ugly
service-worker shoes that I'm not for sale.

ii.

I'm like Melanie Griffith in *Working Girl*,
Ferry, except less cawfee, less schlep,
less red-lipstick-schmear. Listen, the longest
relationship I've had is with my MetroCard,
holding it dear in my pocket. Place a cupped ear
to the ground, hear the skulls that gave in
to sidewalk. Listen to the waves going hallelujah

hollaback. Do you get my spindrift?
Honey nights: song of hustle, of bailout, of being
mad tight—it ferries us over, kills me with dank
kush delight. Your song is not forgotten,
is not lost in frost.

iii.

What is your vernacular? Whatever it is
I'm gacked on it: clouds cracking up, crump
of brown paper bags on beercans.
Listen, let me get a baconegg&cheese, AriZona
iced tea & a Newport behind the ear.
Gimme your liquor, your lotto tickets,
your shredded lettuce. Jackpot, burner phone.
Gimme your lowbrow meow, blue-collar
slang, all the Wu-Tang loving white boys
on the island, where the question is dead-ass
& the answer is dead ass. Your sound is fiberglass,
nylon. Acrylic nails tapping against the windows.
"If you see something, say something." All right,
I'll say it: boat ride of morning or night, boat ride
of keeping the 99% out & we're all praying
that God might pluck us out of this hellhole
with the little anchovy fork of an Ortiz jar.

Lolita's Dissection

In the deli parking lot, we were those bestial babes—
gutting a White Owl, blowing its insides out
onto an undercover cop car.

Without the moon's help, we were becoming
holographic jailbait. *Hey, mister, be a dear & buy us
some beer.* Our mothers were still postpartum.

Don't be short with me! we screamed at the night.
We were euphemisms waiting to happen. A vague rain.
We were transactional sex. Cha-ching! We were kiss-him

because-he's-so-goddamn-boring, a mouth-breather.
Remember how we watched lava lamps through needle holes,
became feline, nectarine fizz in our jewel-like heads? Remember

being stripped lollipop pink & spread
on a strange bed? Love was always like this,
jagged & hooked to a different mouth.

In morning's eggshell, we were those girls who slept late
with valedictorians. We were promising, going places.
We intended to keep our animals secret,

but we were those amphibious nymphs:
        green & splayed
pinned down on a nerd's dissection tray.

Consider the Lobster Telephone

"now look!" it speaks as an object of gustatory
pleasure & pain—menacing antennae as if
some trickster, some mustachioed man

—think of it, *aphrodisiac telephone*:
growing off the black rotary like a tumor

or lusting you into bed—see how the mouthpiece
aligns with genitalia & it holds claws close
to whisper the ocean into your ear—genteel little

conversationalist, keeping you on ice
in the bathtub with champagne—with phony

reluctance, it leads through a phosphorescent terrain
to the bottom-of-the-ocean dwellers, scavengers
living on anything semiconscious, semiprecious

—like the one time you ever won anything
was from a dark tank & named it Ruby,

ran across six lanes of traffic to the harbor, setting
the rubber-cinched creature free—but what is there
to do with half-remembered love?

do memories feel pain or decompose
or moult or hibernate off the New England coast

at twenty-five fathoms? diving suit,
winter sleep deep—some argue when you eat
a crustacean's flesh you taste the repressed:

its desire, the unbearable green anguish—
you carry one home in a brown bag

& in an act of intimacy, reconsider plunging
the knife between its frantic eyestalks
as lobotomy, as courtesy—in reconsideration

the do-it-yourself-boiling-alive-method
appears most humane as you clarify

butter, do your best to ignore
the thrasher, lid-clanker—alarming armor
going tongue-red in hair-raising

needle-screeching suspense
if this becomes too much, walk away

set a plastic timer for twelve minutes
goosebump & shook—look over
your shoulder when the landline *riiiiiiiiiiiiings*

once, then twice
& beseechingly answer "hello?"

"now look: I was carapace & there was nothing
but filth specks—I ate the parts others wouldn't eat
I ate things I would rather not share."

A "FIELD" SYMPOSIUM

on

Ciaran Carson

edited by Piotr Florczyk
& Wayne Miller

Introduction

Piotr Florczyk & Wayne Miller

IN THE PROCESS of emailing about the Jerzy Jarniewicz translations featured in this issue, we began to discuss the brilliant Irish poet, essayist, novelist, and translator Ciaran Carson, whom we both admired deeply, and who died in October, 2019.

Carson is of the generation of Irish (and particularly Northern Irish, though Carson preferred "Irish") poets born in the late 1940s and early 1950s—poets writing in the immediate and massive shadow cast by Seamus Heaney—a generation that also includes, among others, Medbh McGuckian and Paul Muldoon. We lamented our sense that American readers aren't necessarily that familiar with Carson, despite his importance and acclaim in Ireland, where The Gallery Press has been publishing his poetry books from the beginning of his career, and despite the excellent work of Wake Forest University Press, which has been publishing his work in the U.S. since the 1980s. We soon arrived at the idea that we should put together some sort of feature that would both celebrate Carson's legacy and introduce his work to new readers.

Both of us loved for many years *Field* magazine's "Symposium" series, in which invited poets each wrote a response, both personal and critical, to just one poem by the poet whose work was up for discussion. *Field* was, for an astonishing 50 years and 100 issues—from 1969–2019—among the very few truly important literary magazines in America. Its "Symposium" format seemed perfectly suited to our goals for a Carson feature, so we reached out to *Field*'s editor David Walker to see if we could essentially just steal the format for *Copper Nickel*. After discussing our idea with co-editor David Young, Walker granted us permission. Indeed, we are thrilled to be able to honor both Carson and *Field* in this feature, and we hope readers will see our appropriation of the *Field* "Symposium" as a reverent nod to a magazine that shaped our poetic loves and sensibilities for many years. (And it's worth saying, here, that the first 18 symposia are collected in the book *Poets Reading: The Field Symposia*, which came out in 1999.)

So: here we are! What you have in front of you are poems and prose excerpts by Ciaran Carson, each followed by the commentary of a poet who has for some time been captivated by Carson's work.

For those readers who are already familiar with Carson, we hope that the commentaries will enlarge your engagement with his astonishing writing. For those unfamiliar with Carson, we hope you will find his work—as we do—to address history, cities, violence, and the complex meanderings of language and thought both unflinchingly and with a wry sense of humor and play. Our belief is that Carson's work—in long lines and in short, in poetry and in prose—is truly singular and deserves an ever-growing amount of attention in the years to come.

———————

Books by Ciaran Carson:

POETRY

Still Life (2020)
From There to Here: Selected Poems & Translations (2019)
Until Before After (2010)
On the Night Watch (2009)
For All We Know (2008)
Collected Poems (2008)
Breaking News (2003)
The Twelfth of Never (1998)
Opera Et Cetera (1996)
First Language (1993)
Belfast Confetti (1989)
The Irish for No (1987)
The New Estate and Other Poems (1976)

PROSE

Exchange Place: A Belfast Thriller (2012)
The Pen Friend (2009)
Shamrock Tea (2002)
Last Night's Fun: A Book About Irish Traditional Music (2000)
Fishing for Amber (1999)
The Star Factory (1997)

TRANSLATIONS

The Inferno (2020)
From Elsewhere (2014 [Follain & original response poems])
In the Light Of: After Illuminations by Arthur Rimbaud (2012)
The Táin: Translated from the Old Irish Epic Táin Bó Cúailnge (2008)
The Midnight Court: A New Translation of Cúirt An Mhéan Oíche by Brian Merriman (2005)
The Alexandrine Plan (1998 [sonnets by Rimbaud, Baudelaire, & Mallarmé])

Claude Monet, *Artist's Garden at Vétheuil*, 1880

Today I thought I'd just take a lie-down, and drift. So here I am
Listening to the tick of my mechanical aortic valve—overhearing, rather, the way
It flits in and out of consciousness. It's a wonder what goes on below the threshold.
It's quiet up here, just the muted swoosh of the cars on the Antrim Road,
And every so often the shrill of a far-off alarm or the squeal of brakes;
But yesterday some vandal upended the terracotta pot of daffodils
In our little front garden, that's not even as big, when I consider it,
As the double bed I'm lying on. Behind the privet hedge, besides the daffodils
There's pansies, thyme and rosemary. A Hebe bush. A laurel. Ruefully
I scuffed the spilled earth and pebbles with my shoe and thought of Poussin—
Was it Poussin?—and his habit of bringing back bits of wood, stones,
Moss, lumps of earth from his rambles by the Tiber; and the story of him
Reaching among the ruins for a handful of marble and porphyry chips
And saying to a tourist, 'Here's ancient Rome.' So, here's Glandore Avenue.

So different now from thirty years ago, the corner shop at the interface
Torched and the roadway strewn with broken glass and rubble.

There was something beautiful about the tossed daffodils all the same.
I'd never really taken them under my notice these past few difficult weeks.
It's late March, some of them beginning to turn and wilt and fade, heads
Drooping, papery at the tips, dessicated, or completely gone, reduced to calyx.
So many shades of yellow when you look at them. Gorse. Lemon. Mustard.
Honey. Saffron. Ochre. But then any word you care to mention has so many
Shades of meaning, and the flower itself goes under different names.
Narcissus. Daffadowndilly. Lent lily. So we wander down the road of what it is
We think we want to say. Etymologies present themselves, like daffodil
From asphodel—who knows where the *d* came from?—the flower
Of the underworld. They say it grows profusely in the meadows of the dead,
Like a buttercup on its branching stem. And I see a galaxy of buttercups in
A green field, and the yellow of the tall sunfowers in Monet's *Garden at Vétheuil*
That flank the path where the woman and the two children stand commemorated.

Strange how a smear of colour, like a perfume, resurrects the memory
Of another, that which I meant to begin with. 'Asphodel, that greeny flower.'

I'd just found the book I had in mind—*What Painting Is* by James Elkins—
When the vandal struck. *Thud.* What the . . . ? The gate clanged. I looked out
The bay window to see a figure scarpering off down the street to the interface . . .
What a book, though. I have it before me, open at this colour plate, jotting notes
Into a jotter, which I'll work up later into what you're reading now.
'The detail I'm reproducing here is a graveyard of scattered brush hairs
And other detritus,' said Elkins. 'At the centre left, glazed over by Malachite Green,
Are two crossed brush hairs, one of them bent almost at a right angle.
Just below them are two of Monet's own hairs, fallen into the wet paint.'
Brushstrokes laid down every which way. Jiggles. Jabs. Impulsive
Twists and turns. Gestures that 'depend on the inner feelings of the body,
And the fleeting momentary awareness of what the hand might do next.'
You listen to the body talking, exfoliating itself cell after cell. I saw it
Happening just now in the dust-motes drifting through this ray of sunlight.

So everything gets into the painting, wood-smoke from the studio stove,
The high pollen count of a high summer's day *en plein air* by the Seine.

The detail is so magnified it is impossible to tell where it is of, if you didn't,
Like Elkins, know. The visual field looks like a field. Shades of umber, khaki, mud,
And other greens beside the malachite. It could stand for anything it seems
In Monet's garden—or *Garden*, rather—as Poussin's handful of porphyry
Is Rome and of the days of the fall of Rome. I want it to go to the stately tune
Of a Poussin painting, *Landscape with a Man Washing His Feet by a Fountain,*
Say, where a woman sweeps by, balancing a basket on her head, and an old man
In blue dreams full-length on the grass. There are milestones and tombs,
And puddles on the road, and you can just imagine the whispering of the cistern.
A line of blue hills in the distance is contoured like a monumental sentence.
It's beautiful weather, the 30th of March, and tomorrow the clocks go forward.
How strange to be lying here listening to whatever it is is going on.
The days are getting longer now, however many of them I have left.
And the pencil I am writing this with, old as it is, will easily outlast their end.

A Necessary Indolence

Sandra Alcosser

STILL LIFE, CIARAN CARSON'S POSTHUMOUS collection, opens into a garden of roof-high sunflowers before a pink farmhouse where Claude Monet draws one's eye to a path lined by his own blue and white porcelain jardinieres from which red gladiolas exuberantly rise, to a boy and his wagon rendered so delicately they could be phantoms. Carson's "Claude Monet, *Artist's Garden at Vétheuil*, 1880" begins:

> Today I thought I'd just take a lie-down and drift. So here I am
> Listening to the tick of my mechanical aortic valve—overhearing, rather,
> the way
> It flits in and out of consciousness. It's a wonder what goes on below the
> threshold.

There is something deeply inviting in this languid opening. Its tone and scene are reminiscent of the first section of Wallace Stevens' philosophical meditation "Sunday Morning." Helen Vendler commented in an interview with Henri Cole for *The Paris Review* (winter 1996), "I feel close to Stevens by temperament. I feel close to Keats and to Herbert by temperament. They are indolent and meditative writers. I don't mean indolent in personal character, but they like to roam freely in their thinking about a topic, so that Herbert will come back and back to affliction and Keats will come back and back to the sensuous life."

As Ciaran Carson counterpoises human agency within time, he follows a similar path, and isn't that what most poets do—find a place for necessary indolence against, or outside of, time? Christian Wiman writes in *Ambition and Survival: Becoming a Poet:*

> I've never been able to write poetry without having vast tracts of dead time. Poetry requires a certain kind of disciplined indolence that the world, including many prose writers, doesn't recognize as discipline. It is, though. It's the discipline to endure hours that you refuse to fill with anything but the possibility of poetry, though you may in fact not be able to write a word of it just then, and though it may be playing practical havoc with your life. It's the discipline of preparedness.

One senses Carson's nerve-endings, all two billion of them, well-prepared, as, lying down, he drifts from a micro to a macro vision of history, and back again, following a series of graceful turns—from his own double-bed-sized garden where a terracotta pot of daffodils has been upended by a vandal, to a scene of 16th-century painter Nicholas Poussin, who has gathered bits of marble and porphyry from Italian ruins. "Here's ancient Rome," Poussin says to a tourist, to which Carson responds by describing his bit of Belfast:

> . . . So, here's Glandore Avenue.

> So different now from thirty years ago, the corner shop at the interface
> Torched and the roadway strewn with broken glass and rubble.

With a mind, as Steven's writes, "in the act of finding what will suffice," Carson, while expanding his vision, circles back again to the spilled daffodils, a botanical relative of the asphodel, Homer's flower, prolific in the underworld, as he highlights William Carlos William's confessional tribute to his wife Flossie:

> Strange how a smear of colour, like a perfume, resurrects the memory
> Of another, that which I meant to begin with. 'Asphodel, that greeny
> flower.'

Carson then recalls the book he reached for just as the vandal clanged the gate. *What Painting Is* by James Elkind, which provides a visceral assay of Monet's 19th-century canvas of a garden he constructed at the farmhouse he'd rented for his family. "The detail I'm reproducing here is a graveyard of scattered brush hairs / And other detritus," said Elkind, as he noted two of Monet's hairs caught for eternity in the canvas.

While another of Ireland's most highly regarded poets, Patrick Kavanagh, created kindred motion in his great sonnet "Epic," Carson's poem plays through a reader's entire body more like the movements of a sonata, and with great equanimity, he brings his poem to a close.

I was fortunate to have a graduate seminar with William Bevis, a fine speculative Stevens scholar who wrote *Mind of Winter: Wallace Stevens, Meditation and Literature,* an important book about long, disjunct works, not episodic but spontaneous and varied. Because of that seminar, I became initiated into Stevens' meditations, then followed them back to the 17th-century Metaphysical poets and forward to the dialectical arguments of Czesław Miłosz. Even though the meditative tradition became a primary pursuit, too often what was described as a meditation in contemporary poetry, long and rambling as it might be, failed to articulate, or even posit, an irresolvable question. In "Claude Monet, *Artist's Garden at Vétheuil*, 1880," Carson moves about the irresolvable—time and human agency—with such modest, often humorous and intellectually passionate motion that we give ourselves over to the voice and follow its oblique query, until he finally closes with, instead of Stevens' "downward to darkness on extended wings," something far more pointed:

> It's beautiful weather, the 30th of March, and tomorrow the clocks go
>   forward.
> How strange it is to be lying here listening to whatever it is is going on.
> The days are getting longer now, however many of them I have left.
> And the pencil I am writing this with, old as it is, will easily outlast their
>   end.

Because of Carson's refusal to veer from the music, quotidian oddity, and magnificence of the world, "Claude Monet, *Artist's Garden at Vétheuil*, 1880" is a most compelling introduction to an equally compelling collection—"like a new knowledge of reality"—as Stevens notes in the final line of his collected poems. More than that, Carson's *Still Life* is both *Ars Poetica* and *Ars moriendi*. By the time we reach the beautiful weather of late March with its corresponding clocks and have shared his tour of cities and centuries limned by personal memory, Ciaran Carson, poet of great lyric elegance and erudition, will have reached the end of his own long, light-filled days and will be gone by early October.

Nicolas Poussin, *Landscape with a Calm*, 1650-51

For a long time, if only now and then, I'd idly think about the difference
Between 'hawthorn' and 'blackthorn'—were they indeed divergent genera,
Or merely synonymous terms for the same plant?—invariably deferring
The quest until, my conscience pricked by the blackbird I'd put in my poem
Of a fortnight ago to sing from a blackthorn for the sake of consonance, I resolved
To settle the matter for once and for all. So I googled it. *Blackthorn, flowers first,*
Then leaves; hawthorn, leaves first, then flowers. I remembered the tree as
Sprinkled by a hail of tiny blossoms. Not a leaf to be seen. The wood was dark. Cautiously
I put my finger to a thorn: it was needle-sharp and hard. Was this
The thorn that cut one to the quick? I put the question to one side.

For I've been thinking of the stanza as an ample room I want to wander in: Latin
Stantia, present participle of *stare*, to stand, hence Italian *stanza*, a room, a place wherein
You stand; a stopping place, a station. Of the poem as a verbal suite
Of interconnecting rooms—here, I'm entering the virtual London National Gallery tour,
Important portals with massive architraves of blue-grey striated marble that
Successively invite you into spaces you can walk right through or dawdle in
To contemplate a phrase, the line or contour of a painting,
The happenstance of a statue. And it occurs to me that our habitual journeys
To the Waterworks might form such a measure, as we sometimes scan this memorable
Place or that, and dwell on it a while as we have many unremembered times before.

For now, we're on the Antrim Road. It's Easter Sunday and the sun is shining.
We take the usual turn at Hopefield Avenue. Here No. 1 once stood. It was
A beautiful house back then. We'd peep over the privet hedge to peer into it.
A Chinese vase in the bay window. A landscape on the parlour chimney breast.
Now a waste ground. Chain-link fencing. We pause here to visualize once more
The goldfinch we saw two years ago, perched on a thistle-head, plucking fluff
For food. Then to circumvent the House of Cerberus, the chained watchdog
That lies in a circle of its own excrement. We are glad to reach the House of Kids,
The front garden a jumble of primary colours: red, blue, yellow; toy dump truck,
Wheelbarrow, JCB; green garden hose, bucket & spade, and green garden gnome.

And so to the Waterworks. We cross the road and enter by the little Eastern Gate.
We take our customary anticlockwise circuit across Milewater Bridge, left into
Bird Alley: a tall impenetrable hawthorn hedge on one side—just beginning to bloom!—

And a minor Everglades of willow on the other. Birdsong surrounds us,
The trees reverberant with trills and warbles. Gradually we enter a new acoustic:
Here comes Squawk Island, a place so densely wooded that its denizens are not
To be seen, but loudly heard in their cacophony of panic-stricken shrieks
And squeals. But soon we'll be arriving at our usual bench, where we'll be well
Out of earshot. Now we sit to contemplate the water, whether calm or ruffled.
Here we reflect on all we've seen throughout the years, and all there is to come.

And so we come to talk of how we take our bearings from the moment
Of a painting, where everything is at a standstill. Poussin's *Calm*. For some time past
The landscape of the Waterworks has made me think of his. His lake, our pond.
On the Cavehill Road the skyline of serried chimneypots accorded to the crenellated
Battlements of his citadel. Extending the conceit, sunlit rectangles,
Parallelograms and cubes of shade, roofs, bay windows, apertures began
To correspond. The yellow gable of a terrace house took on a new significance—
See that other patch of yellow—there, below the citadel? I looked at
Reproductions, images from books, the internet. The more you looked
The more there was to see to know exactly what there was, and what was not.

For there is more to it than meets the eye. But first, an overview. It measures
Some three feet by four. A generous picture. A great citadel takes up the centre.
A colossal twin-cragged mountain stands to its left. Clouds hang in a sky
The blue of the pellucid lake that occupies the middle ground. On its further shore
A long drove of sheep and cattle. In the foreground a goatherd tends his goats.
These are some of the most immediately apparent features of the landscape.
I think it takes us a while to get the horse galloping off stage right, urged on
By its bareback rider, for it's dark over there in the shadow
Of the framing tree. And what's this curious structure that it dashes past? Seemingly
A washhouse—look, there's a woman leaning over a trough, and another horse drinking
    from it.

For one thing leads to another, as the heads of the unruly goats point
This way and that, directing us to look further. That fire in the middle distance,
What is it for? And what about the lake, that neither crag nor cloud are mirrored in it?
As for the citadel, a piece of its intricate structure appears missing from its
Reflection. Regarding the Grecian frieze of animals, why is the bull of the herd
Not recapitulated? And now—as musicians, we should have seen this before—
Look at the bagpiper bringing up the rear of the drove, about to break into tune!
Look at his cap, tunic, pannier, belt, pipe and drone, etcetera, his complex stoop

And stride into the lateral flow and the light. He drives or follows the entablature
Of animals into the time of day, whatever it might be. And we follow him.

For music is afoot, and we imagine it from what we know of music, tunes
Reiterated over decades, played in back rooms, or upon the stanza of a stage.
Melodies that alter between hearing and remembering, remembering
The friends we learned them from. Missing bits we touchingly get
Wrong, yet somehow work. How many the utterances of *The Blackbird*, each one
Different from the last? And again I hear the mad cadenza of the blackbird in his tree.
The bellows groan and creak, the piper starts up, windblown skirl and parp
Encouraging the beasts into a great polyphony of pastorale. Lowing, bleating,
Undulating to the groundswell of the drone, moving slowly in the amplitude—
The musician driving the stock-still moment steadily into the future.

On Ciaran Carson's "Nicolas Poussin, *Landscape with a Calm*, 1650-51"

Don Bogen

ALONG WITH BEING A WONDERFUL poet and the founding director of the Seamus Heaney Centre at Queen's University, Belfast, Ciaran Carson was a great folk musician. As those who've seen him give a talk or reading know, it was common for him to play a few bars of Irish flute music before he launched into his public presentation. I'll let this anecdote, from the first time I had a chance to talk with him when I was a Fulbright Scholar at the Heaney Centre in Belfast, serve as my preface:

> Setting: Madden's Bar, Belfast. Winter, 2011.
> CC: You know, Don, the blackbird is the symbol of the Heaney Centre. There's always been this connection between poets and birds. We all want to sing like nightingales—or maybe skylarks. Yeah, we all want to be skylarks.
> DB: Right, like in Shelley—"Bird thou never wert."
> CC: Yeah, Don. But do you know what we are, then, what we *really* are?
> (Pause)
> We're parrots, Don. We're fuckin' parrots.

So much for poetic originality. I like to think of that joke as an Irish vernacular version of Eliot's "Tradition and the Individual Talent." Like all the poems in his posthumous book *Still Life*, Ciaran's "Nicolas Poussin, *Landscape with a Calm*, 1650-51" engages the tradition of poets writing about visual art that runs from classical times to John Ashbery and beyond. His distinctive approach is also in line with a tradition of "conversation poems" that goes back at least to Coleridge. Its long but fairly regular lines chime a bit with late Auden or C.K. Williams, as does its relaxed, discursive voice—not the squawk of a parrot exactly but definitely the cry of a bird who knows his flock.

A poem with a walk at its heart, "Nicolas Poussin, *Landscape with a Calm*, 1650-51" is mostly set at a walking pace. I love how it takes its time and leaves plenty of space to move. At the start of the second stanza, Ciaran describes his ten-line stanza as "an ample room I want to wander in." I'll take that as an invitation to wander through the eight rooms of the poem myself.

But first a general point about those rooms: they have symmetries that go beyond their equal number of lines. For one thing, they're all closed, and each begins with either *For* or *And so*. The pattern is three stanzas starting with *For*, followed by two starting with *And so* right in the middle, and then another three starting with *For* at the end. I think of these opening words as something like doors to the rooms. In various ways, each refers to time. When *For* is used as a conjunction to mean *because*, as it almost always is, it looks toward the past, some thought or fact that has led the poem to where it is now. *And so*, in contrast, is a broader opening, maybe not a door but just an archway, with its focus on the ongoing flow of events in the present rather than their causes. There are subtle variations here, but it feels inimical to the dynamic spirit of the poem to dwell on them. Let's get going.

"Nicolas Poussin, *Landscape with a Calm*, 1650-51" opens with one of its longest sentences, taking up just over half of the stanza. It's a wonderful jungle of specific memories from different moments, self-doubt, and deferral. "For a long time" (a bit of Proust at the start) "if only now and then." Ciaran has the wit to follow the lengthy interwoven speculation of the first sentence with one of the shortest sentences in the poem: "So I googled it." We get a blackbird early on, and a nice self-mocking tension between the "virtuous" drive to "settle the matter for once and for all" and the pleasure in "putting the question to one side," as he does, understandably, at the end of the stanza when mortality rears its head.

Stanza two is all about having space to move at different paces: a big stanza, a suite of rooms, a museum site on the internet with "spaces you can walk right through or dawdle in," a familiar walk where memories layer the past. (But it occurs to me I'm dawdling here myself—there's already so much to dwell on.)

In the third stanza *For now* gives us a specific instance of that familiar walk in present tense. This stanza, one of my favorites, is largely in the moment, with the "we" and "you" focusing in now on Ciaran and his wife Deirdre, a fellow musician (she plays fiddle) with whom he shares both this walk and memories of others that occur while the couple are out walking: the past woven into the present. Dense and evocative, the rush of specificity flows over into a catalogue at the end, where the cluttered front yard of the House of Kids grows from a vivid "jumble of primary colours" to particular toys and garden implements.

Then the walk itself flows over into the next stanza, as *And so* keeps the door wide open. There's the hawthorn from the opening question of the poem again, and six lines exploring the "new acoustic" of Bird Alley—birds suggested only by their "shrieks," "trills," and "warbles." The animated world of sound replaces the visual for a moment, and I'm sure there's a blackbird somewhere in that polyphony. The last line of this stanza is the only one-sentence line in the poem. Set precisely at the mid-point of the piece, it gives us the present as a kind of breathing space, Ciaran's own "calm," between past and future: "Here we reflect on all we've seen throughout the years, and all there is to come." Understated and balanced, with a fine iambic turn in the middle, this line evokes the rewards of a long marriage better than anything I know.

Then another *And so* leads us from life in time to art "where everything is at a standstill. Poussin's *Calm*." And the poem starts up again with another translation of Proust's *Longtemps*: "For some time past." I love the humor of this stanza, as the poet stretches to find correspondences (a nod to Baudelaire?) between the urban landscape of the walk and the fairly bizarre pastoral scene of Poussin's painting. The whole stanza is a tribute to the imaginative energy of metaphor. Are these two worlds—a domestic walk in Belfast and a seventeenth-century painting in an on-line museum—really related? Maybe in some mysterious Baudelairian way, despite the straining for visual parallels—"For there is more to it than meets the eye" as the sixth stanza announces.

After noting a number of prominent features in the painting—the citadel, the mountain, the lake—the poem begins to speed up. You can see it in the double meaning of "get the horse galloping": *get* as *see* or *understand*, but also *get* as *make*. It turns out a long gaze at something that can't move, a painting, actually leads to motion of a sort. We are moved by visual art, but we also make *it* move as we spend time with it.

And what we're spending is ongoing energy, "For one thing leads to another." As the poem keeps accelerating, questions about the painting—the purpose of some of the details, the apparent flaws in its attempt to reproduce life—that strangely non-reflective lake, among others—gather until we finally notice the bagpiper. A conversation, a walk, an ekphrastic commentary are all turning into a dance.

Because "music is afoot" in the last stanza. Sound animates the visual—we're now in the human version of Bird Alley. There's time weaving and looping with the changing wealth of memories it provides. There's the tune called *The Blackbird* and the blackbird's "mad cadenza" in a tree—art and life. There's the relentless "groundswell of the drone" as we move toward our end but also the "amplitude" of space ahead, with "The musician driving the stock-still moment steadily into the future." The poet is that musician—Ciaran's last line hangs in the air as a perfect closing note.

An ekphrastic tour de force, a meditation on time, and a moving love poem, "Nicolas Poussin, *Landscape with a Calm*, 1650-51" shows Ciaran's work at its most dynamic. Like *The Blackbird*, it deepens every time you go through it.

Soot

It was autumn. First, she shrouded
The furniture, then rolled back the carpet
As if for dancing; then moved
The ornaments from the mantelpiece,
Afraid his roughness might disturb
Their staid fragility.

He came; shyly, she let him in,
Feeling ill-at-ease in the newly-spacious
Room, her footsteps sounding hollow
On the boards. She watched him kneel
Before the hearth, and said something
About the weather. He did not answer,

Too busy with his work for speech.
The stem of yellow cane creaked upwards
Tentatively. After a while, he asked
Her to go outside and look, and there,
Above the roof, she saw the frayed sunflower
Bloom triumphantly. She came back

And asked how much she owed him, grimacing
As she put the money in his soiled hand.
When he had gone, a weightless hush
Lingered in the house for days. Slowly,
It settled; the fire burned cleanly;
Everything was spotless.

Instead Instead / On Ciaran Carson

Marianne Boruch

EARLY IN 2012, WHEN I was about to leave for Edinburgh, Ciaran Carson got wind of my Fulbright there, inviting me to read at the Seamus Heaney Centre in Belfast. Since Northern Ireland is part of the UK and brief city-jumping allowed, even encouraged within assigned Fulbright regions, off I went—delighted—for a few days' visit.

I mention this to explain why my husband and I were even *in* Belfast at a table of a cozy place for supper, waiting to meet this amazing Irish poet. Certainly Northern Ireland is rich with poets. And was then as well—Heaney, Medbh McGuckian, Sinéad Morrissey, Michael Longley among others. Into that warm and welcoming place (it was winter, after all) walked—more like *lurked toward* us—a guy about my age bent forward in a wrinkled Columbo raincoat, looking quite furtive, and—I have to say it—a shade comic, which only added to my pleasure. It was Ciaran. Who took the seat across from us.

"I am rereading Proust," he blurted out, first thing. "I know everyone is saying that these days, but I really am!" And with that, a most strange and lovely conversation began. (I know *lovely* is probably the most overworked glad adjective in the Commonwealth, but cross my heart, this time it proved accurate.)

And I only mention *that* because in reading again so many poems for this meditation on Ciaran Carson's work, I'm convinced Proust is key. Or at least the *idea* a lot of us have of Proust. That is to say, *memory* is key (locked in that bite of now near-cliched tasty *madeleine*—but going way beyond) and how so much of our memory, personal and communal, gets erased violently or just out of exhaustion as years pass. Yet how it creeps back, so eternal-seeming, because we're stuck with remembering no matter what, however down to its bits and parts. More: this poet takes on two of poetry's great subjects: time and knowledge. But how this dual gravity is *earned*, as people like to say now—*that* means everything.

From his first book, *The New Estate*, the poem "Soot" keeps haunting. But why?

On the surface, it's a simple, credible narrative. An upper-middle-class matron hires a chimney sweep to clean out what might be a dangerous blockage of soot, ash, maybe twigs, rat bones, all kinds of crap up there. The details of this commonplace interaction that get laid out carefully: autumn and its dark, the room stripped as a defensive move against what damage this sweep might do, the carpet rolled back "as if for dancing." The caste system is clear (and universal really) but this woman's what-to-say awkward chitchat about the weather is ignored. The hard-working sweep will not engage, thank you, and goes straight to it in silence, kneeling, his "yellow cane creaked upwards / Tentatively." Of course any reference to this medieval but necessary ongoing trade brings back William Blake's innocent/experienced double-whammy take on his young sweep, surely another kind of haunting that Carson must have hoped for. Good poems are echo chambers after all.

What fascinates though might fall into the "point of view" territory of the fiction writer (so-called "third person limited," yes?), which in turn governs how we readers peep-tom all this, our own POV. We see as she does. The woman *shrouds* the furniture, and grows *shy* as this chimney sweep enters. The whole room abruptly feels suspect and vulnerable, "newly-spacious," even "her footsteps sounding hollow." Sympathy grows for her and yet we feel for him who keeps to the work at hand, apparently peering up the chimney in a rain of soot, then for real asking that she step outside and look. And the repair *is* happening; she sees "the frayed sunflower" up there, "[b]loom triumphantly." She absorbs this fact through image real but imagined via metaphor in open air, she alone on watch while inside he must be still cranking away, equally solitary. A weird sort of symmetry. A success, sort of.

The fact that we know by heart what probably will happen makes it an old story— nothing new here, right?—and in return, she will "put the money in his soiled hand." It's she who notices that his hand is marked by the work, thus we do. And each will go about whatever they must attend to, later in the day. The point is we lose him. It's technically over; narrative ends. But poetry doesn't.

Here's the thing, really two things: *story* is what we remember, *poetry* what we discover. In fact, the room *is* altered in spooky, secret ways. First "a weightless hush / Lingered in the house for days." Fair enough, I guess, though presumably the carpet's unrolled, back as it was, the chairs un-ghosted, everything "spotless" now. But the past is never past, especially in Belfast, beloved city of so many wounds where this poet was born, then lived a life. And it is wounds that make poems.

It's like years later, in Ciaran Carson's brilliant signature book *Belfast Confetti*, in his poem "Turn Again" where

When someone asks me where I live, I remember where I used to live.
Someone asks me for directions, and I think again. I turn into
A side street to try to throw off my shadow, and history is changed.

Because in my copy of "Soot," the mundane but extraordinary happens: I must turn the page. My own hand lifts the poem into whatever's next where a final stanza looms up. That accidental pause and turn makes literal the shift to future time and season, to a new *space* of mind. The woman learns that the soot she swept up will feed the flowerbeds. And in the rain, could make its way down

> . . . to lightless crevices,
> Sleeping, till in spring it would emerge softly
> As the ink-bruise in the pansy's heart.

There is a curious quiet astonishment here and only a rare, lasting poet, a brave one, would keep going like this straight into transformation. Unlike Carson, many of us—dutiful reporters of the human story—would stop happily enough, going silent when the conventional narrative fades out.

When I think of this poem, everything arrows in and widens and deepens with that *ink-bruise*. And the most unprepossessing flower ordinarily doomed by diminutive cuteness becomes history and prophecy, warning and solace. The pansy: a startling redefinition of hurt and survival.

Which is an honest-to-god epiphany. I stare down at my hand as if holding it there.

Hamlet

As usual, the clock in The Clock Bar was a good few minutes fast:
A fiction no one really bothered to maintain, unlike the story
The comrade on my left was telling, which no one new for certain truth:
Back in 1922, a sergeant, I forget his name, was shot outside the National Bank. . . .
Ah yes, what year was it that they knocked it down? Yet its memory's as fresh
As the inky smell of new pound notes—which interferes with the beer-and-whiskey
Tang of now, like two dogs meeting in the revolutionary 69 of a long sniff,
Or cattle jostling shit-stained flanks in the Pound. For *pound*, as some wag
Interrupted, was an off-shoot of the Falls, from the Irish, *fál*, a hedge;
Hence, *any kind of enclosed thing*, its twigs and branches commemorated
By the soldiers' drab and olive camouflage, as they try to melt
Into a brick wall; red coats might be better, after all. *At any rate,*
This sergeant's number came up; not a winning one. The bullet had his name on it.
Though Sergeant X, as we'll call him, doesn't really feature in the story:
The nub of it is, *This tin can which was heard that night, trundling down*
From the bank, down Balaklava Street. Which thousands heard, and no one ever
Saw. Which was heard for years, any night that trouble might be
Round the corner . . . and when it skittered to a halt, you knew
That someone else had snuffed it: a name drifting like an afterthought,
A scribbled wisp of smoke you try and grasp, as it becomes diminuendo, then
Vanishes: For *fál* is also *frontier*, *boundary*, as in *the undiscovered country*
From whose bourne no traveller returns, the illegible, thorny hedge of time itself—
Heartstopping moments, measured not by the pulse of a wristwatch, nor
The archaic anarchists' alarm clock, but a mercury tilt device
Which 'only connects' on any given bump on the road. So, by this wingèd messenger
To promise 'to pay the bearer' is fulfilled:

As someone buys another round, an Allied Irish Banks £10 note drowns in
The slops of the counter; a Guinness stain blooms on the artist's impression
Of the sinking of the *Girona*; a tiny foam hisses round the salamander brooch
Dredged up to show how love and money endure, beyond death and the Armada,
Like the bomb-disposal expert in his suit of salamander-cloth.
Shielded against the blast of time by a strangely mediaeval visor,
He's been outmoded by this jerky robot whose various attachments include
A large hook for turning over corpses that may be booby-trapped;
But I still have this picture of his hands held up to avert the future

In a final act of *No surrender*, as, twisting through the murky fathoms
Of what might have been, he is washed ashore as pearl and coral.

This *strange eruption to our state* is seen in other versions of the Falls:
A no-go area, a ghetto, a demolition zone. For the ghost, as it turns out—
All this according to your man, and I can well believe it—this tin ghost,
Since the streets it haunted were abolished, was never heard again.
The sleeve of Raglan Street has been unravelled; the helmet of Balaklava
Is torn away from the mouth. The dim glow of Garnet has gone out,
And with it, all but the memory of where I lived. I, too, heard the ghost:
A roulette trickle, or the hesitant annunciation of a downpour, ricocheting
Off the window; a goods train shunting distantly into a siding,
Then groaning to a halt; the rainy cries of children after dusk.
For the voice from the grave reverberates in others' mouths, as the sails
Of the whitethorn hedge swell up in a little breeze, and tremble
Like the spiral blossoms of Andromeda: so suddenly are shrouds and branches
Hung with street-lights, celebrating all that's lost, as fields are reclaimed
By the Starry Plough. So we name the constellations, to put a shape
On what was there; so, the storyteller picks his way between the isolated stars.

But, *Was it really like that?* And, *Is the story true?*
You might as well tear off the iron mask, and find that no one, after all,
Is there: nothing but a cry, a summons, clanking out from the smoke
Of demolition. Like some son looking for his father, or the father for his son,
We try to piece together the exploded fragments. Let these broken spars
Stand for the Armada and its proud full sails, for even if
The clock is put to rights, everyone will still believe it's fast:
The barman's shouts of *Time* will be ignored in any case, since time
Is conversation; it is the hedge that flits incessantly into the present,
As words blossom from the speakers' mouths, and the flotilla returns to harbour,
Long after hours.

Ciaran Carson, "Hamlet"

Troy Jollimore

Ciaran Carson's "Hamlet" is set, as the first line informs us, in The Clock Bar—a place where time, it seems, is out of joint. "As usual, the clock in the Clock Bar was a good few minutes fast." You'd think that if you could find an accurate clock anywhere it would be in a place named for one. But then, there's a difference between regular time and bar time. Between sober time and after-a-couple-of-drinks time. Maybe more than a couple, depending. Just how many drinks have been consumed prior to this point? The usual number. What we are drinking? The usual. With whom? The usual suspects, presumably. Telling the usual stories.

As usual. What usually goes on in a pub, along with the drinking, is the storytelling; and it's that, if it's anything, that is warping and distorting local time. Stories are time machines. In stories, the past, like a ghost—and, as it turns out, this is a story about a ghost—"flits incessantly into the present." History repeats itself, or is repeated. Same old story. Repetition is fundamental to stories, a story being by definition something to be repeated. Poems, too: repetitions of words, of sounds, of structures—the long line, for instance, in which "Hamlet," and many of *Belfast Confetti*'s poems, are written. "Hamlet," the final poem in this collection, allows the poet, like a jazz musician improvising on a theme, to return to and riff on many of the elements from the poems that precede it.

Storytelling is explicitly evoked in the poem's second line, a line that begins with the words *A fiction*, reminding us that the story we are about to hear, like any story, while not necessarily false, is an artifice, something made, whose relation to the truth may be ambiguous. And quite possibly beside the point. If there is an idea of bar time, whose relation to ordinary, outside-of-the-pub time is ambiguous, difficult to ascertain, there is also, surely, an idea of bar truth, whose relation to ordinary truth is, let's just say, equally complex.

True or no, the story inside this poem is barely begun before it gets diverted—or, rather, we get diverted, for the mention of the National Bank immediately summons memories so forceful and vivid that they "interfere with the beer-and-whiskey / Tang of now." Current sensory experience being, as usual, no match for the onslaught of recollection. Though the *which* here is rather ambiguous: is it the memory, or the smell of the pound notes, that is doing the interfering—or is it precisely the smell of the pound notes that is being remembered? Hard to keep straight: we can't really tell, it seems, the past from the present. Same old story: it all seems so real.

For creatures like us, afflicted with prodigious capacities for imagination and memory, questions about what is real, and what is merely remembered or imagined, possess a certain urgency. *Is it, or is it not?* Or, where memory is concerned: *Is it, or was it?* Which is why, perhaps, we are bound to treat ghost stories with a certain gravity. As Barnardo asks Horatio, on being confronted with the ghost early in Shakespeare's *Hamlet*, "Is not this something more than fantasy?" Imagine a race of creatures much better than we are at distinguishing reality from fantasy: they wouldn't have such a thing as literature, whose very possibility, and power, depends on its ability to make imagined things seem real. As real as the rock Samuel Johnson, irritated at Bishop Berkeley, kicked. As usual, the attempted philosophical refutation failed. But the story persisted.

The image of Doctor Johnson kicking that rock naturally calls to mind the game of "kick-the-tin," about which Carson has the following to say in his book *The Star Factory*:

> Kick-the-tin, a hybrid of tig and hide-and-seek, employed an empty tin can as a release-mechanism, which, if kicked away from its central location, allowed players time to find new hiding-places while 'it' retrieved the can and replaced it on its spot. Thus the can was a kind of clock with differential radii, depending on the angle and length of the kick: it recalls the vatic tin-can ghost of the Lower Falls, which was heard tripping down the gutter, but never seen, any time there might be trouble in the offing. It was first heard in the twenties, when a policeman was shot dead outside the National Bank on the corner of Balaclava Street; since its habitat has been demolished, it has not been heard, but its memory lives on, even within the minds of those who'd never heard it, *since it had acquired the status of a story*.

The status of a story. Emphasis mine, as usual. The same old story, indeed, that's about to get told in "Hamlet," though the idea that the can is itself not only a ghost but also a clock adds a bit of connective tissue the present poem has elided, and it's worth mentioning that the consequent page of *The Star Factory* contains a description of a ghostly clock, even more out of sync than the one that adorns the Clock Bar: "a broken Westclox alarm-clock with luminous numerals and hands [that] was a fixture in one of the tin-roofed catacombs of Mooreland." (To be fair, the stalled Westclox must have displayed the correct time twice daily. The Clock Bar clock, by contrast, *never* reported 'actual' time.)

Meanwhile the hands of the Clock Bar clock go round, and the same old stories go round, and the barman (who has, one can be sure, been around) comes round, and "someone" does the inevitable and "buys another round." The story of the policeman killed outside the National Bank finally gets itself told. Incidentally, we should note that it shows up not only in *The Star Factory,* but also earlier in *Belfast Confetti,* in a prose piece titled "Schoolboys and Idlers of Pompeii." There, pre-echoing his remark in "Hamlet" that the slain man, "Sergeant X, as we'll call him, doesn't really feature in the story," Carson observes that the tale "does not concern the policeman; rather, it is about the tin can which was heard that night rolling down Balaklava Street into Raglan Street, and which was heard again for years after, whenever there was trouble in the offing; thousands heard it, no one saw it." "Hamlet" adds a further detail: "when it skittered to a halt, you knew / That someone else had snuffed it."

You almost feel bad for the policeman, superseded by a ghost. But for each of us there's a can that, sooner or later, skitters to a halt. We all snuff it; it's stories that survive, not us—unless, of course, we have the luck to be turned into one. That is, into a story. I almost wrote 'good' luck, but then thought again of the violent circumstances of Sergeant X's end, and remembered that it tends to be the violent snuffings that get transformed into stories. As for *this* story, we might well find ourselves asking what Barnardo asked regarding *his* ghost: is it real? "Is not this something more than fantasy?" As a version of *Is it, or is it not?,* this question is a clear cousin of the one Hamlet famously poses to himself later in *Hamlet: To be or not to be?* Perhaps, indeed, Hamlet himself vaguely suspects that he, Hamlet, does not really exist. If ever a fictional character had the self-aware wherewithal to puzzle this out, surely it's him.

Meanwhile, all this talk about snuffing has reminded us that the "*undiscovered country from whose bourn no traveler returns,*" a phrase Hamlet utters just a bit later on in that same monologue, and which is quoted in Carson's "Hamlet," is, of course, death, nonexistence, the void; and that the phrase "strange eruption to our state"— also quoted in Carson's poem—is spoken by Horatio and refers to the appearance of Hamlet's father's ghost. Which surely, in turn, reminds us that at the end of Act One, Hamlet, having conversed with the ghost, subsequently curses his own existence—or, rather, the event that led to it, his birth. And why? Because "the time is out of joint," and his sad fate is to be "born to set it right."

If only he could have averted his future—as that bomb-disposal expert attempted. But which future? One timeline has our sapper rendered jobless by technological progress, facing a future of uselessness and idleness, while in another he perishes on the job, blown to bits. By the same blast, perhaps—admittedly, this is pure speculation—that stopped the clock of the *Belfast Telegraph* in an earlier poem, "Gate." "Difficult to keep track," as that poem has it—it's all in the way you tell the story. Which fragments you assemble, and the pattern they make. Or as "Hamlet" puts the point:

. . . So we name the constellations, to put a shape
On what was there; so, the storyteller picks his way between the isolated stars.
But, *was it really like that?* and, *is the story true?*

Was it really like that? Is the story true? Is not this something more than fantasy? To
believe or not to believe, isn't that the question, really? So we have, a few lines later:

. . . Like some son looking for his father, or the father for his son,
We try to piece together the exploded fragments. . . .

Which is what we have been doing all along, it would seem, whether we realized
it or not. As for the bomb-disposal expert, he seems to face a grim fate either way.
Perhaps his error, like Hamlet's, was to be born at the wrong time, with the wrong
fate. At any rate, what's the point? Find your father, avenge him, or don't, everyone
still ends up dead. The future, as usual, will arrive, and do what it will, regardless of
our efforts. Indeed, according to the clock at the Clock Bar, it already has.

Except that the clock at The Clock Bar no longer tells anyone anything. In an
earlier poem, "Question Time," The Clock Bar is itemized in a list of "vanished
public houses." Gone, then, along with the National Bank and Sergeant X, who
once stood outside it, and held his hands up too, I wager, in a futile effort to ward
off the future. Or were those the hands of a clock, that we have only mistaken
for a man? In the realm of memory everything that happens happens repeatedly,
long after hours. And somewhere, anyway, an unseen tin can is skittering to a stop.
Somewhere an long-delayed flotilla is about to arrive. And somewhere, although
everyone is, as usual, ignoring him, a barman is calling *Time, folks. Time.*

from *Shamrock Tea*

Paris Green (pp. 1–3)

PERHAPS I WILL return one day to the world I first entered. For now, I wish to record something of it, if only to remind myself of what I am.

The first things I remember are the colours of my bedroom wallpaper, and their chalky taste under my fingernails. It would, of course, be years before I learned what the shades were called, which leads me to my first paint-box. Hooker's Green, Vermilion, Prussian Blue, Burnt Sienna: I knew stories must lie behind those names, and I resolved to discover them some day.

As I learned to speak, I understood that green was the colour of jealousy. But I did not know yet that Napoleon, on the isle of St Helena, was supposed to have died from breathing the fumes of his bedroom wallpaper, which was liberally tinted with the arsenic-laced pigment known as Emerald, or Paris Green; nor did I know that a green moon shone in the sky for weeks after Krakatoa disintegrated on 28 August 1883, the feast day of St Monica, mother of St Augustine.

In the *Confessions*, Augustine speaks with awe of the vast cloisters of his memory, which is an immeasurable sanctuary for countless images of all kinds. Perplexed by time—since the present has no duration and past and future do not exist—he concludes that the measure of time must be memory; hence a long past is a long remembrance of the past.

In Church liturgy, which is a measure of time, green is the colour of hope, and the priest wears green vestments on the Sundays between Whitsuntide and Advent. When Nero, in his savage persecution of the Christians, had them sewn up in the skins of wild beasts, and exposed to the future of dogs, he is reputed to have peered at the spectacle through a prism of green beryl, which has magnifying properties. Otherwise, green is the colour of the planet Venus, and therefore of love and fertility.

The Greeks thought green to be associated with Hermaphroditus, son of blue Hermes and yellow Aphrodite. Green is ambiguous. It is the colour of aliens, or of creatures who dwell in the underworld, as illustrated by the following legend:

On 20 July 1434, at the hour of tierce as told by the great Belfry of Bruges, in Flanders, two green-skinned twin children—a boy and a girl of about thirteen—materialized from a storm-grating in the town square, clothed in garments of what appeared to be frogskin. They were dripping wet. Crying bitterfly, they were brought to the nearby house of Arnolfini, a respected Italian merchant. Questioning them in various languages and dialects, he found they responded well to Attic Greek. In their land, they said, it was always twilight. It was called St Martin's Land: that saint was much revered there, since he had descended from the upper world and made them Christians. Yesterday they had been tending their flocks of dragons and had followed them into a cave. They heard a sound of distant bells, in which they discerned the voices of angels calling to them. Led by the voices, they had climbed up a flight of steps roughly hewn in the rock, to emerge in a brilliant light.

The children were baptized. It was quickly established that they would eat no food save beans, and after several weeks of this diet their green hue noticeably diminished. Shortly afterwards, they boy died. The girl, who was somewhat wanton, lived long as a servant to the Arnolfini household. There is no further record of her fate; but it was noted, and rememberd by the people of Bruges, that the day on which the green children had first come into this world was the feast of St Margaret of Antioch.

On Ciaran Carson's *Shamrock Tea*

Paul Perry

IT'S TWENTY YEARS SINCE CIARAN Carson's *Shamrock Tea* appeared—a dazzling novel which shows Carson's encyclopedic interest and knowledge of art and literature off to a breathless degree. There are echoes within of Borges, his labyrinths, and garden of forking paths, and of course the bibliophile in Carson is there with references as diverse and far ranging as St. Augustine to Rilke. A poet's novel in many ways, ekphrastic, and composed more with shape and form in mind rather than plot and character, rather like one of Italo Calvino's "cubist" novels, but one that remains quintessentially Ciaran Carson. I often think of the book as an embodiment of the man Carson was, or to put it another way, a look into the great poet's mind.

And what a mind; Carson's love of language is apparent, and not only because Wittgenstein is a character in the novel, but also because of the attention to detail, and the litany of colors which give each of the 101 chapters their titles, including Whiskey, Redcoat Red, and Milk. The opening chapter is PARIS, GREEN. "Perhaps I will return one day to the world I first entered," writes Carson. "For now, I wish to record something of it, if only to remind myself of what I am." This notion of recording a world to remind one of who one is, is to my mind something of Carson's, and the writer's, more generally, project in literature. Green as a color has a heft—of identity, nationality, and as one of the colors of the Irish tricolor, of course. And yet in this opening chapter it is a Paris Green—a green so diverse it conjures "The Greeks" who thought green was associated with Hermaphroditus, and invokes Augustine, and of course Arnolfini, who, with his wife, is the subject of the early Netherlandish painter Jan van Eyck's portrait the protagonist in this magical novel enters.

In fact, *Shamrock Tea* has all of Carson's preoccupations: Belfast, the name Carson, books, and painting, Jan van Eyck's "The Arnolfini Portrait." The Irish Border Commission comes up as we travel through time, and *into* a painting, in a mind-bending, hallucinatory and joyous narrative. "You must go back into the past in order to retrieve the future," he writes. Not that Carson is ever afraid of the earnest and sincere point and having lived through the entire Troubles in his beloved Belfast, he often will make you sit up with statements embedded in this fantasy like, "The border remained as it had been, a device for creating a viable economic unit which could be ruled by a Protestant majority."

It's fitting in many ways that Carson's life-long love affair with the visual arts was captured in his last collection *Still Life*, each of whose poems is about a painting, and that last tender farewell of a book could also be seen as a companion piece to the prose of *Shamrock Tea*. Endless curiosity into the "mystery of being" and the nature of memory are features of the novel. I have a special interest in the novels written by poets. These writers, like Ciaran Carson, approach the genre with a completely surprising, and often new way of seeing and doing "it." But that doesn't mean that Carson is ever afraid of a good yarn and will gladly weave one for you. But he did so with brio, and brilliance.

Every poet I know loves Ciaran's work, but fewer novelists know his novels. I think that's something of a shame. As we look back on his life and work, perhaps that will change. I want the novelist to read his poems, sure, but I'll also recommend to them his novels. Dapper dresser that Ciaran was, intellectually subversive, fun, and always good company, *Shamrock Tea* testifies to the notion "*le style c'est l'homme même*." And if, as he writes, that "time is memory," surely, his work will never be forgotten.

Dresden

Horse Boyle was called Horse Boyle because of his brother Mule;
Though why Mule was called Mule is anybody's guess. I stayed there once,
Or rather, I nearly stayed there once. But that's another story.
At any rate they lived in this decrepit caravan, not two miles out of Carrick,
Encroached upon by baroque pyramids of empty baked bean tins, rusts
And ochres, hints of autumn merging into twilight. Horse believed
They were as good as a watchdog, and to tell you the truth
You couldn't go near the place without something falling over:
A minor avalanche would ensue—more like a shop bell, really,

The old-fashioned ones on string, connected to the latch, I think,
And as you entered in, the bell would tinkle in the empty shop, a musk
Of soap and turf and sweets would hit you from the gloom. Tobacco.
Baling wire. Twine. And, of course, shelves and pyramids of tins.
An old woman would appear from the back—there was a sizzling pan in there,
Somewhere, a whiff of eggs and bacon—and ask you what you wanted;
Or rather, she wouldn't ask; she would talk about the weather. It had rained
That day, but it was looking better. They had just put in the spuds.
I had only come to pass the time of day, so I bought a token packet of Gold Leaf.

All this time the fry was frying away. Maybe she'd a daughter in there
Somewhere, though I hadn't heard the neighbours talk of it; if anybody knew
It would be Horse. Horse kept his ears to the ground.
And he was a great man for current affairs; he owned the only TV in the place.
Come dusk he'd set off on his rounds, to tell the whole town-land the latest
Situation in the Middle East, a mortar bomb attack in Mullaghbawn—
The damn things never worked, of course—and so he'd tell the story
How in his young day it was very different. Take young Flynn, for instance,
Who was ordered to take this bus and smuggle some sticks of gelignite

Across the border, into Derry, when the RUC—or was it the RIC?—
Got wind of it. The bus was stopped, the peeler stepped on. Young Flynn
Took it like a man, of course: he owned up right away. He opened the bag
And produced the bomb, his rank and serial number. For all the world
Like a pound of sausages. Of course, the thing was, the peeler's bike
Had got a puncture, and he didn't know young Flynn from Adam. All he wanted

Was to get home for his tea. Flynn was in for seven years and learned to speak
The best of Irish. He had thirteen words for a cow in heat;
A word for the third thwart in a boat, the wake of a boat on the ebb tide.

He knew the extinct names of insects, flowers, why this palce was called
Whatever: *Carrick*, for example, was *a rock*. He was damn right there—
As the man said, *When you buy meat you buy bones, when you buy land you buy stones.*
You'd be hard put to find a square foot in the whole bloody parish
That wasn't thick with flints and pebbles. To this day he could hear the grate
And scrape as the spade struck home, for it reminded him of broken bones:
Digging a graveyard, maybe—or better still, trying to dig a reclaimed tip
Of broken delft and crockery ware—you know that sound that sets your teeth on edge
When the chalk squeaks on the blackboard, or you shovel ashes from the stove?

Master McGinty—he'd be on about McGinty then, and discipline, the capitals
Of South America, Moore's *Melodies*, the Battle of Clontarf, and
Tell me this, an educated man like you: What goes on four legs when it's young,
Two legs when it's grown up, and three legs when it's old? I'd pretend
I didn't know. McGinty's leather strap would come up then, stuffed
With threepenny bits to give it weight and sting. Of course, it never did him
Any harm: *You could take a horse to water but you couldn't make him drink.*
He himself was nearly going on to be a priest.
And many's the young cub left the school, as wise as when he came.

Carrowkeel was where McGinty came from—*Narrow Quarter*, Flynn explained—
Back before the Troubles, a place that was so mean and crabbed,
Horse would have it, men were known to eat their dinner from a drawer.
Which they'd slide shut the minute you'd walk in.
He'd demonstrate this at the kitchen table, hunched and furtive, squinting
Out the window—past the teetering minarets of rust, down the hedge-dark aisle—
To where a stranger might appear, a passer-by, or what was maybe worse,
Someone he knew. Someone who wanted something. Someone who was hungry.
Of course who should come tottering up the lane that instant but his brother

Mule. I forgot to mention they were twins. They were as like two—
No, not peas in a pod, for this is not the time nor the place to go into
Comparisons, and this is really Horse's story, Horse who—now I'm getting
Round to it—flew over Dresden in the war. He'd emigrated first, to
Manchester. Something to do with scrap—redundant mill machinery,
Giant flywheels, broken looms that would, eventually, be ships, or aeroplanes.

He said he wore his fingers to the bone.
And so, on impulse, he had joined the RAF. He became a rear gunner.
Of all the missions, Dresden broke his heart. It reminded him of china.

As he remembered it, long afterwards, he could hear, or almost hear
Between the rapid desultory thunderclaps, a thousand tinkling echoes—
All across the map of Dresden, store-rooms full of china shivered, teetered
And collapsed, an avalanch of porcelain, slushing and cascading: cherubs,
Shepherdesses, figurines of Hope and Peace and Victory, delicate bone fragments.
He recalled in particular a figure from his childhood, a milkmaid
Standing on the mantelpiece. Each night as they knelt down for the rosary,
His eyes would wander up to where she seemed to beckon to him, smiling,
Offering him, eternally, her pitcher of milk, her mouth of rose and cream.

One day, reaching up to hold her yet again, his fingers stumbled, and she fell.
He lifted down a biscuit tin, and opened it.
It breathed an antique incense: things like pencils, snuff, tobacco.
His war medals. A broken rosary. And there, the milkmaid's creamy hand, the outstretched
Pitcher of milk, all that survived. Outside there was a scraping
And a tittering; I knew Mule's step by now, his careful drunken weaving
Through the tin-stacks. I might have stayed the night, but there's no time
To go back to that now; I could hardly, at any rate, pick up the thread.
I wandered out through the steeples of rust, the gate that was a broken bed.

On "Dresden"

Stephen Sexton

WHEN IT COMES TO CHOOSING a single poem to write about, an impulse moves me to choose the one most like him. I think that means like him in expression or manner or voice, or in style or form. I think it's an elegiac impulse. I read *The Collected Poems* of Ciaran Carson often, or rather, I fetch it from the mantelpiece as I would a dictionary. Often, this follows some flash of good thought or flourish of language I think I've come up with, to discover the same good thought, or its cousin, somewhere within the book's 32 years. Everything, however, is like him: the translations from the Irish and French and Italian are like him, so are his sonnets, so are the fractured, skeletal poems of later career. "Dresden," though, is representative of the style he's perhaps best known for: meandering, rangy, long lines broken by the typesetter's right margin before they break themselves. This poem comes from his second book *The Irish for No* (1987), published 11 years after his first book; time he spent travelling around Ireland and elsewhere, playing traditional Irish music. Sometimes I imagine, during those years, a moonlit night somewhere in rural Donegal, at a crossroads, a handshake might have taken place. The poet of this book bears little resemblance to the poet of the first book, *The New Estate* (1976). The transformations are all his.

"Dresden" is among the first of Ciaran's great poems. Unfolding over its five pages, and various digressions, is a recollection of its speaker's staying, or nearly staying the night "in this decrepit caravan, not two miles out of Carrick / Encroached upon by baroque pyramids of empty baked bean tins," a guest of the poem's central character, one Horse Boyle, who is also very much a *character* in the other sense. The first lines are these: "Horse Boyle was called Horse Boyle because of his brother Mule; / Though why Mule was called Mule is anybody's guess." There's a comic and iconic ring to those lines, but more significantly, they introduce the kind of haphazard, contingent logic by which the poem reckons toward the point its speaker is trying to relate; proceeding not quite at the speed of memory, but following its directions. The ways Carson's brilliant, rhizomatic imagination draws from its innumerable experiences; sensory, linguistic, synaesthetic, is one of the pleasures of his writing. Most often, "Dresden" proceeds by sonic association. The thought of the sound of those toppling baked bean bins is

> more like a shop bell, really,

> The old-fashioned ones on string, connected to the latch, I think,
> And as you entered in, the bell would tinkle in the empty shop, a musk
> Of soap and turf and sweets would hit you from the gloom. Tobacco.
> Baling wire. Twine. And, of course, shelves and pyramids of tins.

There are several instances of this kind of logic: the poem is a riffle of scenes; stories within stories. News of a defective "mortar bomb attack in Mullaghbawn" prompts Horse to tell the story of Young Flynn who was caught smuggling gelignite across the border and imprisoned for seven years, during which "he learned to speak / The best of Irish." ("*Carrick*, for example, was a *rock*.") Horse, digging in stony earth, "the grate / and scrape as the spade struck home" is reminded of broken bones: "that sound / that sets your teeth on edge / When the chalk squeaks on the blackboard." Subsequently, a schoolteacher comes to mind, one Master McGinty, who was from Carrowkeel, "a place that was so mean and crabbed, / Horse would have it, men were known to eat their dinner from a drawer." This is the kind of meandering conversation some readers denigrated as "mere pub-talk." "If that's the case," Carson says, "I'm very happy with the comparison. Any poetry that confines itself to the merely literary is half dead. And I enjoy pubs a lot more than poetry readings."

For all its jabbering humor, the poem reveals itself as one with an empathetic pulse, somewhat uncommon across Ciaran's poems. Elsewhere, violence is reported with an aloofness and a dark humor. Horse Boyle, we learn, four fifths of the way through the poem, joined the RAF and became a rear gunner who "flew over Dresden in the war." He is haunted by his part in its destruction.

> It reminded him of china.

> As he remembered it, long afterwards, he could hear, or almost hear,
> Between the rapid, desultory thunderclaps, a thousand tinkling echoes—
> All across the map of Dresden, storerooms full of china shivered, teetered
> And collapsed, an avalanche of porcelain, slushing and cascading

Horse remembers too a figurine of a milkmaid from his childhood, knocked from the mantelpiece and shattered. Her hand and pitcher of milk, along with tobacco, war medals, a broken rosary, are kept in a biscuit tin. Despite Horse's edge of jocularity, he's a man living in ruins approximating, consciously or not, the devastation of Dresden. His pyramids of empty baked bean tins are, beyond artful junk, mausoleums; the broken milkmaid is a dreadful precursor to his bombing missions. This instance of childhood clumsiness is what sets the story going and "the milkmaid's creamy hand, the outstretched / Pitcher of milk, all that survived" reverberates in the tinkling of china, "delicate bone fragments," the spade in stony earth, and reverberates through the anecdotes of the poem, surviving the associative leaps of logic that are its sinews, and is offered, eventually, to us.

The Irish for No, and the book that follows, *Belfast Confetti*, are books of the Troubles in Northern Ireland and its society, its impermanent architecture and its topography altered by decades of bombs and murders. The books are also particularly concerned with borders and boundaries and thresholds, both permeable and impermeable. History, memory, language, are as inextricable here as they are anywhere else, and there are moments in "Dresden" where I'm not quite sure who is saying what: the speaker and Horse and Young Flynn seem to blend together, their voices and personalities intertwine. Reading this poem again, new edges and angles show themselves. I'm struck, for example, by how the poem is composed of leaps and digressions, yes, but also by the number of thresholds it traverses: not just the tinkling bell on a latch in an ancient shop, Young Flynn in prison, or, at the end of the poem, the speaker's exit through "the gate that was a broken bed." There are thresholds of people and time too. I've never thought about how intimate the poem is.

It would be about now in our discussion Ciaran would say something like "it's all metaphor anyhow," and we'd think about wrapping up our discussion of whatever poem lay before us in our workshop. That would make it a Friday afternoon sometime between late 2011 and early 2019. Those were the years of my most dynamic transformations: afternoons of etymology and metaphor and stories and jokes and singing where, with Ciaran and my fellow students, little by little, I was becoming most like myself.

from *The Star Factory*

Owenvarragh (pp. 97–101)

AT THE BACK of Moreland Drive was a plot of undeveloped land that would become Owenvarragh* Drive; beyond that, fields of grass and buttercups dotted with cows' clap, that I remember harvesting with a coal shovel and a tin bucket as manure for our back garden. The undeveloped half-acre was, for us children, a foyer or rehearsal space for that rural hinterland beyond us, containing its essential elements in miniature: here, a small tributary of the Owenvarragh River ran between blackthorn hedges, where we built tree-parlours. Ensconced in them, invisible to adult eyes, we made up secrets for ourselves, which remain untold, and so intricate as to be untellable. We dug fist-sized catacombs in the clay banks of the stream, and installed in them the bodies of frogs, mice and birds, returning to them years or weeks later to disinter their clean white skeletons.

The small stream was enormous in its details of meander, its microscopic reefs and deeps and sandbars, the purl of its current round an imposing stone; sometimes, flood-borne minor Mississippi rafts of twigs would form a log-jam and a rippling dam of water became pent behind it, where we would launch paper-boat flotillas and bomb them with clay pellets.

Beyond this adjunct of our new estate lay the Cows' Field,** its boundary marked by a tall electric pylon protected by storeys of barbed wire and skull-and-crossbones signs. When it rained, the pylon buzzed with intimations of mortality and suicide, and the cows would low and moan as they staggered up off their knees in an almost integrated body to find uncontaminated pastures on the margins of the force-field. Years later, people would claim compensation for the cancers allegedly induced by these Eiffel Towers.

South of the Cows' Field lay the Jungle, demarcated on one side by the Owenvarragh, and on the other by the railings of Musgrave Park Hospital, which occupied a low plateau above the river, looking like a derelict RAF aerodrome with

---

* From *abhain bharrach*, barred river, the bars being stakes or staves; and the Owenvarragh, in its lower reaches, from Stockman's Lane to where it joins the Lagan, becomes the Blackstaff. *Barra* can also mean a sand-bar, or *fearsad*; so these waters—Blackstaff, Owenvarragh, Farset—form an etymological confluence.

** So-called because it was invariably inhabited by cows.

its rows of isolated Nissen huts, each one of which was a hospital ward. Making our way through the jungle, we were subliminally aware of this near-necropolis above us, and its empty gravel walks whose order contradicted our meanderings. Although the Jungle was a mere strip of river bank some ten or fifteen yards across and some four hundred long—a bonzai zone of low, implicated scrub and thorn— we kept finding *terra incognita* in its labyrinth; or, exploring different routes between known places, we saw them from a new perspective. Here were tiny glades carpeted with moss and microcosmic galaxies of flowers; pools in them, sometimes, flickering with embryonic fish and water-bugs; dense undergrowths of ferns; rank columns of umbellifers, and phalanxes of bulrushes. One loop of the river was almost completely ceilinged by over-arching trees: this was a secret place of mine, where I would sit alone for hours on a minor sand-bank, studying the compass-needle flickerings of dragonflies, entranced by the languid fish; once, I saw a kingfisher dive like a blue bolt through the clerestory of branches and break the surface water in an eye-blink, before coming up, almost instantaneously, with a struggling silver flash in its beak. It was easy to imagine dim organ-music in this miniature cathedral, where leafy bifurcations met and whispered in confessionals, allowing tremolos of light to penetrate its shades.

I knew that if ever I was on the run—an IRA man, say—I could retreat here, to the heart of the Jungle; here would be my final See, or siege. Here I'd be absorbed and camouflaged, protected by its genius, with whom I'd long communed. Incorporated by its teeming ecosystem, I'd become a detail of its verdurous glooms and winding mossy ways, whose divarications, and the routes and tributaries between them, were innumerable.

Yet, others must have had the same idea: scouting the territory, we would come across small clearings dotted by the charcoal interims of camp-fires, where important pow-wows had occurred throughout the long campaign of summer. Some of these we recognized as our own residue; around others, still warm to the touch, we found scattered cigarette-butts, evidence that others, older than us, had been here previously; and we felt a Crusoe wobble of fear, like when he saw a footstep on the sand of his supposed desert island. For we knew that the Jungle was an intermediate ground, that it contained a demarcation between Catholic and Protestant territory, though where precisely this border might be, or where we might infract it, no one was prepared to say. No map delineated it. We were given no specific caveats against it by our parents, since, after all, they only knew the Jungle by our non-committal reports; yet, we got osmotic rumours of the broader picture, where the Protestant majority might view our new estate as the tip of the iceberg of the Falls Road minority community, expanding under demographic pressure westwards into lush farmlands and the ornamental parks of planters' houses.

Making our way westwards through the Jungle, we felt the force-field of home gradually diminish, till, its signal imperceptible, we were exposed like aliens on the margins of our known world. This point was marked by the hospital rubbish tip, which spilled down from its elevation in a cornucopia of dead flowers, blood-ied bandages, Roman-toga tumbling drapes of bed-linen, disgorged orange rubber tubing and discarded hypodermics. Staggering up its scree, we were archaeologists of the avalanche, finding dead Ever-Ready batteries, rusted scalpels, odd shoes, crutches, Bakelite, plugs; once, we disinterred a practically intact radio. We dreaded to imagine the hospital activity that lay behind this waste, the Frankenstein interi-ors of morgues and incubators palpitating with galvanic zig-zag sparks.

Contemplating these inner dimensions, we were also implicated in the wider landscape, finding new bearings and perspectives as the skyline of Black Moun-tain, a long mile or so to the North, shifted to accommodate our purposeful me-anderings, whose river-source lay in the mountain. The sky seemed bigger here; unbalanced by it, we would get a dizzy, pleasurable tremor of agoraphobia. After a repast of camp-fire cabonized potatoes and scorched woodsmoke-perfumed toast, we would sprawl on our backs and gaze into the hemisphere above, seeing pictures in its lagooned archipelagos of moving cumulus and jigsaw-puzzle sky. On rare cloudless days, it almost hurt to look into the huge blue levels, where the diamond point of a jet scored a silent white line miles long, and amethyst became forget-me-not....

Owenvarragh

Connie Voisine

In Ciaran Carson's *The Star Factory*, a wonderful short essay, an encomium really, called "Owenvarragh" maps a particular landscape of his childhood. He describes Owenvarragh as "at the back of Mooreland Drive" and "a plot of undeveloped land" that by the time he was writing this essay (the late 1990s) was called Owenvarragh Drive. It also was, to his child self, a place as big as imagination itself.

Wanting to enter that space from my home in New Mexico, I google. I can find Mooreland Drive, a mere block-long street ending in a green patch called Casement Park. The two most magical places for young Ciaran, a small unnamed tributary and its source, the Owenvarragh River, are not to be found, not on Google Maps, StreetFinder or the Property Pal mapping system. A whole river and its tributary—gone? Where is this place of Ciaran's where "[e]nsconced in [tree-parlors] invisible to adult eyes, we made up secrets for ourselves, which remain untold, and so intricate as to be unintelligible." I shouldn't be surprised, as the reconfigurations of Belfast City have filled up many books of poems, novels, and histories, and Ciaran found this subject especially rich.

Ciaran often discussed poetry in the context of traditional music—he was a flute and whistle player and his wife Deirdre a fine fiddler—tracing the transmission of each to the intimacies of the "small back room." Much in the way the small back room sets the community of the moment knee to knee to play a tune, "Owenvarragh" is filled to its brief capacity. The glimpses, fragments, half-anecdotes and missing rivers knock against my knees as I enter those tree-parlours.

Cut to December 19, 2011, the day my family and I arrived in Belfast for my Fulbright semester, the first time we lived there. We were invited to the Queen's University English Department holiday party, exhausted but trying to stay awake, the common advice for jet lag. While pulling my five-year old's face out of the icing on a tray of cupcakes, I introduced myself to Ciaran and him to my husband, saying, "Rus plays fiddle." Rus said, "Old time, mostly." This set Ciaran off on a meandering tale of his travels in Appalachia where he stumbled onto a small back room and he heard such lonesome, mournful singing, the murder ballad, "Oh, Bury Me Under the Weeping Willow." Ciaran started singing it, Rus sang harmony, and they sang it with joy into each other's ears, because the room was loud, having found a connection.

To write this piece, I purchased a used copy of *The Star Factory* online, since mine was in quarantine in my office at school. As I read "From Abby Road to

Zetland Street" (an essay where Ciaran quotes letters purchased in an auction room, one to a navy man, Jim, from Gertie, and a letter to the same Gertie, perhaps, from some illegible suitor), an actual letter dropped from *The Star Factory*'s pages. This letter was on elegant stationary that announced its writer as Maurice Sunderland, who had many initials after his name indicating that he was an architect. Some research, Google again, indicated that Sunderland (1926-2002) mostly practiced in Canada and was the original designer of the Mall of America. The letter hopes that Leslie might enjoy the book, as Maurice did, though the Belfast described is very different from the one he remembers from his childhood. This Carson fellow, he says, is rather "medieval in his wanderings." I think Ciaran would have liked that story, beginning as it does in coincidence, but creating complicities across lives, time, and place.

On *The Star Factory*

Tess Taylor

Sitting here, on a now-bright California day between winter rainstorms, in the tenth month of a pandemic, I am long-deprived of travel. In the lockdown months, I've been confined to taking notes on the smallest details of my neighborhood: The sound of its underground creek, the collapsing wagon wheel in front of the Old West Gunshop, the kestrel I've seen hunting near the Sunset Mausoleum. Perhaps that's why I've been savoring again *The Star Factory*, Ciaran Carson's labyrinthine and palimpsestic memoir of his childhood in Belfast, which allows me to travel through time and space, and also reminds me of the intense detail by which someone else's words can help a reader light up their own life.

Now as I sit, fingering pages on a damp green morning—(California's rainy season feels, for a few months, a bit Irish)—it seems to me that Carson, an incurable collector and admirer of *things*, and a lover of the trails onto which things direct you, might want me to pause first and admire the book itself, and the way its presence invites me to travel back to the fall before I was first slated to travel to Belfast as a Fulbright. I was then after a straightforward historic narrative of the city—a rough timeline of facts, mind you—and I asked the poet Sinéad Morrissey for recommendations. Instead of offering something with any clear through-line (I've since realized that the clarity of agreed-upon history is bit anathema to Belfast's life), Morrissey suggested I read *The Star Factory*, Carson's rather remarkable idiosyncratic tour of the city's linked and branched sites—the stations where, for him, memory, history, and pathway await decoding.

The book begins, unceremoniously enough, on a chamber pot, or rather in front of one, where Carson-the-boy is listening to his father tell a story. It's a tribute to Carson that not only has he invited us into this rather unorthodox space to begin a book, but that within a few gestures he's also made it feel actually regal to be there. In fact, it may be ceremonious after all: The father is smoking a cigar and Carson is considering the "ancient magisterial importance of the chamber pot, where courtiers and Privy Counselors await the outcome of his majesty's deliberations like a plot, and perfumes of Arabia are sprayed discretely round the room." So much for straight-ahead history, but, by God, I'm entranced.

The angles of vision stay compellingly strange, and the magisterial air builds, rarely out of the essential grandeur of the things explored, but rather out of the force of the explorer's curiosity. There are no ideas but in things, said William Carlos Williams, but Carson is also intent on capturing the phantasmagoria things partake in, the dreams that attach, refracting at last an entire world-view accrued from flotsam and jetsam. In Carson's hands, no thing (not even the ping pong ball foraged out of the old Chesterfield) is actually minute, but has its place in the arc of history, the world of the mind, and the flow of a writer's insatiable curiosity. "Magisterial import" is thus bestowed by Carson himself. Indeed, who but Carson could linger so long over the humble postage stamp, reminding us that it is the document and glue which binds us (even uneasily) to place and nation and Empire? Here is Carson, in three sentences, opining on just one stamp:

> The 2 ½ d blue-black definitive commemorative of 1941 is best known as the Gunman: it depicts a Gulliver-sized Volunteer armed with a bayoneted rifle, poised at his post above a Lilliputian GPO; the stamp has a somber border like a death notice . . . Banal, pious, badly drawn, next to worthless in monetary terms, the Gunman is not a beautiful stamp, but it fascinates me. I love the blue-black ink that seems to have a tint of bottle-green in it, so that it summons up the dull enamelled frames of the Royal Ulster Constabulory bicycles armed with upright handlebars, three-speed Sturmey-Archer thumbswitch gears, stirrup breaks and faltering hub-dynamo lamps; the colour of gunpowder, broken slates or magnets; the ooze-blue glad of the Lagan at low tide; coke smoke from the Gasworks; livid, live-lobster blue; rubber bullets, purple cobblestones, a smear of rotting blackberries; cinder paths at dusk, when no one walks on them; the black arm-band of the temporary postal worker.

Oh my—that glorious, thing-and-clause-filled third sentence! That sentence whose cobbled and waterfalling purpose seems to be to gum together all the associations of one color of one postage stamp, and which, in so doing, refracts an outer world of cobblestones and bullets, livid lobsters and tidal ooze, hub-dynamo lamps and gunpowder! We must now pause and wonder: Does the thing hold the ideas, or do the ideas inhere the thing? We can also note how in Carson's hand a sentence about just one thing becomes divagation and world-making at once, one dense node on which Carson builds his "alternative hologram of the city," or assembles his own "vastly complicated interactive model airplane kit"—a landscape, somewhat like Freud's Rome-as-subconscious, of spongy portals and upthrust connections. We are inside a logic that delights in places lost and re-found, in naming the parade of Belfast's streets (Odessa; Balaclava; Raglan), in savoring lost landmarks. Station by station, essay by essay, we collect and tenderly examine core samples of Belfast. One such meditation is devoted to the now-lost Smithfield Bazaar, a crowded and intriguing urban flea-market, which was bombed in 1974, and replaced by the far more bland Castle Court shopping mall. In their movement over such landmarks,

Carson's linked essays channel Baudelaire ("The old city is gone / the shape of a town / changes faster, alas, than the heart of a mortal"); echo Walter Benjamin ("Not architecture alone but all technology is, at certain stages, evidence of a collective dream"); and offer to Belfast a bit of the love that James Joyce spent his career offering Dublin ("When I die Dublin will be written on my heart"). Sinéad had known best: *The Star Factory* was a perfect introduction.

I have woven my memory of reading the book into my exploration of it, and perhaps this is part of Carson's point—that the objects or cities or books we encounter become somewhat inseparable from the self who encounters them, that they attach to us, too, weaving in and through us. In any case, Carson's meditative essays on such attachments weave together by unexpected skeins. He writes,

> it strikes me that [the] hook-and-eye principle is applicable to my own method of writing, where I have to make a link or bridge from the end of a chapter to the head, or body of the next, sometimes in quite an arbitrary fashion; it is also part of the ever recurring problem of getting sentences to follow each other like a troupe of circus elephants, trunks hooked into tails, or the tall-tale filing system . . . where 'in the 10th century . . . the Grand Vizier of Persia, Abdul Kassem Ismael, in order not to part with his collection of 117,000 books when traveling, had them carried by a caravan of four hundred camels trained to walk in alphabetical order.'

Elephants, camels or caravans aside, here is my one, well-traveled copy of *The Star Factory*, carried first with me from California to Belfast, and then back to California again. I do not wish to part with it, particularly because it now holds Carson's inscription to me: "To Tess with very best wishes for meeting in Belfast on Bloomsday, 2017." The inscription (itself at a shrewd coordinate of place and literary time) calls up the day Carson honored me by letting me run a workshop alongside him. The workshop was a special thing: his gift, as an emeritus professor, to the Heaney Centre. Unlike other workshops in the Queen's program, that were (as they are nearly everywhere) structured around topic, or segregated by age, Carson's workshops, held at the Friday-afternoon-cusp-of-the-weekend, were a delicious communal craft-and-thought space open to anyone of any age, graduate or undergraduate, enrolled in the university. The only prerequisite was wishing to know something about the poet's path. There was no great agenda or reading list, and the only point was to come and share poems round in a circle, and talk about how they worked, what valences were alive in them. Carson, who had served on the Arts Council for many years, and had disbursed funds and advocated for pathways for artists, also ran a similar free workshop that was open to the public. This feels important to remember: While Carson-the-writer was capturing the tangled portals and pathways of his own memory, and finding a way to build up the mythic presence of his fractured but beloved city, Carson-the-teacher was intent on leaving a path for others, helping young writers find foothold on the pathways of a craft that had been practiced in Belfast at least since the writing of the 9th century Irish poem "'The Blackbird of Belfast Lough" which Carson translates thus:

the little bird
that whistled shrill
from the nib of
its yellow bill

a note let go
o'er Belfast Lough—
a blackbird from
a yellow whin

It is fitting that, just as I was writing, a lemon yellow California warbler dove into a live oak just outside my office window, offering me a bit of time to think about the middle distance, the way a book like *The Star Factory* makes one's own life, wherever one is, feel richer, more *seen*; more overheard, as it were. Writing like that makes life's music feel more full of notes. It is not that I have ever been a boy in Belfast in the 1950s—far from it. It is rather that in capturing both place and experience with such density and verve Carson also invites his readers to find, wherever they are, more richness and possibility in their own lives. As I look up, I see mercury storm clouds banking off the green hills and promising the afternoon's rain, and I see them freshly as emissaries of the ocean, the faultline, the season, the currents that sweep down from Alaska. I feel more aware of the convergences at the place where I now perch and live.

After I returned home, I hoped to find a way to invite Carson to come and read in Berkeley. It was not to be so: Carson grew more ill and could not come, and then left us. I have not been back to Belfast since 2017. Apparently, this winter, as the pandemic was on, there was a gaudy light show up at Belfast City Hall, called, of all things *The Star Factory*. Will some later writer glance off its memory with wry humor? Perhaps. For now, even sitting here, I have a sense of having voyaged some, and also how the book, with its aliveness to possibility has offered me both some fantastic escape, and the challenge of caressing more deeply what life I have got, right now. For that, I am very, very grateful.

EMILIA PHILLIPS

from The Queerness of Eve

Book III

Not halves of a whole.
Not mirrors. Not puzzled
together in the missionary
position. Not a gunpowder
keg and a gun going off.
You scoff, but I wasn't
the fruit to his pit,
a tangle for his nit.
No, Adam and I,
we were more
like brothers
from our quickchange
infancy forward. Big-footed
babies with steel wool
scrubbing our pits,
our groins. His face a full
burning bush. Unpleasant
to kiss. My peached
upper lip rubbed raw
by indifference. I flexed
my bicep in the wellspring
pool. God said, For godsakes,
don't name the animals
if you're going
to eat them. The slaughter
will be harder.
(He would know,
I know now.)
Adam named the one that stood
on his foot, *Cow.*

I called her *Tallulah*.
I burned her dried dung
for a cook fire.
But I didn't know how
to cook. I had no mother
to teach me
her bridewell.
Adam was, for all intents
and purposes, my beard—
always dripping
with juice. Always
saving some for later.
But by him, I had citizenship
in the country
where I watched
eagles knot themselves
in spitfire aerials.
If you think about it,
we were the first
domestic animals.
I wore a collar of black-eyed
Susans and so did Adam.
We were as different
as we weren't. Who desires
who doesn't?
I asked, shoving mint
into his mouth.

Book IV

Woman always settled
on me like snow
on warm ground. Briefly.
Some mayfly
tender. But my body's weirder
than archetype, more
pulsed than
perfection. If I had been
marble, I would have
lost interest.
Who says Adam's
manlier?
Who became my nickname
for God.
I also called him
When, *What*, and *Where*.
Why just two
of us? Why does Adam
have nipples
if he can't provide
for his children?
How do I unsilly
a never-asked
question?
How do I make silence
my gender?

Book VI

My brain expanded
like yeast dough
proofing in a covered
bowl. I began
on my hands
and knees, but soon
slouched like a willow.
Eventually, my spine
was as straight
as the definition
narrow. And God shook out
the pterodactyl
like a wet umbrella.
Inside out, it became
the mute swan—
I didn't dare feed it
crumbs from my open
palm, but I watched
it double-s over
the wellspring pond,
and this was the first
moment
I realized there could be
more than one
of anything, the swan
and anti-swan
in symmetry,
imperfect only
for the ripples
glassing away
from its body.
God made man
in his own image,
so they say.
So I made a beloved
in mine.

Book VIII

How to make a name
from no language, a language from no
name: harness it
to the oxen
body, make your tongue
a blunt plow. The first word
that wasn't Godgiven
was what I called
her—*Stranger*,
which could be translated
in your tongue
as The One Who Never
Dies. I learned to
write by watching
the orbweaver
rubix her imperfect
mirror, the light
the first flies she ever
caught, all wings.
And, still, her hunger.
Still, the waiting.
The first almond blossoms
curled like magician's fingers
over the lost bronze
coins. Who says it had to be
fruit I took from the tree?
The centuries have been
playing a game
of telephone. I know everything
you know,
by now. I know God
hurled the Garden's key
into the sun. But, back
then, the forbidden
tree grew like the future—
wild as alternate
endings, as a conspiracy

of meanings. This is
not a happy
story. No, this is not
a story at all.

JASON KOO

The Rest Is Silence

I've been sitting at this window in MiKro
for the past hour and a half on a Friday afternoon

in Hamden, watching folks come in to start
their weekends, and every single one of them

has been white. I came here to unwind
after a phone interview a few colleagues and I

conducted with three job candidates,
all white. I was the only one participating not

white. All of the other seven finalists
the other subcommittees are interviewing

are white. All of the other subcommittee profs
are white. We will likely hire three new

white profs to join a department in which all
but one of its fourteen full-time profs (hi)

are white. At no point will we talk, unless I
bring it up, about the problem of adding

three new white profs to this all but all-white
department, because our job applicant pool

(according to HR) yielded a 7% diversity rating,
3% below the national average but deemed

"acceptable." There were 93 candidates, so six,
maybe seven people of color self-identified.

In my advanced poetry workshop this semester,
every student is white. In my intro to poetry course,

17 out of 18 are white. These percentages
are typical. They've been so since I started here

in 2012. They are, apparently, "acceptable."
Less than 7% diversity. When I got to this bar,

not many people were here, I was feeling good,
I like the hickory-smoked chicken wings, locally

brewed IPAs, but as one by one every new white
person filed in, I felt myself shrinking into a tinier

%, becoming more and more miKroscopic.
I'm not surprised. I've been to this bar many times,

it's my favorite bar in Hamden, I like to come here
after work to have a beer and work on things

before hitting the road back home to Brooklyn.
Always it is all white except for me—it's like

our thing. Mind you, not almost all white, *all* white.
6:30 now and the happy-hour weekend crowd

is pouring in, the place is packed, I look up
and watch every new white customer walk in

with a peculiar, dangerous sort of pleasure,
like I'm itching a rash. I'm lucky this doesn't

bother me that much, I know when I come here
I'm going to leave and drive back home to Brooklyn.

But imagine if I lived here. When people at my school,
students and faculty alike, ask me why I don't

live here, why I commute an hour and a half
from Brooklyn, they don't understand how this

is a racist question. Imagine if I told them that.
Man, how can you bear that commute?

Man, how can you bear that racist question?
Look around you in this bar. Look at every single

person walking through that door. Let's count
how many people look like me by the end

of the night. Do you ever do that obligatory
room check, turning to scan the faces around you

to see how many non-white ones there are? No?
Well maybe don't ask me about my commute then.

It's that never having occurred to you that this room
might be a problem, might make some people

uncomfortable, might make them, consciously
or unconsciously, change their behavior, their very

personality, that reveals your racist blindness—
no, that's not the right word, it's too strong,

ableist, suggests there's something wrong
with you, some flaw, whereas you don't think

there's anything wrong, it's a racist innocence.
And you're not wrong, what's so bad about

what's happening here? Are these bad people?
Is anyone saying some racist shit or not serving me

or causing me physical harm? Am I not being
included like everyone else, am I not being

treated equally? I couldn't call you a *racist*.
You're not *doing* anything. I would never tell

you to your face you're asking me a racist question
or explain you're enjoying a racist innocence

(except in this poem), I wouldn't want to do that
to you, you're too innocent, it's not your fault,

I'd immediately feel like an asshole. And that's
the problem, isn't it, innocent? You go on innocent,

places like this go on innocently looking this way.
What's the bar supposed to do, institute some kind

of diversity quota? It's a business, these are the people
who live here, these are its customers, it needs

to make money, there's nothing racist about that.
Right? It's not turning people of color away or not

serving them, the people who work here are all
nice, I've never had a problem other than seeing

white person after white person walk in without
interruption, which is not against the law, maybe

I'm just a whiner, overly sensitive, I don't have
to drink here, I don't even live here, what's the bar

supposed to do, offer free beer to people of color?
Host People of Color Night? That would be absurd.

Right? Hire more people of color to change
the complexion of the room and attract more

customers of color? That would be against the law,
potentially, if it were found the bar hired POC

over more qualified white candidates, and let's be
real, how many POC work in the craft beer industry?

Compared to white folks? Especially in this area?
You'd have to go out of your way to find someone

when there are all these super-qualified white folks
already available to hire. And they're all so nice,

hard working, experienced, most importantly
they love beer, they're passionate about it,

it's the one thing in their life they care about
the most, they'd fit right in here, they'd hit

the ground running, whereas a person of color . . .
would they even be happy? Would they want

to stay? Wouldn't they have other interests,
aspirations? This job is not easy. It's mostly grunt

work, a person with aspirations might find it
difficult to endure, especially if they already feel

out of place. All of this reasoning makes sense
even as I sit here feeling more miKroscopic

sipping my white beer. What's funny is how absurd
diversity initiatives seem at a bar that do not

at a university, offering free beer to bring POC
into this space seems hilarious in the imagination,

especially when I picture furious white customers,
whereas offering financial aid at a university

does not. What's funny is what's not so funny,
how diversity initiatives at a bar only seem absurd

because not enough people are talking about them
to give them traction, admitting POC or women

into a university let alone giving them financial aid
seemed as absurd if not more so to white gents

not so long ago. And by absurd I mean so against
the natural, historical inertia of the norm

as to seem like a physical violation, that inertia
is the bedrock of all true power, the saturation

of the same so-be-it that has always been, what makes
a 7% diversity rating "acceptable," what can we do

about it, these are the people who applied,
we don't know how many of them self-identified,

this is our demographic, it's not our fault
POC are not taking advantage of this opportunity,

we made it available to everyone, what are we
supposed to do, redo the whole job search?

Change the qualifications? Cast a wider net
with our advertising? Change the whole way

we do business? Who's going to do all that work
and spend all that money? You? Of course not

me, I'm not in charge here, if I were, the whole
business would be built differently from

the ground up, inclusivity and diversity
would be part of the very fabric of how we do

things, we wouldn't need to pay for outside
assessment of our diversity or hire a Chief

Diversity Officer or construct a strategic plan
for increasing diversity, a plan that slyly gives

a company convenient cover if anyone
should point out the factual lack of diversity

among their ranks and the problems arising
because of that, now there's official language

"proving" the company takes diversity seriously
and is doing something about it, a simulacrum

of diversity including a definition that expands
its meaning beyond race and gender to include

class, ability, sexuality, age, religion, education
and pretty much anything under the sun,

so that looked at this way, diversity has already
been achieved, there's no need to do anything

despite what the strategic plan seems to suggest
by its existence, if not by what it actually says,

the company brilliantly grows so inclusive
by the letter of its own law as to become more

exclusive, as now white job committees can
hire more white employees to entrench their own

"diversity." There is a "yesterday I find almost
impossible to lift," as Elizabeth Bishop said

at the end of her career, not talking about race,
but I feel it mid-career, or perhaps pre-career,

as whatever career I have always feels like a prelude
to an actual one, and this because of race,

I can say something about our lack of diversity
to my department, how for us and our school

this starts with race, as we don't have a gender
issue and race is the most easily visible form

of diversity missing here, making any POC
uncomfortable and strangely causing even more

discomfort to white folks when the subject
is brought up, they won't go out of their way

to increase racial diversity but they'll go out
of their way to talk about this problem, acting

like they want to do something, saying,
"We need to have a conversation about this,"

then having meeting after meeting
where talk replaces action and postpones

the problem for another meeting, but will talk
of any kind change the room around me?

Look at where I'm sitting. Imagine me
saying something. What would the reaction be?

Who would I say something *to*? Another
customer? The bartender? The manager?

The owner? Where would I even start?
At least at a university there's some kind

of intellectual and political context for what
I'd like to say, but at a bar? On a Friday night?

There might be some talk here and there
about the problems of race in America,

but no one wants to hear that the problem
is them, especially on a Friday night, what did

they do, they're just trying to kick back
and have a good time. And truthfully I don't

think they are the problem, the problem
starts so far in back of us, in all the yesterdays

that have built up this room and others
like it without question, there's no moving

the massive weight of them without total
cataclysm, or by tiny, incremental, all but

imperceptible shifts that feel like waiting,
or doing nothing, so saying something

feels, in the end (because there is no end),
like silence, except now you're full of unrest

because you've caused unrest, you've ruined
everyone's happy hour, starting with your own—

I just want to sit here after work and eat
these hickory-smoked chicken wings and drink

these locally brewed IPAs, not so ruefully aware
of how doing so participates in and bankrolls

this hand-crafted whiteness, how my tastes,
which feel so particular to me, are informed

by whiteness, whiteness of a certain kind
that I perceive as cool and try to embody

with my own Asian slant, this bar, I know,
appeals to me because it looks and feels like

Brooklyn, starting with its being housed
in a renovated historic building (or at least

what looks like such a building), the name
is Korny but this is the closest you're gonna get

to Brooklyn in Hamden, I recognize all
the Brooklyn design touches, how Brooklyn

itself is an import for any place trying
to commodify its local, historic identity,

and this is a white Brooklyn, I'm such
a sucker for it, much as I say I'm becoming

uncomfortable with all the white people
walking in, obviously I feel more comfortable

here than anywhere else in Hamden, I keep
coming here though this keeps happening,

something about this place feels inclusive,
or inclusive enough to keep me consuming

rather than speaking out about its problems,
except in the space of this poem, and let's face it,

a poem is a more acceptable way of breaking
silence, it can be ignored (especially one this long)

and doesn't ruin anybody's happy hour, in fact
it goes well with happy hour if read for some

indie reading series at your neighborhood bar,
I can even see it working here, though there

might be some initial discomfort, everyone
likes to be challenged politically and made

uncomfortably aware of our nation's problems
when there's a time limit, booze and packaging

as art and entertainment, it's a good discussion
starter, "edgy," an edifying hors d'oeuvres

to clear the conscience before the evening's
inanities, and I'm not *too* angry, which helps,

look at how I've already qualified my complaints
by showing how I'm complicit in everything

I'm complaining about, reassuring whiteness
that there's no real problem here, everyone

can go back to their drinks, plus I'm Asian
American, white folks don't find my kind

(that) threatening anymore, at least not since
Executive Order 9066, I might not feel I fit in

but I fit in, Asian American is the new white,
or the closest to white of any POC, which I

find troubling, to say the least, how many
times do you see a room full of white people

and the only, or the most, POC present
are Asian? I almost wonder if we even count

anymore, I see this so often, I only don't see it
here because *I'm that one present*, just as I am

in my department, the problem is not much
better in New York City, during meetings

of the 2019 Whitman Consortium consisting
of 70+ organizations planning to celebrate

the bicentennial of Whitman's birth, I was
the only POC at the table, a couple others sat

on the margins but they were not the heads
of their organizations, only I, Asian American,

got to sit in the circle with all the esteemed
white heads representing some of the most

prestigious literary wealth in the country,
we shared how we were going to celebrate

the "Poet of Democracy," the "one white father"
in June Jordan's estimation who shared

the "systematic disadvantages of his heterogeneous
offspring trapped inside a closet," and all I

could think was *This is us 200 years later?*
What would Jordan have thought of this room?

There were plenty of women in charge, but all
white. A few gay men I knew, white. And me.

And I had to create my own organization
and build it big enough to gain white approval

to get a seat at that table. I didn't feel proud
of this, or like I had any power, but small,

smaller than I usually do when I'm dreaming
big dreams alone or among my peoples

because I'm not seeing the stakes of the game
laid out with such physical reproof, there

was no moving any weight at that table,
someone asked if the Consortium was going

to say anything about Whitman's problematic
views on race and another person said yes

thank you for bringing up that issue and
another said I think it would be best to get out

in front of this, as if it were a PR problem,
I put in my one cent about the importance

of getting people of color involved, especially
young ones, connecting Whitman to those

"heterogeneous offspring" Jordan imagined
he stood for, but I didn't say it in just this way,

I didn't mention Jordan's quote, I didn't want
to come off as confrontational, in fact I don't

remember exactly what I said, it might as well
have been silence for all the difference it made,

I've taken part in event after event celebrating
Whitman over the past few months and save

for the one I myself organized, there were no
or almost no POC speaking or performing

other than me, and perhaps more alarmingly,
almost no POC present in the audiences,

and these events were in New York City, not
Hamden, I went to speak in support of a coalition

trying to get Whitman's last standing NYC home
at 99 Ryerson St considered for landmarking

at a Landmarks Preservation Commission hearing
on six proposed LGBT sites (not including

Whitman's), and I was the only POC offering
public testimony in our group, I did that

obligatory room check and saw just one
older Asian gentleman and one black woman

at the otherwise white table of commissioners,
another black woman sitting off to the side

of the table who presented research on why
Audre Lorde's last home in Staten Island

should be landmarked, and one black man
wearing a Vietnam Veterans cap sitting

with the rest of us in the public, he rose
to speak on the Lorde case, we'd already heard

several prepared statements of support
delivered by smart white folks representing

LGBT interests but I was most interested
in what this man had to say as the lone black

man in the audience, I assumed he was
going to offer support but then got a lesson

in the complexities of identity politics
that Lorde spent a lifetime trying to work

out, he didn't *not* offer support, he said
he wasn't against landmarking the house

but he *was* against the LPC writing him,
the owner of that house for over twenty years,

to say he'd built an illegal deck at the back
of it, the house was already designated

as "historic" by the LPC in 2004 as part
of the St. Paul's Avenue–Stapleton Heights

Historic District and thus already protected
from major alterations, hence this letter,

you might wonder why the house had to be
landmarked if it was already protected

and I assume this was to give it some kind
of additional protection, honor its cultural,

not just architectural, significance, and also
to mark it as a political "win" for the LGBT

community in the year celebrating the 50th
anniversary of the Stonewall Uprising,

but this man didn't care about any of that,
he didn't mention Lorde once or show pride

in what the house represented, he took pride
in that deck, how much money and time

and care he'd invested in it, he said if you'd
looked at the back of the house (not pictured

in the slideshow) when he'd bought it, you'd
have seen a window that looked like it was

originally a door, probably leading to a deck
that had been removed, all the other houses

on his historic block had decks except his,
so in his mind he'd been doing the work

of restoration, not alteration, he was the one
who'd painted the house the way it looks

today, who'd kept it so convincingly "historic,"
he didn't know why he was being penalized

and he was worried landmarking the house
would make it even more difficult for him

to save his deck, he got the loudest applause
of any speaker in the room but I wondered

what the LGBT contingent thought of him,
whether they felt sympathy or perceived him

as a threat, Lorde herself would've been
keenly aware of all the ironies in play, white

LGBT activists like those she often clashed
with over race working to honor her role

in their cause and race again irritatingly
getting in the way in the form of a black man

troubling their unified front, protecting
his own interests and exposing the whiteness

of their own, a man she may have clashed with
too, who didn't seem to know or care at all

who she was, who might've seen her sexuality
as a betrayal of their own unified black front

against white interests, I don't know who
Lorde would've sided with or if they were even

opposed but I doubt she would've been for
having her home landmarked if it meant

this black Vietnam vet would have to suffer
the loss of his deck, I think she would've been

suspicious of any coalition of white interests
advancing upon a black citizen's autonomy,

and she definitely would've said something,
she would've braved the return fire, though

I don't know if she would've said anything
about this bar, if she would've thought it worth

the unrest, but maybe calculations like this
prove our difference, my greater alignment

with whiteness, my ability to choose rest
or unrest, when for her, the rest was silence.

SRUTHI NARAYANAN

A Test of Fire

THE GARBAGE-PICKERS SPOTTED HER FIRST.

Perched like sooty crows atop mountains of trash, the men watched as fifteen-year-old Devika Giridharan approached from behind an alley. The bruises on her arms and neck were visible from a distance. Her fingers gripped her abdomen. Her tattered skirt, a bright peacock blue, was stained with blood.

It was far too common a sight.

Abandoning a sack of dried-out pens they'd been sorting, the garbage-pickers began crawling down from the piles, calling out to Devika: "We're here, child, we're here."

The men flanked Devika, supporting her trembling frame as they guided her home. As they walked deeper into the heart of Awadh Nagar, the news of what had happened traveled faster than they did. By the time they arrived at the Giridharan house, every woman from within a quarter-mile radius had gathered in front of the threshold.

"Let us handle this," we said to the garbage-pickers, gently yet firmly. Rarely was it within a man's realm to understand such pain, or know how to soothe it.

And so the men departed, fixing their collective gaze on some faraway point, their hands braced against their waists.

•

WE DIDN'T KNOW his real name. It wasn't of particular importance, especially when he touted his alias as a kind of trumpeting proclamation.

The critical fact was that, over the course of a decade, the man known as K. K. Raghav had attacked nearly two hundred women from the Awadh Nagar slum.

It didn't matter what precautions we took. We forbade one another from leaving the slum unattended, we rushed through our outdoor chores in the dark before sunrise, we scrounged money for locks to put on our doors—but he still came after us.

Devika's mistake had been succumbing to thirst. Bit by bit, the story came out: in the midday heat, unable to tolerate her parched throat, Devika had ventured out alone to the water pump. Raghav's gang followed her silently for several yards before surrounding her. When she attempted to fight back with slaps and kicks, they beat her unconscious.

"She was always a plucky girl," Jia Rao murmured.

"And isn't she still?" Ganga Giridharan glared, wiping her daughter's brow with a corner of her sari. "She's just a child. Who will marry her now? Who told her to go to the pump alone?"

Ganga herself had been attacked by Raghav's gang several years prior—as had the woman boiling water for tea, and the unmarried sisters from the shack with the blue door, and the elderly widow chanting prayers in the corner.

We reached into our kitchens and brought forth various remedies: ghee to use as a salve, copper vessels of water to rinse her face, turmeric milk for a quick recovery. We lifted Devika's skirts and gently applied coconut oil between her legs, working silently.

The widow Krishnajee broke the silence. "I don't have the energy to watch this happen again. I'm seventy-four." She had taken over preparing the evening meal for Ganga, and was allowing the lentils to burn.

Ganga leaned forward, holding a tumbler of water. "Drink," she whispered, tilting the cup towards her daughter's lips. Devika only took a few sips before turning away.

•

"Teacher Madam is so much taller than Teacher Sir," a boy in the back row whispered. "She can pluck the mangoes in the highest trees and give them to him."

The other children squealed with laughter, even while silencing him. "Be quiet! We want to hear!" Above their heads, cars sped over the bridge with crowing honks.

Varsha Chennaiya turned a page, lifting the book towards her face so the children wouldn't see her smiling. "Book Six of the Ramayana tells the story of Goddess Sita's kidnapping. Who kidnapped Goddess Sita?" Varsha's brother Harish stood at the back of the class, waiting for the children to shout out the correct answer.

The school took place under the abandoned overpass: two roads merging into one created a vast, triangular open space below the bridge. A crumbling wall stood several feet before the fork in the road above, and served as a makeshift chalkboard. Varsha had become used to feeling the vibrations in her hand as she wrote on the wall, when traffic was low and cars on the highway could drive at full speed.

"Ravana kidnapped Sita!" the children shrieked in unison. They sat in four rows, cross-legged on lengths of torn cloth.

Varsha adjusted her glasses. "When the ten-headed demon Ravana kidnapped Goddess Sita, Lord Rama's entire kingdom wept for her. She was a beloved symbol of chastity and virtue, and everyone feared for her safety." Despite knowing the story by heart, the children listened with rapt attention. "When Lord Rama learned that Goddess Sita was being held captive in Ravana's castle, he stormed the castle with his army of crowned monkeys, ready for war."

There was a crash and the children screamed, whirling around to see Harish banging two metal pipes together, mimicking the clashing sounds of battle. They fell apart giggling as Harish waved the pipes over his head.

It was then that Varsha noticed the absence of the Giridharans—eight-year-old Abhi, twelve-year-old Karunesh, and fifteen-year-old Devika. Devika was the oldest member of the street school, and often helped reign in some of the more energetic younger children.

Harish lowered the pipes. "Who knows the story of the monkey god Hanuman?"

The students stretched their hands in the air with full force, in their unrestrained way, begging Harish to choose them.

•

Several streets away, past the large Prince Jewelers billboard and the rows of posters advertising an action movie, stood a windowless shack underneath the feathery leaves of a neem tree. This shack was freshly painted in mint-green, and a row of stones had been methodically placed at the entrance to create a makeshift threshold.

Inside the shack, Asha Nagendra sat on a woven jute mat, unpacking a suitcase of textbooks. She wore a red-and-white printed salwar, her hair in a neat bun.

The Nagendra family stood apart from the other slum dwellers of Awadh Nagar. Bhaskar and Shubha Nagendra, both call-center workers, had put all four of their children through formal schooling by way of careful saving and back-to-back shifts answering phones. One by one, their children left the slum—Asha was preparing for her final year of postgraduate study in Mumbai.

Speculation swirled as to what caused K. K. Raghav to leave the Nagendra family alone. Many of us believed it was a perverse form of respect for their educated status, a boundary of sorts; they were the one family that remained unharmed to-date.

"She's studying hotel management," Meenakshi Ghosh had reported, back when Asha had first left for Mumbai. "It's a three-year program."

"She'll work for American tourists," came the tittering reply from Jia Rao, before she was quickly hushed. It felt unseemly to speak of Asha's schooling with anything other than reverence, and so we commented on other things—how her visits back to the slum came fewer and farther between, how the timbre of her voice had developed an artificial over-polish, how the sunburst-shaped bindis she favored over traditional round or teardrop shapes were like a gunshot between her eyes.

Asha had come home to an empty shack, her parents busy at the call center, and so it was Prabhakaran Raj and his ten-year old daughter Vidya who came by to welcome her.

"You must come home and eat with us," Prabhakaran insisted. Sweat beaded on his dark skin. "Vidya has started learning how to shape chappattis, she would love to cook for you." He sat cross-legged next to Asha, leaning against the wall.

"The artist is using her talented hands to cook?" Asha grinned at Vidya. The girl rocked back and forth on her heels, weaving two blades of grass together in an attempt to mimic the pattern of the jute mat. "That's very kind, Uncle, thank you."

Prabhakaran glanced at his daughter, and then added, his voice low, "And . . . if you feel unsafe, please stay with us until your parents return. We have plenty of room."

Asha laughed. "If he's planning to come to our house, I wish him luck. I'll be fine, please don't worry." She reached into a suitcase and pulled out a stack of wrinkled salwars.

Prabhakaran winced. "You've become quite brave." He said "brave" the way he might have said "reckless" or "stupid."

Asha registered the shadows under Prabhakaran's eyes. Her parents never discussed the attacks in their letters, but she didn't think for a moment that they had ceased.

"We can't keep letting this happen, Uncle. There has to be some kind of . . . due process, some kind of consequence."

Prabhakaran opened his mouth, searching for the right words. Then he sighed and stood, his stomach shaking under his thin cotton shirt. Prabhakaran motioned for Vidya to get up. "Would you like to show Asha the drawings you've been working on?"

•

THE SUN BEGAN to set on Awadh Nagar, and the corrugated tin roofs gleamed orange in the evening light. Devika was asleep in the Giridharan shack, Ganga lying at her side. We stood outside the threshold, rustling our saris and clearing our throats.

Jia Rao spoke first. "Does Ganga want to go to the police?"

Even those few who might have dared to report Raghav knew better than to bother. Beyond turning a blind eye in exchange for money and liquor, police officers did little in response to complaints. Occasionally, they even alerted Raghav.

Silently, we recalled the young bride who was attacked on the night of her wedding, and then again the following day for filing a report. We thought about the housewife who'd had her breasts cut off for complaining to the police. We remembered the woman who ended up dousing herself with kerosene after Raghav forced himself on her in front of her daughter. After she'd burned herself, the smell of charred flesh permeated the slum for days.

A moment passed before Meenakshi Ghosh whispered, "It's her daughter."

"How does that make a difference?" Ambika Mevani clucked her tongue. "They'll do another courtesy arrest and his goons will be here demanding bail money by tomorrow."

Without warning, there was a swoop and a dive and a koel bird flew from a branch, landing neatly on Jia's shoulder. She screamed and reflexively swatted it, the flat of her palm landing with an unsettlingly muffled thud. The bird widened its eyes and chirped in her ear, revealing a pink mouth. It did not fly away.

Jia began jumping up and down, slapping her arms; Meenashki rushed forward, waving her hands, and only then did the bird depart in a flurry of black feathers.

We burst out laughing. "She yells like an ox," Ambika cackled. Crescents of sweat had bloomed under her arms.

"Why didn't it fly away?" Jia's voice was a mix of horror and mirth.

"That's more than I've seen you move all year, Jia," Meenakshi teased.

Nighttime seemed to arrive all at once—the sky was dark, the moon made grainy by thick clouds. A grunt broke the silence, and we turned to see the widow Krishnajee lowering herself to the ground, using her hands to brace herself before allowing the weight of her body to hit the floor. She crossed her legs and began massaging her feet, her eyes closed.

One by one we followed suit, pulling our saris tightly around our bodies as we sat down on the dirt road.

•

VARSHA STOOD NUMBLY in front of the children as Harish handed out cracked slates. Karunesh Giridharan had informed her that his sisters would no longer be coming to school, then told her about Devika's attack. Though Varsha had heard the news, she'd listened to Karunesh speak, his already quiet voice taking on a dull monotone.

Varsha looked down to see seven-year-old Gopi Prasad pulling on the hem of her sari. Gopi sat as close to the crumbling chalkboard as possible, squinting with poor vision. Vidya Raj sat on her other side, writing diligently on her slate.

"Teacher Madam, why did Ravana want to kidnap Goddess Sita?"

Gopi and Vidya were two of just six girls who came to the street school—four, now that Devika and Abhi wouldn't be returning.

"Ravana wanted Goddess Sita to be his wife," Varsha said. Parents of young children often glossed over the demon's motives when telling the story, merely saying he was "a bad man" until the time came to elaborate further. Varsha thought briefly before continuing.

"Lord Rama had fought Ravana's demon sister, so Ravana decided to kidnap Goddess Sita as revenge. But Goddess Sita wanted to go back home."

Harish returned to the front of the class. "Goddess Sita prayed earnestly, and eventually Lord Rama came to rescue her."

Gopi released her grip on Varsha's sari. "But what if Lord Rama hadn't come?"

Varsha glanced at Harish, and then crouched down until she was eye level with Gopi.

"Then Goddess Sita would have fought back. She would have saved herself."

•

Vidya Raj sat on the floor of her hut trying to light a match. The day was windy, and the flame wouldn't catch. She squinted, holding the match closely between her eyes and examining the charred wick.

A deafening blow suddenly shook the walls of the hut. Vidya dropped the burnt-out match. There was a second bang on the door, followed by a third. Vidya cowered near the back wall, closing her eyes and rotating her body until she was facing the wall.

Perhaps if she couldn't see him, he might not see her.

Several streets away, Prabhakaran stood on the second-highest rung of a ladder, repairing the thatching on the pharmacy roof. As he weaved thick straw into a corner of the roof, he heard a high-pitched shriek pierce the air.

Contrary to what Prabhakaran had always believed, fear did not seize a person all at once. Fear takes its time traveling through one's body, moving upwards and outwards, patiently touching each limb and ligament before moving along. By the time Prabhakaran reached his hut—by the time he saw, having run as fast as he could but not fast enough, that the door had been broken down, that two men with leering eyes and dirty scythes guarded the threshold—the panic had only just begun to mount.

The men didn't try to stop Prabhakaran as he tore into the hut, momentum overtaking his body to the point where he nearly tripped over himself, his legs like pinwheels. K. K. Raghav stood in the middle of his house, towering over Vidya. She was kneeling on the ground, tears scurrying down her face. Raghav had her braid wrapped around his hand and held a scythe to her throat.

With his trimmed moustache and ironed polo shirt, K. K. Raghav could have been any stranger in the street, or someone's young bachelor uncle; his thinning hair was neatly combed, his frame relatively slight compared to the men who guarded him. He was an upper-caste man, and this gave his actions a sobering air of preordained destiny; he had come across the Awadh Nagar slum with a hierarchy already in place. Raghav looked up and merely nodded upon seeing Prabhakaran.

"Baba!" Vidya screamed. She tried to stand, and Raghav yanked her back. Vidya's neck whipped backwards, and she cried in pain as her feet flew out from underneath her.

"Shut up," Raghav said calmly.

Prabhakaran took a step forward. A prickling heat coursed over his skin. "I'll get you as much money as you want," he murmured, realizing belatedly that Raghav's men had surrounded him and were wiping their scythes on their jeans. He cleared his throat. Tears jumped into his eyes. "She's only ten years old."

Raghav laughed—a loud, bark-like laugh. "Such a small girl, and she has you wrapped around her finger? Like a puppet?" The men joined in the laughter. Raghav pivoted around Vidya and walked towards a corner of the shack, dragging her with him. Her thin frame quaked with sobs. Raghav examined a section of the wall, which was papered with Vidya's drawings: sketches of flowers, parrots, and palm trees. "Five thousand rupees."

"I'll get you the money," Prabhakaran repeated.

Raghav whirled around, twisting Vidya's hair in his hand. "You agree so quickly?" He turned to his men. "Undress him."

Prabhakaran felt the men grabbing him, ripping the dhoti he wore around his waist, tearing his shirt in two. He heard Vidya, in a shrill whimper, repeating the same verse of her morning prayer over and over. He saw Raghav attempt to move forward, shackled by the hair wrapped around his hand, and—almost as an afterthought—lift up his scythe and slice through Vidya's braid. She fell to the floor.

Raghav's men pressed the pointed ends of their scythes into Prabhakaran's naked waist. He drew a sharp breath, feeling blood trickling down his thighs.

K. K. Raghav took three slow steps towards Prabhakaran. His eyes gleamed like the black backs of beetles. "Aren't puppets supposed to dance?" Raghav threw the length of braided hair at Prabhakaran's feet; it landed dully, like a dead snake.

Prabhakaran was only partially aware of the door closing behind him, darkening the shack's interior.

•

At dusk, Asha walked up the steps of the district police station and banged on the door; her staccato knocks echoed sharply through the air.

After several moments, a police officer opened the door. His khaki uniform was wrinkled and his eyes were red. Asha caught a whiff of alcohol on his skin.

The officer raised his eyebrows, taking in the kurta with pants Asha wore in lieu of a sari. She stared right back at him, challenging him to speak first before speaking herself.

"My name is Asha Nagendra. I'm here to report a physical assault. K. K. Raghav attacked my neighbors this morning."

The officer leaned against the doorframe. "Yes?"

Asha blinked, then continued. "He broke into their home, stripped Prabhakaran Uncle—Prabhakaran Raj—and made him dance naked in front of his ten-year-old daughter." The officer remained silent. "He cut the little girl's braid off with a sword, then ransacked the place." Asha's voice quivered as she recalled the sight of Prabhakaran, cowed and ashamed, knocking on her door earlier that afternoon.

The officer was young, his creamy skin a contrast to his bloodshot eyes. He gestured for Asha to enter before sitting behind his desk and taking out a notebook. "Any injuries?"

Asha approached the desk, which was littered with papers and manila folders. A kaleidoscopic glass paperweight sat uselessly off to the side. "Prabhakaran Raj has some bruises, and two large gashes on his stomach. And his daughter's hair, as I mentioned."

The officer continued writing. "Okay."

Asha took another step forward. "Do you have any plans to deal with this?" She hesitated briefly, then placed a fifty-rupee note on the desk, lifting the bill through the air slightly higher than was necessary.

The officer chuckled. He didn't look at the money. "Madam, it sounds like you're asking me to arrest a man for giving a girl a haircut."

Asha planted her palms on the desk, attempting to quell the rage that was rising. "Sir, I'm asking you to respond to assault, battery, rape . . . this is a problem you've been ignoring for years." She swallowed. "For someone to terrorize our town—our people—for so many years, and to see absolutely no consequences, and now he's attacked a father with a little girl to look after . . . for you to do nothing, it's . . . horrible. It's horrible."

The officer stood abruptly, the pages of his notebook fluttering. He leaned towards her, and a lock of curly hair fell on his forehead. He looked like a schoolboy. "Have you ever been personally harmed by Raghav?"

Asha briefly considered saying yes.

"No. I haven't."

The officer sat back down. "I've written everything down, and I can see that you're very upset." He reached for the paperweight and began rolling it around on the desk. "It's getting late. I suggest you go home before it gets dark."

Asha started to speak, but the officer had turned away and opened one of his desk drawers. He removed a shiny green bag from the top drawer—Haldiram's Bhel Puri Mix—and poured the snack into his cupped palm, then tipped his head back and dropped it into his mouth. A stray peanut tumbled onto the desk. Asha glanced down at his notebook and saw that he had only written "Raghav," "Asha Nagendra," and "braid."

"Thank you for your time," she said bitterly, before turning to leave. She tossed her dupatta over her shoulder, allowing the door of the station to slam behind her.

As soon as Asha had retreated from view, the officer stood, wiping mustard oil on his pants before pocketing the fifty rupees. He picked up the receiver of a black rotary phone and dialed. Though he was alone, he kept his conversation quiet and short.

He then hung up the phone and opened the top drawer of a metal filing cabinet, rooting around for a few moments before pulling out a pair of nail clippers.

•

GANGA GIRIDHARAN EXITED her shack in the middle of the night and stood on the threshold, unwinding her hair from its bun. She took deep, heaving breaths, pulling at her hair and feeling the satisfying ache on her scalp.

Devika had woken in the middle of the night, screaming. Ganga's first instinct had not been to go to her side, but to start screaming herself. For several seconds, mother and daughter cried out together in anguish before Ganga was able to wipe the sweat from her face and tend to Devika.

Now Devika slept on her side, her younger siblings lying in a tangle against her back. Earlier that evening, Abhi had tearfully asked Ganga what kinds of things Raghav would have done to Devika, and Ganga had nearly slapped the little girl across the face. Instead, she took her to the back of the shack and gave her a small banana she'd placed on the prayer mantle as an offering. "Eat this. Keep up your energy."

Ganga locked the door behind her and started walking. She walked by rows of shacks, taking the route towards the water pump she knew Devika preferred— along the perimeter of the slum, in order to pass a banyan tree with a broken trunk, rather than the direct route through the slum's center.

If Raghav were to find her, Ganga would have no excuse. She was alone at night. She was away from the slum. She wasn't carrying any weapons. Each time she passed an alley she looked back and forth, waiting to see him standing in the shadows.

Ganga walked the full distance from the slum to the water pump without seeing a single person. The sky was light by the time she arrived. Ganga cupped her hand under the pump and lifted the lever just once, splashing the water on her face.

•

"I FORGOT TO wash my blue sari," Ambika sighed. We were walking from the water pump towards Meenakshi's shack, balancing baskets of damp clothing against our hips.

"Is it because you're wearing it?" Jia reeled back to dodge Ambika's playful slap.

"I have two blue saris, smartass." Ambika shifted her basket from her left side to her right. "The patterned one is still at home."

As we approached the edge of the slum, we heard shouts coming from the direction of the Nagendra shack. We paused briefly, and without discussion began walking faster, straining under the weight of our laundry, our legs hitting our baskets with each step.

K. K. Raghav was banging on the front door of the mint-green shack. Two men had perched themselves in the neem tree directly above the roof, scythes raised high.

"Open the door, Asha." Raghav's hair was wild, like it had been chewed. "I wanted to thank you for taking the time to visit the police yesterday."

"She did what?" Jia hissed, nearly dropping her basket. We stood several paces away, half-concealed by a tall mound of trash.

"She's going to get herself killed," Meenakshi growled.

We heard Asha's crisp reply from within the shack: "I'm not afraid of you, Raghav. No one is."

Ambika let out a horrified groan, and K. K. Raghav turned towards the sound. We automatically moved closer together as his gaze fell on us.

Raghav's eyebrows lowered and he raised his voice, directing his words toward us. "Asha! Come on out. Your friends are here."

Raghav reached into the pocket of his jeans and pulled out a bottle of clear liquid. The front door of the shack opened a crack and Asha peered out, mere moments before those of us at the front of the crowd had identified the bottle. Acid.

"Stay back, Asha!" Jia screamed.

Raghav turned back around, meeting Asha's gaze through the opening in the door. Wordlessly, he held the bottle up.

In response, Asha pulled her head back, sucked inward, and spat a wad of mucus at Raghav. Then she slammed the door, locking it with a deadbolt.

The pounding on the door resumed almost immediately. We cried in fright: "Keep the door locked, Asha!" "God help her!"

•

"DO YOU REMEMBER what happened after Goddess Sita was rescued?" Varsha paced in front of the class, her hair clipped back haphazardly. "Lord Rama began to question her virtue. He wondered what it meant that his wife had lived under the roof of another man, and he hesitated to welcome her back home right away."

Gopi Prasad was now the sole female student present at the school. She picked at her lips with her fingers, gazing at Varsha.

"Goddess Sita was heartbroken, and decided to perform an agni pariksha—a test of fire—to prove her purity once and for all. With Lord Rama as witness, she jumped into a roaring blaze, her palms pressed together in prayer."

Varsha closed her eyes, inhaling deeply. Her voice began to shake.

"Goddess Sita's devotion was so strong that she remained unharmed, even as the flames consumed her body. She had passed the fire test. But by then, it was too late. Goddess Sita had endured and endured, until she simply couldn't endure any more."

•

Asha ran to the back of the hut, to the portable stove her parents used for cooking, and turned all four dials to the far right. The smell of gas began to crawl up the walls and skitter across the floor. She got down on her hands and knees.

She heard Raghav's voice, mingled with the banging on her door: "Locking the door won't protect you. Your parents won't protect you. The next time you see your mother, her body will be on the train tracks."

Asha waited until dark shapes began forming in her field of vision. She thought about the police officer who had asked her if Raghav had ever raped her, and who was prepared to dismiss her otherwise. She pressed her forehead to the ground, tasting the earth.

Then she stood and grabbed a match, bracing herself against the doorframe as she threw the door open. The floral perfume of the gas hit Raghav, and his eyes begin to water. Asha saw a group of neighborhood women hovering near a garbage mound, watching.

"Do you smell that?" Asha held up the match. "Go ahead, break the door down. See what happens. I'll blow us both up if I have to."

And reeling from the smell of the gas, K. K. Raghav did something unprecedented: he took a single step back.

It was like a gun had gone off. Whether spurred by Asha's actions or encouraged by Raghav's response, the group of women began to yell, dropping their laundry baskets:

"Do you think we'll let you off so easy, Raghav?"

"You've taken away our peace! Ten years!"

"Fucking pig!"

Asha saw the women screaming, and saw K. K. Raghav looking back and forth—first at the group, then at her. She didn't lower the match.

After a moment Raghav let out a chuckle, guttural and low, and began walking away from the shack. Two men leapt down silently from the neem tree, scythes swinging. Asha withdrew slightly, but kept the door open. She wanted to watch the men leave; she wanted to know whether she'd won or lost.

And then, his retreating figure giving no betrayal of his next move, Raghav whipped his body around and flung the bottle of acid at Asha.

Asha threw her hands up to protect her eyes, but the bottle did not hit her face—it fell short, smashing on the stones at the shack's entrance. The corrosive acid, clear as clean water, splashed across her bare feet.

Asha was only able to process the next few minutes in flashes. There was her vision blurring and her feet giving out from underneath her. There was a glimpse of K. K. Raghav disappearing down an alley. There was the searing pain, the feeling of raw electricity traveling up her legs, her nerves seizing. There was the sight of two women frantically wrapping her feet with wet saris, several more running back from the water pump with buckets.

She would not remember screaming.

When she came to, she found herself surrounded by women. Meenakshi Ghosh was sitting cross-legged, supporting Asha's calves on her knees. Ambika Mevani and Jia Rao were on either side, pouring water over Asha's sari-wrapped feet. Jia was weeping softly.

"Why are you crying?" Asha asked, dazed.

Jia turned her face away. She continued flushing Asha's feet, unable to wipe her eyes. When she finally spoke, it was in a near whisper: "You were the only one."

When Ambika unwrapped the first sari, Asha saw a swathe of skin fall off her right foot. She watched as it floated to the ground, cradled as if by some invisible breeze.

•

WE CONCLUDED, AT the end of it all, that this could only be a woman's job.

The men in our lives certainly suffered with us; they wept, prayed, and bled for us. Many tried in vain to fight for us. But a task like this couldn't be carried out on the basis of secondhand rage.

After Asha Nagendra was brought to the hospital, and after she had gone on official record as being the victim of an acid attack, K. K. Raghav was taken to the police station. He was put in a holding cell for the night: "For the safety of all parties," according to the police report. A hearing was scheduled for the morning of August 13th at the district courthouse—yet another courtesy arrest, another slap on the wrist.

On the morning of the hearing, we reached into our kitchens once again.

The courthouse was a behemoth of a building. High walls, lined with jewel-toned broken glass, separated the lawn from the streets. The entrance's grand staircase was made of the same white marble as the floors, catching the light of the courtroom's chandeliers.

That morning, nearly one hundred women gathered in the courtroom. Only half of us fit in the gallery area, marked off for the general public by a wooden railing. The rest of us crowded in the foyer and spilled onto the top steps of the marble staircase.

At nine o'clock, K. K. Raghav was escorted into the courtroom, handcuffed and accompanied by two police officers. We waited behind the railing, shaking yet steely, our palms resting on the waists of our petticoats. As he walked to the front of the courtroom, Raghav's eyes slowly traveled across the gallery area, looking at each woman one by one. His gaze landed on Ganga Giridharan, who stood at the edge of the crowd.

With a serene smile, K. K. Raghav said in a clear voice that echoed through the courtroom: "Like mother, like daughter. Both of you like to fight."

The flimsy wooden railing broke as we rushed from the gallery area, wielding the items we'd taken from our kitchens, concealed in our skirts. The two police officers pulled out their batons, and in doing so momentarily let go of Raghav. The unmarried sisters from the shack with the blue door grabbed his arms, dragging him to the center of the courtroom. Later, they would tell us how limp his body had been.

Our actions were mechanical, possessing a rehearsed quality. In many ways, we'd done this a hundred times before.

Ambika Mevani slashed his arms and legs with a kitchen knife.

Meenakshi Ghosh used a butcher's cleaver to cut off his fingers.

Jia Rao took a star-shaped blade meant for grating coconut and drove it straight into the center of his forehead.

The widow Krishnajee flung red chili powder into his wounds.

And with a howl that shook her entire body, Ganga Giridharan shoved a serrated knife down into Raghav's groin. She hacked and twisted, blood flowing over her hands, cutting through his pants until she had sawed through the mound between his legs.

By the time the police officers had returned with backup, K. K. Raghav was dead on the marble floor. His blood had coagulated with the chili powder, forming a thick paste. The stumps of his hands were still in handcuffs.

A senior police officer beat his baton against the wall in an attempt to silence us, bellowing: "Who is responsible for this?" His mustache quivered.

We began yelling in unison:

"I did it!"

"I murdered him!"

"Arrest us all!" Ganga stood, drenched in blood, and flung K. K. Raghav's severed penis at the officer. We emitted a roar, holding out our wrists, demanding to be taken in.

A young officer turned to his superior, a single boyish curl clinging to his sweaty forehead. His words came out parched: "Find Asha Nagendra and bring her here."

•

VARSHA AND HARISH stood in front of the class. There were no girls left at the street school. The day was unexpectedly cool, and a soft wind blew under the bridge.

Eventually, Harish spoke. "The various interpretations of the Ramayana disagree on whether Goddess Sita was actually harmed during her imprisonment. Some say she was so pure that the demon Ravana was physically unable to harm her. Others avoid the question."

Despite not being at the courthouse on August 13th, Asha Nagendra was arrested under suspicion of orchestrating the murder of K. K. Raghav. She was removed from the hospital and placed in a cell at the district police station, awaiting a trial for weeks on end.

Harish was waiting for Varsha to speak. Her voice came out like a choke. "Goddess Sita's fire test symbolized a breaking point. But this breaking point didn't come when she was being held captive, when she was almost definitely being assaulted and tortured. It came when her purity was challenged. Goddess Sita did nothing wrong, but she was being held responsible for the demon Ravana's brutality and her husband's doubts, even after she was returned to her throne."

Varsha closed her eyes, feeling desperation seize her. It was crucial that the boys heard and understood her, that she choose her words carefully—and yet, Varsha knew that whatever she said would be utterly insufficient.

"She didn't want to do the agni pariksha." Varsha opened her eyes to see the boys listening intently, their slates resting in their laps. "Goddess Sita passed the fire test, as she knew she would, and we can even consider her actions to be a form of rebellion, or a type of quiet violence. But it wasn't a choice. It was a decision, but it wasn't a choice."

Varsha removed her glasses and allowed the tears that had been welling to fall, pleading: "Do you understand?"

STEPHANIE ROGERS

Fat Girl Cascade

Please don't close your eyes. I want to see
          your eyes, where light reflects me there,
                    my body thin, a pin-prick figurine

for once. Hold me for a moment
          in the gleam. Meet my gaze.
                    Please don't close your eyes. I want to see

the way my body changes, how it shrinks
          as you move away. Stay far away.
                    Your eyes, where light reflects me there,

can hold me all night long but don't come
          close. Just let me watch the way I slink,
                    my body thin, a pin-prick figurine.

JESSICA JACOBS

*"'One nation shall prevail over the other nation.' . . .
refers to Jacob and Esau . . . [and] is understood as an al-
lusion to the divine soul and the animal soul respectively,
who are constantly warring with each other."*
—Rabbi Schneur Zalman of Liadi

In the village of my body, two people

vie for the throne, box-sprung and
gold-leafed though it is. The firstborn—
lusty, muscled, veins cantillating
with sunheat, field and flesh, she is all
hunger: for a mess of stew, for
a burger, she'd give anything, even
her birthright, that divine protection:
those who curse her are cursed
and those who bless her get
God's *attaboy*, God's divine
pat on the back. The second is hermetic,
blanched as a leek and wilting
at her texts, a root vegetable plucked
from darkness into darkness,
immaculate poet of the tents.
The small Solomon in my gut
notes how each runs
on the same clean-burning
will, which in a mortal body
is like pure light
through a dirty window: it spatters
particular shadows. And of what worth
is such a birthright anyway? What
would it mean if one part of myself—
vigor to the point of violence,
or giving to the point
of giving in—if one were blessed

beyond the other, given
license to govern and multiply?
My belly growls, small Solomon
whispers, *It feels better
to be kind than right.* In a clearing
between my ribs, I plant
a shade tree—ideal spot for treaties.
Hope it grows to block the two
rusting water towers on my village's
opposing sides: the first tagged
MIGHT MAKES RIGHT, the other
airbrushed *the meek shall inherit.*
The tree will wait there, bannering
its leaves, until my two women
can agree to dig one well from which
both will draw: *balance*, etched on one side,
on the other, *incorporation.*

MARIANNE BORUCH

The Art Historian Told Me a Fish

on command produced a coin in the fresco.
Saint Peter walks over to plead for

the temple tax all twelve of them needed
plus the one who urged him to talk to the fish

in the first place. So I saw that radiant creature
half out of the river, mouth open, the coin not nearly

as lit as the fish got to be. The paint those days
copied sunlight exact . . . Apparently what I missed

in catechism for as lapsed as I am—*fallen away*—
I'd remember if told the Renaissance

recorded and framed such a story. People imagine anything.
But truth too can be quirky. Four centuries later

some thought the platypus fake, dim England's brightest
certain the bill sewed on, the pouch a clever addition,

and fur—on this weirdling with duck feet? As for the fish
and its coin, a painted saint in clear supplication, not

by a long shot a Dreamtime story, I'd admit to
the Indigenous Elder, nothing next to

how that enormous rainbow Snake loosened its coil
to lie down and make a river. Or the Songlines,

the Ancients chanting into the real thing each valley
and mountain as they walked the length of a continent.

Well, you take what origin you get. But surely it *means*—
my delight in how a man is bent to a fish in gratitude,

the fish doing its selfless job *to get the show on the road*
my mother's raised eyebrows might have said. The way

I first looked at a platypus, his dive into mud and gloom—
ie: charmed! And so signaled her ghost.

STEVEN ESPADA DAWSON

Every Word Is My Mother's

favorite fruit. I'm convinced
a billion moths are skulking

towards their final curtain. Outside
my window each flash of blue

is a small death, too, that proud bug
zapper swung above a neighbor's porch.

Mom says she's scared of ladders,
not heights, something about her spine

pressed up against the world.
While standing outside her hospital door

a crowd of doctors promised me
there is no such thing as dying

of old age. Everyone finally croaks
from something more precise—

a heart's clumsy rhythm, a liver's
constant gathering, a tumor's slick

migration. I want so badly to write words
with a future attached. I'd kiss each one

goodnight, tuck them deep inside
my friends' dimples. I haven't forgotten

there is so much that is perfect.
A lover's well-perched hand, Saturn's

galactic pizza cutter. Every smile now
is an accident I want to apologize for.

Over the phone, I hear her, my mother
plucking rubies from a pomegranate.

In Spanish, they're called granadas,
from grenade. When I ask why

she tells me they explode.

orchard

the first oncologist   of many
    pinched his fingers together
as if to say microscopic
the tumors first   wander
-lust the field
from breast to ovaries   finally
brain   he uses fruit now
to explain their swell
    fruit is easy to picture
ripening
in two weeks a cherry pit
becomes a cherry in eight
years an apple seed   becomes
an orchard   your body   unable
    to harvest itself
eventually the kernel
budding   behind your
right eye is a grape
-fruit quivering
    on its stem

ALICE TURSKI

The Congee Test

My mother's congee may look strange to you at first but really
is just seven portions broth of the bones boiled with one cupful
of rice for the white marrow and white starch she calls
silk and we call velvet. It's not as strange as the sea and
its giant squids and anglerfish; its coloring, though pale,
has never reminded you of the sea's wife the
moon even with her black hair pulled back *oh
what a nape* and bound in a hairnet like a good
professional. Call it, if not the plaster of tide
schedules or our undigestible beak—left behind
in a sperm whale—a pond for shorthand if you
can hold your favorite pond in both hands to serve
my blondish auburn boyfriends their dinner, when cast
aboard our leafed-out table you'll also find
our slipperiest chopsticks, our inmost bowls
and oval plastic plates, their red temple
drawings hidden in piles of delicacies
we never ate, not really: horse meat and shark fins,
most of the tendons of a pitbull mutt
in black vinegar.

So, if my appetite surprised you
after nights of reassurance; I moan
when you moan. If I stroked your hand *thank you
for this bag of Werther's original* then swallowed you
and your smile, all of us smiling, remember it was
all an accident: me meeting you and you finding
me very beautiful. I'm as confused as you.
When you balked then bucked
I looked away, gave you your privacy,
a paper towel halved, a stroke
underneath the table, understanding
your test in these textured treasures.

When she saw me watching, she held
up something small and grey by the tips of her
chopsticks and said, "This one would not eat the shark
though she flailed on the sea's floor for three days to be served
on this table." You were home, scoring loaves of bread—*I told
you, we don't eat sourdough*—and she was standing in moonlight
at the sink sifting leftovers to catch us for the shark pieces
we had laid to rest beneath a blurred, pockmarked
congee face. Nothing so cute as a pond and a poor
burial for things born in deep waters. I turned,
as ethics demanded, from my mother who could not
understand how things in this country
were very gruesome.

But now, what if I told you I have just
lied and the whole time it was me.
To be honest, I've grown tired
of the games I play, choosing between duck
tongue and the tongues of blond boys,
replacing more and more of a recipe's
all-purpose white with whole wheat until
collapse, or it overproofs. These days,
I sit in front of my T.V. and dream
about butterscotch, butterscotch coating
my throat, butterscotch dripping down
the tail of my back,
butterscotch in my pants.

CINDY KING

Mortality Forward, Mortality on the Nose

Sunshine. Every day, sun. A thrust through
the turnstile to the unforgiving heaven, desert of forgetting—
your childhood, adolescence, most of your adult life.

The walk in the park, not much mortality in that.
You need fitness—heart, lungs, abs.
The other list: cigarettes, anti-depressants, box wine,
all those micro-mortalities accumulate in the bloodstream.

Didn't you ask? You didn't ask. My father died last year.
He was a butcher; Hell is for vegans.
Those pink rocks looks just like pork chops.
I know all about his *I-told-you-so's*, nothing of your *I'm-so-sorries*.

I keep walking in sunshine. No prophesies
required. No sunscreen or shade.
Crosswalk. White light. Man made of stars.
The RV that nearly hit me. *Murderers*,
I shout from the middle of the street.
Oh, if only I had a teenager to be ashamed of
me, to see his mother, sultana in cheap sneakers.

My father used to say, *Clean your plate. God put animals on earth for us to eat.*
Who's eating them now? What's eating him?

God, what gives? Cleanliness isn't godliness anymore.
Is there a he, she, or it (anyone) at the end of this goddamned prayer line?
My dad, he'd pick up if he had a phone down there.
As it was, his last pro-mortality, a burger he ate
with my ghost child. Offspring of a 9-month pregnancy scare,
eating with my father.

Fear is to rage what blade to whetting stone,
shame the utensil he most avoided.
Regret a carcass dismembered.

Drumstick, music, with something he'd fill my plate.
My mother tells me he wasn't drafted, he
enlisted in the army at the height of the War.
He wanted to kill, she says.
He wanted to go to college.

CHRIS SANTIAGO

Golden Age

It used to embarrass me when my father talked
back to the TV.

Since my mother died he doesn't talk anymore
but falls asleep enwombed

by voices: anchors,
procedurals, the invisible labor

of foley artists. My teacher
gasped when the *Challenger*

exploded on live TV. We had to wait
for the set to warm up

from a white hot pinprick of light.
It was so heavy the librarian warned

it could crush us. We watched as the column
of smoke split in two. *Gasp*

comes from Old Norse *geispa*
& shares a base with *brag, bluster,*

& *babble*. My second week of
teaching Kindergarten a girl came in &

said she saw a plane on TV
fly into a tower. By the end of the day

a colleague had rushed in & announced
that we'd started to bomb

Afghanistan.
We are still bombing Afghanistan.

My father turns the volume up
to 77, 78. Each morning I have to crank

the volume back down.
His hearing loss could be described

as severe to profound. Still he must feel
bathed in those shifting backdrops,

those faces, *profound* from the Latin for before
the bottom. In order to remember

what to capitalize in *McAuliffe*
I think of how it contains the chemical

symbol for gold. The noise
of the television soothes everyone

on the other side of the house; it tells us
someone is watching but not watching

us, not the room where we can finally
make love undetected. I was taught to be silent

when praying. She was taught to pray
out loud, the way our sons

threw up their hands when we could solve
any unhappiness by lifting them: *up*

they would say. *Up.* The crew
of the *Challenger* were likely conscious

the whole way down. I want
to lay like this a little longer,

before getting up, before
erasing all traces

of intimacy. Sometimes I go back out
& pour my father a finger of Jura

& he pretends he hasn't been sleeping.
I've been doing this since I was a boy,

sneaking out after bedtime & over
my father's shoulder watching the Cold

War unfold. The atomic
number for gold is 79. *God*

he says when there's a protest,
a wildfire, a shooting.

God as though
there were someone else in the room.

TYLER BARTON

to continue

THE NATURE OF JEB'S EMPLOYMENT is that he zips around the city, undressing young trees. The ones with the green plastic skirts, which apparently protect the young trees from the horror of dog piss. Once a tree turns ten, it's time to remove the skirt. The city has eighteen thousand trees. If you're thinking Jeb probably just spends a lot of time sitting around parks sipping flasks or eating weed-infused Rice Krispie treats, you'd be wrong, because Jeb also puts the skirts on, and there are new trees all the time. In the whole world, you don't even want to know how many more trees there are than humans, don't get Jeb started. Also, Jeb is sober. Well, California sober. That's why the Rice Krispie treats.

Jeb believes this job, which saved his life, is such an apt metaphor for humanity. You're protected (or at least you should be) for the first few years alive, but then eventually you're strong and tall and old enough to handle whatever piss the world pours on you.

Jeb knows what that's like too, because his father ran for state representative as a democrat, and someone once threw a wine-bladder full of piss at the windshield of their pick-up truck. They were stopped at a red light, in fact, Jeb's favorite red light, the one in town with the little white sliver in the middle everyone said was a camera. Jeb always smiled for it, except that day, because though the piss exploded on the windshield, his father immediately put the wipers on, which thwacked the piss wildly around and into Jeb's open window. Jeb still feels a pang of shame for throwing up. If a body was ready for the world and working correctly, it would not vomit after contact with a bit of stranger's piss. *I'm fine*, Jeb kept saying between heaves. His Dad was pale, but also fine. They went home and jumped in the inflatable pool. He didn't mention this memory at the job interview.

Jeb does his job well, honest, but he has some secrets. For example he's running an experiment to see if a tree can grow just fine despite this piss protection, so every eleventh tree on Locust street, you'll see, is naked.

And at the far corner of Buchanan park, where the treeline meets the fence for the fashion factory, there is an oak that's now seventeen years old, and Jeb never took its skirt off. The roots and trunk bulge against the plastic, like muscles in a tight tee. Some days when he's cutting through the park on foot for work, he steels himself against what could be, any second now, the ugly sound of the skirt popping open or, for some strange reason, exploding.

But Jeb's actual hypothesis is that the tree will grow through the plastic, the way branches can grow through a fence, or around a powerline . . . or like this one weird sculpture he saw as a kid with his father, where an artist had affixed a porcelain fist to the trunk of a young tree. It looked as if the disembodied hand were gripping the trunk for safety, fingers dug deep into its flesh. The question that the sculpture asked was: where will this hand end up in ten, twenty, fifty, a thousand years? Guess. Talk to your father about it. Jeb went back to that sculpture park a few months ago, alone, and found the tree, or what he thought was the tree, and he swore he could see it when he squinted, a glint of white up in the canopy. The tree had grown just the way his father said it would, like an elevator for the hand.

GREY WOLFE LaJOIE

work

WE MOVE INTO A DOUBLE wide set out over the river   jules looks after the baby
and i go to the funerals   the doves have to come back each and every one   if
even one dove is lost than i cant break even and cant replace it   you have
to think about all the weeks of traning. the food i feed them. all the expenses
right out of the gate. the tagging the registering   i dont do this just for
God after all i do this for jules and for the baby. i tell myself exactly that each
morning. i remind myself   you are doing this for jules and the baby

the other day at maude hewitts funeral a owl i mean a very large owl was siting
in a oak stairing and i mean stairing at my little birds   just waiting for me to
let them out owls being a natural predator to the dove of course   so i refused
to release and the family   the hewitts   began to scream into my face
well   that did not exactly convinse me   yelling at me right infront of all those
unhappy morners   some people have no contol whatever   the doves looking
up at me wondering what it was all about   that noise   i did what i thought
i had to do for my livelyhood i put them up in the truck and drove off   let
me be clear i do not wish to be a crual man i do not wish to take from no one
but i have seen what a owl or a hawk can do to a dove in mid air and it is not
a pretty sight   if those people had got to see such a sight it would do them
no spritual favor   charles said im not sure i can give you another buriel you
can not keep acting this way these people are   sensative.   sensative to what
i wonder? to who? you handed your grief over to some stranger,   i want to say
        i want to say   they took your beloved and washed her body which a long
time ago you would have washed yourself   they took her body and put
spiked contact lenses over her eyes   to hold the lids shut forever   and glued
her mouth up   and filled her with formaldihide   to make her look less dead
you people   i want to say   you people think *i'm* taking something
you already gave it   away
        but i dont say none of that   i just get in my truck and close   the door
being careful not to slam it   and i drive away

Translation Folio

JERZY JARNIEWICZ

Translator's Introduction

Piotr Florczyk

ONE WOULD BE HARD PRESSED to find—on the web or in print—truly disparaging comments about the art of translation. Certainly, there are plenty of gripes and quibbles about the quality of a particular rendition, or the threadbare arguments about translators being copyists at best, but by and large the field of translation is seen as benevolent. After all, translators bring the world to us and thus make it more hospitable—what's there to criticize or even discuss? Plenty, actually. For instance, while translation is a dialogue between languages and cultures, which makes it generative in and of itself, it is equally true that for every voice carried over into another language there are others who are subsequently shut out. What's worse, newly translated authors are often viewed as stand-ins for their country's literature in general, which fixes its reception for years to come.

Well, I decided to open my intro with that brief self-flagellation because it's important for translators to be cognizant of their choices (what and who to translate), and I think that Jarniewicz, who's not only a poet but also a searching theorist and practitioner of translation, would agree. His dividing of translators into "ambassadors" and "legislators," where the former aim to introduce foreign classics into a new cultural realm, while the latter set their sights on upending the target literature by exposing it to hitherto unknown formal and linguistic trends, has been hugely influential. As a Polish poet being translated into American English, he would seem to have a straight shot to the heart of the American reader, since the reception of Polish poetry in the U.S. has been nothing short of spectacular. Indeed, the works of Czesław Miłosz, Zbigniew Hebert, Wisława Szymborska, and Adam Zagajewski have not only been received with open arms but have also entered the bloodstream of American poetry; their translators have succeeded as the legislators of Jarniewicz's theory and for that deserve our gratitude. However, did the near uniformity of the poetics practiced by the aforementioned authors help or hinder the chances of other Polish poets to be translated and embraced in the States?

The popularity of the poets representing the so-called Polish School of Poetry at the expense of non-traditional or experimental poets is a good problem to have, some might say, and I would agree. Still, where does Jarniewicz belong? He was born in 1958 and came of age as a writing artist during the gonzo days of Poland's transformation from a communist backslider into a capitalist teacher's pet. Unlike most Polish poets I know, he writes erotic poems that never veer into kitsch—or when they do, the move is deliberate, echoing various pop cultural borrowings that bolster rather than lessen his erudite pedigree. Formally, his poems are always taut, emphasising a kind of rapid delivery that hints at Jarniewicz's love of linguistic slippages. With his words careening down the page at breakneck speeds it's easy to miss the switch, which is to say, sometimes the beginnings of his poems have little in common with the endings. To achieve this effect, he frequently employs the enjambment.

Traditionally, Polish poets have been expected to play the role of a sage or bard, but Jarniewicz, in my view, writes for himself first and foremost. Doing so doesn't prevent him from pursuing the ineffable like the rest of us, as evidenced by "27 Floors," in which he alludes to the Grenfell Tower fire. This split between private peregrinations and public utterances, which his predecessors have mastered to the tee, stems at least in part from his engagement with the work of British and Irish authors, whose books he translates and teaches at the University of Łódź. But let's not get too involved with trying to explicate Jarniewicz's poetic lineage. American readers are not dumb. We realize there are other voices and—to paraphrase John Ashbery—other traditions out there. Where Jarniewicz belongs or doesn't belong within Polish letters, or, god forbid, to which American poet might we compare him (comparing translated authors to original voices is more common than we realize!), is a moot point. His smart, funny, and surprising poems, with their "lazy bends and mock estuaries," which reward repeated readings, tell us he belongs with us.

27 Floors

Got your email, Paweł, about writing
something for you for tomorrow, a poem, perhaps,
because it's your birthday, but since daybreak a tower block
has been burning on the TV channel Piotr says represents the regime.
Kensington, isn't it? I lived there
briefly, when visas were still required, and miners picketed
outside the Northern mines, that's why, again and again, if
I recall correctly, the electricity was cut and
I wrote letters home only in the light
of day or didn't write them at all. A poem, meanwhile,
won't get written, because I don't even know what to say
when you ask how to handle the guy who
hooks up with his students, but none of them wants to
testify. Poems will find their time, your time
will see poems. A leap from the window,
when the rooms are on fire and the city falls into a stupor,
can't be an escape nor a premature
declaration of will.

Rorschach

That's not true, it's just coffee, as you see,
spilled on the table. So obtrusively nobody's
in its attempt to imitate the classic test,
where one can discern approximately
everything, if only anyone cared to look.
Its lazy bends and mock estuaries
form into a map more clearly present
than the words blurted out upon waking,
which now, given the aftertaste of coffee, mean
just enough to be met with a shoulder shrug,
raised eyebrows and googly eyes, and a wish to
keep on living, even in the unknown,
before the coffee stain takes on in your eyes
the shape of a brain or a spider.

Here Comes the Rain, Here Come the Cats and Dogs

I desert, you desert, he
deserts—the teacher made me conjugate
at the blackboard, when as an example for an infinitive
I stupidly blurted out: to desert. To eat, to drink,
to sleep—my peers volunteered around me, truth be told,
with more mature suggestions. I wanted
to show off, I admit, with a subversive word,
but to make me crawl like that straight
through conjugation? I considered it a harassment
and a harbinger of torture. Only beetles and ladybugs
took my side.
       I had to flee for a long time through
guerrilla forests and fenced-off estates, through
Siberian mud and the highways of Midwest, before you, love, would embrace me and
hide me under the kitchen floor. It's safe here,
with enough space for two, and we only have to make love,
covering our mouths, when the tongue, this loot for
scalpers, hungers loudly for love
syllables. I go AWOL, you go AWOL . . .

A Neogothic of Yellow Brick

In May the cathedral on Piotrkowska Street was burning.
It was my first fire, if you don't count
the fire in films and on TV. You're about to be
born, I was at the cathedral, the cathedral
goes up in flames.
                              Then we both tried
to live on fire, like those yellow lizards, which,
obviously, don't exist, but our fire was also
of another order. It was kind, nourishing,
but we exited extinguished, without eyebrows and without skin. Such
nakedness, as if a Trojan deleted the folders
with photos of us making love, leaving only the screen
intact. About this cathedral people were saying that
it wasn't a fire, but communists.

translated from the Polish by Piotr Florczyk

DANIELLE CADENA DEULEN & SHARA LESSLEY

Until

I'VE BEEN THINKING ABOUT LIGHT as a medium, a presence amidst the photographer and the thing photographed—how it loves the surface of everything: the hibiscus-thin membrane of eyelid, crumbling frescoes, as much as road-kill slick with blood, and moss like hair in trees. But it cannot delve deeply. It loves, especially, the chemicals in paper, perhaps, because paper is almost all surface. This isn't, alas, my own thought. It's borrowed from a conversation with a friend. I didn't hear most of what she said. She spoke her points clearly, but they were as intricate as an organism and I have a mind like a hummingbird. One bloom leads me to another. I meant to listen attentively, but kept thinking *it loves the surface of everything*, and of her eyes as she spoke (so large, aqua, tender), and the warm surface of the rough wooden table, and how I wished you were there with us because I missed you. I'm always missing you. On the back deck that overlooks her tiered garden and pots of basil, habanero, thyme, we were melting because it was a humid summer in Cincinnati. The Midwest is so far from Jordan, from where we sat on your balcony when I visited that spring so long ago. Though I couldn't see them from where I sat, I knew the flowerbeds alongside her house were spiked with white hostas, which seem to rise from nothing after the hard winter. Such a surprise—how just before spring all the foliage looks gone forever, then from the dark earth blooms these terrestrial stars. When I first learned the flower's name, I misheard it as *hasta*—Spanish for *until*. Also, *to, through, during*, depending on context. It's a connective word, a bridge between the beginning of a thought and its completion.

•

THOUGH I couldn't see the bridge from where I sat, the balcony became it. Our emerald-iron railing that held back Amman's adjacent apartment buildings somehow becoming the massive cable-stayed bridge that connected the expanse of Wadi Abdoun. While the weeks-old baby slept in bassinette beside me, I climbed the concrete Y-shaped tower that stretched two-hundred-thirty-three feet above the valley floor. A fantasy or dream, of course, but one I couldn't shake. My mind, after all, is nothing like a bird—rather, it fixes and stays put—so that, although our balcony was just a single story up, day after day in those hazy postpartum weeks it became the s-shaped traffic-congested bridge that existed both in mind and miles across the city. While the baby slept, I kept picturing the pale gray span of deck, the bridge's hidden tendons and segments, the stress it was designed to bear. In the garden below, our neighbor's fruit trees were just beginning to yield; jackdaws picking at scraps of whatever soft thing the branches let go. Seed and flesh, I suppose. The baby slept. Impossible, it seemed, the railing lowering itself, the breeze one afternoon lifting my heel—or so I thought. Why not? Why not make myself fall? Across the street, mothers pushed strollers through the bright dry light. From the balcony I couldn't see them, but knew the patterns they made circling the park's outer ring. All was quiet. All calm. Beneath his hibiscus-thin eyelids, my young son slept. I sat beside him. A photo might be made of it.

•

EVERY day should feel like a photograph, but it doesn't. Every day with my children should be like a kite festival along the bright shore of the Pacific, the wind leaning against everything solid—the squinting faces of people, even the cement boardwalk with its metal rails leading downstairs to the beach—the exposed taut tendons and segments of the kites trembling in midair. We drove the hour there on a Sunday, past fields of ferns and purple lupine timid beneath sky-scraper-tall pines, until we arrived at the edge of the earth. The sandy threshold of it. A line of fliers with sharp kites worked to move them in formation, forming Os and Vs and spirals against a blue sky. Others had somehow filled their impossibly large nylon creatures with wind and pulled them up: a flying gecko the size of a house, a rainbow centipede as long as a semi-tuck undulating its body, teddy bears and sunfish, jellyfish and whirly-gigs—and whales that seemed the size of actual whales, but flying. I should have taken a photo to send to you, all of us sunlit and staring up. There's something about looking up that feels like worship, even for something as mundane as a kite. I should try to hold that in my heart. I shouldn't let my days splinter and slowly erode. I shouldn't let the faces of my children in their delight fade. But I do. Most days are not festivals, or even photographs of festivals. Most days I stand in the waves waiting for the gray day to slip away. Most days I'm just waiting until I can lie down—until I become wind, water, light.

•

CHESTNUT and white-headed, Red Kites will eat the carcasses of shrews and sheep, bed down to rest in pilfered wool. When we moved to England, looking up became a game: spotting the elongated feathers and forked tails mid-flight as the birds soared over highways, hedged-in country roads, meadows sprawling from dusty footpaths. Like ideas moving toward completion. The black tips of their wings writing something we couldn't quite make sense of. How many hours did I squander those years, thinking *until* or *toward* or *through*? Kites were once endangered, you know: eggs gifted in glass boxes; the birds' breeding impeded by modern pesticides; before government measures of protection were enacted, what was left of the population hunted almost to the point of extinction. A lowly thing, loathed. Emblem of scavengers. Carrion lovers. The word a kind of insult, shorthand for thief. *When the kite builds*, warned Shakespeare, *look to your lesser linen*. Our son's striped blue sock; the hand-me-down scarf I gifted my daughter. Imagine these sun-bleached, care-worn items tugged from their clothespins in the garden now lining a pair's first nest. A part of us elsewhere, but home nonetheless. Those seasons far from the country that birthed me, I think I'd forgotten astonishment doesn't necessarily feel miraculous. Case in point: Kites could have easily gone the way of the Dodo, their remains locked up for display in a museum in Oxford. Instead, one drawn-out afternoon our son counted twelve. Then thirteen. We hiked the chalk trackway, taking turns holding hands. In holding patterns over woods dating back to the last Ice Age, fifteen Kites! Our oldest scrambled ahead. The sun dipped down. Eighteen! Nineteen! Twenty-three!

•

Until is always a threshold—the wish for a threshold. When I was a young woman and my body was still mine I often found this threshold-wish in my mouth. *I am working this job until . . . I will stay with him until . . .* All of it—everything in my life—potentially transitory. The wish was for the threshold of a doorway I could walk into and stay. Stay still. Something permanent, real. Something that would anchor my kite of a heart—*please someone catch me, keep me from flying away*. That's all I wanted. When I was a young woman and my body was still mine, I believed love would save me from my drifting loneliness. Not the lesser loves (as I understood it then) of family and friends, but a great romance. I searched for the hand that would grasp me: always handing myself over too quickly, too eager. *Love me now. Make me real.* And for a while I'd feel the uplift, the hot light on my face, the wind driving me forward, but this always preceded the drop—finding myself alone again, feeling less real, less permanent than before. I'm making it sound easier than it was. It's probably more accurate to say that I was torn, or, I allowed myself to be torn over and over, and after those years, I wasn't sure there was anything left to call a self. I wasn't sure that I wanted to live. I try to remember this when I begin to romanticize those younger years: all that freedom. When I feel buried beneath the mundane and the needs of my family, I try to remember that when I was a young woman and my body was still mine, I was alone in the world. I was free, yes, of course—but so free, it hurt.

•

ALL my life, in the quietest place inside, in a room forbidden to anyone or any-thing but fear, I've felt like Tippi Hedren the moment she realizes that Hitchcock's winged things aren't mechanical. For days, she takes her mark in the attic where gloved men hurl pigeons and ravens trained to attack. ASPCA requires an on-set hospital to care for the injured sparrows and crows. How much grief will her body show? Her sheath wool dress stitched with fabric bands to which live gulls are attached. In my mind's forbidden corner, the camera advances, retreats; its eye swings toward a hole in the ceiling. Maniacal birds surge through. I don't know if I've ever felt that kind of freedom—that *uplift* you describe, reckless as driving wind—but I know what it is to be torn. To worry you're nothing but a body. There are moments it goes so far, I can almost hear my synapses firing. Is life more than a reaction shot? Something beyond the brain's erratic patter of flight-or-flight re-sponse? Hedren whimpers, collapses: a week trapped in the climactic attack for an edited minute on screen. "I have . . . to . . . get out of . . . here," she keens in Marian Daniels's half-broken speech, but who can guess what the self behind the actress's mask is thinking? On the floor in a heap or standing upright composed, no one knows what I'm thinking. A fleeting remembrance of winding coastal highway. Some scattered seeds. Is physical or psychological pressure more taxing? I couldn't say. Only, that what began as fable or romantic fantasy, Hitchcock later shot as a threshold: nature's body pitted against a woman's, a pair of lovebirds hatching the plot.

•

BUT to be a body is miraculous enough: to be in this body at this time, thinking and feeling, and communicating with you in your body—the odds against it are staggering. I can hear your synapses firing from here and the sound is gorgeous! The problem is not that we're only bodies, but that we're told over and over that we're *only* bodies, trained to think of the self as two selves: the physical or the men-tal, and pit them against one another. I blame Plato's Ideal Forms, and Descartes's Mind-body split, and even Lacan's Ideal-I—the perception that the physical is some simulacra of a truer, spiritual form—that the "real" is spiritual, and therefore exists in a form we can't perceive. Ironic. That what you can *feel* is the unreal world, while the real remains forever "untouchable." That's what they taught us, anyway, every Sunday. A gray church with beige walls and girls in dresses with ribbons in their hair. I wanted to be one of them. I wanted the dresses—what my family couldn't afford—but also to smile and sing and lay my fist like an emblem over my heart. An emblem of what? I didn't know, though I'd seen the Sacred Heart float before Jesus in Abuela's house—or, the image of Him, at least, His shining chambers wreathed with thorns and topped with a crown of fire. The only man I could trust to tell me the truth. He never spoke. One Sunday the girls with ribbons and I made papier-mâché tombs, laying the wet pulp like a silent palimpsest over the rude structures of chicken-wire. Before we sealed the last torn scrap of pastel tissue-paper we were given a tiny plastic Jesus cast in all white: a ghost, a holy spirit. I wanted to take him home, to place him beneath my pillow as I slept—my only God, my only gift—but the teachers refused my pleading, promised if I placed him where he belonged that he would return to me by Easter. I sealed my Jesus in his tomb. It's an unheroic story: a girl who was tricked and lost her trinket. When I opened the tomb on Easter, of course, my Jesus was gone. The teachers cheered *Hallelujah! A miracle!*—and we were supposed to play along, but I sat there with my mouth screwed shut, imagining them staying up late to open each child's tomb, take Jesus away, then seal it back up. I knew, then, that they were all liars—stupid and cruel—and that I'd take any physical thing that would lie in my hands over any lie that would leave the truth empty.

·

I, on the other hand, would've bought the miracle. However obvious. However manufactured. Given the things that were happening, the secrets I was keeping, I would have done just about anything to believe there was something better, something more. That I was worth sacrifice, not sacrificing. Eight years old. The room smelled like unfinished chores, my dance bag dropped to the floor; dried sweat and a hint of rosin clotting the air. Scattered across the carpet, whatever I'd walked in with—damp towel, school uniform, ribbons embossed with ladybugs or geese, my little books of saints. How many hours did I spend pouring over Father Lovatik's paperbacks, each cover stamped with a seven-celled grid from which God's blended family of martyrs gazed out? The Brady Bunch for the holy, my father, un unbeliever, teased. But unlike the house where I grew up, in the pages of those books suffering held meaning—one that merited recognition and even reverence. Take twelve-year-old Agnes, for instance, dragged naked through the streets in the first century and then tied to a stake for refusing to marry the son of a city official. They say no fire would touch her. That every flame, every spark, every last ember turned away. They say any man who tried to touch her was blinded. Sprawled my stomach, the book beneath me, I stared at her pale face. Then prayed. Maybe my mistake was holding as still as possible, believing what happened to girls like Agnes was sanctioned. Maybe it was appealing to any Father for protection, given the cruelty of my own. But what do I know? Like I said, I would've bought the miracle. After weeks on my knees, the eight-year-old me half expecting an armor of long thick hair to cover her body each time she took off her clothes.

•

YES. Yes. I understand what you mean—that constant want for protection. Love from an Old Testament God, who would blind your betrayers. Because you needed something above the earthly father—there had to be *something* above the earthly father—someone more powerful who might intervene. Of the stories I knew, my favorite was Daniel in the Lion's Den. I made my mother read it to me again and again. Daniel was raised to high office by Darius, as you probably remember, the King. People were jealous of Daniel and made the king decree that only his name should be spoken in prayer. A regular man. An earthly father who demanded his subjects pray to him and if not, they would be thrown into a den of lions. Daniel prayed to his God and was thrown into the lions' den while Darius, who loved him, wrung his hands. I had questions. How did they make a den of lions? How could a king be tricked into killing his friend? If he was the king, why didn't he just change the law that *he made*, or open the door, instead of standing outside of it, listening for the snap of his friend's neck? *To worry*—to seize, especially by the throat, with the teeth and shake, as one animal does another. To be throttled by worry. But it was a worry of his own making. He sounded like a stupid king. A weak king. One who couldn't see what was right in front of him: jealous rivals circling, licking their lips for a kill. Daniel's God sent an angel to shut the mouths of the lions all through the terrible night and I liked to think of this too: the dim bodies of beasts, the musky sheen of their pelts in the moonlight, the soft thud of their paws in the dust as they moved toward and away from Daniel, sniffing his body, listening to the thrum of his blood. None of them opened their jaws. The next day, the king commanded that Daniel be released, that those who had conspired against Daniel would be thrown there in his place, along with their wives and children. With their wives and children. That part always worried me.

•

NOT long after our son was born, I began sketching Amman's feral cats. While the baby napped, I'd watch them watching us. Sprawled near the base of the dumpster. Beneath pomegranate trees. Along the park's rusty fence. I know nothing about drawing. Perhaps therein, the pleasure: the chance, in the pressure-filled weeks of early motherhood, to make mistakes that didn't count. Dragging a charcoal pencil across the page, I'd shade the scraggly band of tabbies that canvassed the nearby alley. A *clowder*, you call them, meaning a pack. But also a *glaring*—their retinas eerily flushed as they stalked their prey after dusk. Maybe that's why when you mention Daniel, it's not the man that I imagine but the surge of light set off in the stone-sealed den: the lions' amber-green pupils refracted and flaring as the angel descends. *Tapetum lucidum*, it's called. From the Latin, "bright tapestry"; meaning, the iridescent retro-reflector amplifying an animal's vision, bettering its chances to hunt at night. The truth is I have little talent for drawing, but remember the texture and light of particular moments as if they were imprinted on parchment. Early one morning, for instance, two men in thobes dragging plastic bags into the deserted street. I heard the cats—a dozen and a half at least—before I saw them: their nails clicking across the broken sidewalk; their high-pitched mewing rushing in waves toward the mound of scraps I guessed were the butcher's. Had I ever known real hunger?, I wondered, my son strapped tight to my chest. I still can't explain why I couldn't bring myself to leave until they'd finished feeding, until the last mouthful of flesh disappeared, except to say that seeing the strays this way I understood that if pride obliterates itself so, too, must certain forms of love. The mob clawed and lapped at fat and gristle. Whiskers glistened. A spotted shorthair grimaced then sniffed. Forced out from the pack, the smallest cat crouched to lick the dust. As its pink tongue flickered, a surge of neurons fired in my nipples—my milk let suddenly down. The men had long since disappeared. Beneath the bench where I sat, a matted grey bunted its head against my leg. I clutched my baby tighter. There was no one else around.

•

THE air here is turning colder. The leaves of the White Oak towering over our house have turned an unlovely shade of russet and curl at the tips like little claws as the wind drags them over the sidewalk—that faint scraping sound. The whole world looks hungry. *I'm starving*, my three-year-old son says when he feels that ache, and I wince. "Don't say *starving*. You don't know what it's like to starve. You're just a little hungry. Here, eat this pear." He shakes his head, "I want cake." When I tell him we don't have cake, he cries outright. Is this a normal developmental power struggle or have I spoiled my children already? I don't remember ever demanding cake from my mother. I remember how careful she was about food, how good at making the best of whatever we could afford. "The Latino Effect," a sociological term to describe the cultural imperative to eat real food, so Latinx families suffering from poverty remain healthier than other poor families—unless they adopt the American diet. Abuela taught my mother and my mother taught me: only real food and no food wasted. Still, my son demands cake. Have I gone wrong in my desire to provide him plenty? I remember standing in the hallway, out of sight from my parents fighting about money, then following my mother down the aisles of the Food Bank, her tender face wincing at the cans of meat before placing them in our basket. We didn't starve. We didn't starve because she was careful and because she waited tables at a pancake house to make up for my father's lavish addictions—alcohol, marijuana, cocaine—whatever kept him numb to the world, whatever transiently filled the greedy vacuum at the center of his mind. The psalmist says, "My soul shall be satisfied as with marrow and fatness," but my father never looked to religion for guidance. The spirits he sought all fit in a bottle and filled him with unrepentant rage. After he left us—that's when we went hungry, but we didn't mind. Our empty stomachs meant he couldn't reach us anymore. It meant there would never be another night he kept us up with his screaming, his fists swinging through the air. In the morning, after one of those nights, my head hurt. The sharp winter light rattled through every window on the bus to school, tapping at my eyes. I remember stepping off the bus and the wind needling my ears, the sound of dry leaves scraping the ground. I needed to describe it. The need to describe what I saw, what I felt, is a hunger I've never shaken. That girl I was believed that words were magic—that if I could find the right words in the right order the hex hovering above my life might lift. My father would be generous, kind. My mother would be happy. We'd feast. But looking over the brittle, matted grass in the fields, the ice-puddles fracturing at their edges, I could only summon these words: *The whole world is starving*.

•

AFTER my mother sent him packing, my father showed up just once for supper. A mercy invitation, perhaps, or some attempt on her part to ease the transition. In either case, a perfect example of the work she's always done as a woman—that is, to tidy things up by comforting the person who hurt her most. My mother has always been a romantic. A passionate teacher of music and art. A keeper of secrets. A reader of sagas set in the South. A believer in redemption. *We don't have to do this*, I told her, as his truck rattled up the driveway. Stirring stew with a wooden spoon, she tested a bite then added some seasoning, bent to the floor to pick up the Cheerios my brother had flicked from the tray of his high-chair. *We're fine*, I added, though it was perfectly clear she'd heard me. But was anyone fine in that house? Better off, no question, without him. But fine? The kitchen's motif was strawberries: sprawling clusters across her oven-mitts and cross-stitched apron, an oil painting of a spilled bushel, a chipped cookie jar that opened via leaf-cap, a set of Mikasa dishware most likely purchased on layaway. Stamped across coffee mugs and plates, on the crimson set of shakers she kept in the windowsill, those strawberries—or so it seemed to me as a child—looked so happy as they shamelessly wore their seeds on the outside for anybody to see. While I ate, I liked to make a game of counting the wallpaper's bundled heart-shapes, imagining myself in some far-off woodland where it was safe for things to grow wild. Had my mother ever been happy? What about me didn't she know? That night, he came in through the garage, as if the house and all its possessions were still his own. I offered to serve; when their backs were turned, spat in his bowl. We sat. He asked to pass the salt, adding—I remember this clearly—with an almost-tenderness, a word he rarely used: *please. Of course*, I answered. He lifted his spoon. From across the table, I looked at my mother and smiled.

•

SOMETIMES vengeance is beautiful. Sometimes it is not. I suppose it depends on which side of the vengeance one sits. I've been hacking a lot lately, though merely from illness—nothing grand or redemptive about it. Yet, my horoscope says the full moon tonight will work to my advantage, romance-wise. The romance that will arise will be tender and profound. "Life-changing," it says. I feel faint, but not from love. A cluster of bacteria has anchored itself in my chest like an inscrutable ruin. Stonehenge, but less famous. Maybe I'm a priestess, a crone. I cough wet dust. I cough the residue of faulty spells. I don't know what minor deity I have angered, but it's vengeful. The full moon will rise, I believe, beneath a thick layer of clouds and I'll never see it. I wonder if that matters for the horoscope. For the full moon to touch me tenderly, must I look into its face, have the time to look into its face, have the youth to think it matters at all in my life? My hair is gray beneath the dye, and my body is no longer admired by potential lovers. With my experience, I could reach out my hand, stretch it up through the clouds and atmosphere, hold that tender moon in my palm, but I'm certain it would only whine and call me Mama. Maybe it's the full moon or my fever, but I keep thinking of the face of a former lover, how I used to hold it in my hands. He's with a younger woman now, one who looks like me a decade ago—this fact both homage and insult. I smile and cry and cough, feeling the magic of the night erasing all desire from my body.

•

A team in coveralls asks about the heart's engine. *Has the vehicle been in an accident?*, they want to know. *When did the alignment start pulling east?* As in most dreams, they say these things without ever speaking. The heart in question is 80-horsepower, fuel-injected—like the kind that rattled my mother's Ford Escort LX Wagon the miles we drove toward her divorce. From the glassed-in waiting room, I can see its metallic blue frame across the garage. Hood up. Finally at rest. The head mechanic insists, however I deny it, you can't separate the heart from the body that holds it. She waves a clipboard, demands to know the places I've been, the routes my mother and I have taken, but the answers are like moving through smoke. I've trouble breathing. My eyes sting. The neon-green billboards are meaningless and bright. Maybe I'm just distracted. I can't get past the fact that the mechanic is a woman who looks just like my mother. That the workers, eager and dirty-gloved, look like me. I was never a child who played with cars, never dragged my brother's Hot Wheels across the carpet, sputtering sounds like *vrooom*. I wanted out, of course—of my room, of that house, my hometown, but had no real map for leaving. The dream, I know, is cliché: something about desire, a thing too far gone. I, too, am a tired piece of my mother's story—a woman going places who, I'm ashamed to admit, can't even change a tire. On the screen of the dream, the workers who look like me go about the business of trying to fix something that can't be repaired. Cars, meanwhile, zip past the shop, presumably toward someplace better. Only, their drivers can't see they're looped on some sort of asphalt track. Like my mother and me, they move at varying speeds in the same direction not understanding why they'll never arrive.

·

THERE's a team of astronomers in Australia whose life work is observing the movement of stars. Imagine that. A whole life spent waiting, looking up into the dark. The earth, which they have no love for, spins beneath them, guiding the trajectory of their observations. They stare at the stars and they stare at the blackness that holds no stars—either out of reach of their powerful telescopes, or the negative space made by the gravitational maws of black holes. There's one spinning at the center of our Milky Way Galaxy with the half-romantic name, *Sagittarius A*—the constellation that dot-to-dots a centaur archer. There is no unified system for naming black holes, and the astrophysicist who discovered and named *Sagittarius A* didn't give a convincing reason for his choice. I always thought the name was misleading: the image of the archer taking aim, an extroverted arrow latent with flight, while black holes are the most significant introverts in the universe—dragging the whole of space and all its stars into themselves. And then this: those astronomers in Australia, looking, ever-looking through their powerful telescope caught sight of a runaway star, twice the mass of our sun and ten times more luminous, speeding out of the center of *Sagittarius A* at a staggering velocity toward an area of space we can't yet see. This isn't supposed to happen. As far as the physicists knew, nothing can escape the threshold of the event horizon—not even light. Black holes don't fling stars out of themselves. They only consume, swallowing down and down to the singularity, where time and space bend into impossible proportions. Yet, here's this star, loosed like an arrow from the center of our archer-black-hole. Where did it come from? Where is it going? I ask you this, my friend, as an aim toward what I want most to believe: that we can't yet imagine where our paths lead, that something astonishing could happen at any time. That we think we know everything ahead of us, until we don't.

BRETT ELIZABETH JENKINS

Marrying the Wind

I proposed to the wind and the wind said yes
but now we are encountering extreme difficulties

putting together our wedding registry.
The wind wants feathers, dust bunnies,

confetti. It has no interest in candelabras. The wind
wants only things that can be carried

on its soft voice. I want all the seasons
of Breaking Bad. The wind cannot appreciate

Walter White, but it may like to carry away a cloud
of smoke. I am unsure if my love can be held

in the wind's arms. Nothing is softer than the wind's arms—
it loves to hold hands with my hair. But I want to fight

about this espresso machine the wind doesn't want.
The wind cannot pick up the registry scanner

so I am forced to do all the booping.
Cornmeal *boop*. Flour *boop*. Wood shavings *boop*.

I buy a Diet Coke and the wind takes the receipt.
I scream into the wind and the wind screams back.

Divorce Registry

New sheets, any kind. Cat food. A place for me—
a lake to jump in, anything to call mine. Kleenex.
Two coffee mugs, or any other thing to hold
with both hands. A name for this stone I carry
around in my stomach. Curtains. Something
to let in light. A broken watch. Spices, spice
rack. Body pillow. Hammers, or chainsaws—
whatever makes noise. Something blue.
Something blue. Something blue. Something blue.

STUART FRIEBERT

The Blue Sofa

Their marriage collapsing, Mileva and Albert
haggled about it in voices so loud neighbors

just shook their heads, the air that had been
charged with reverence for the Einsteins soon

souring. Would she sit on it ever again, once
it arrived in Switzerland at her new lodging?

Why are we made with such desires? Rubbing
her eyes, she rolled a cigarette between fingers

brown with stains, licked it with puffy lips, while
he snapped his fingers as if to light it, driven to

mock her it seems. That's as far as I get before
wishing painters got after the sofa. What would

Klimt, Beckmann, Nolde or even Klee have done
with it? The smoke's so deep you can only see

them from the waist up, Klimt cursing, Beckmann
muttering contempt for everything nationalistic,

Nolde feeling some love for Mileva, while Klee sat
down, "Let's see, here a perpendicular, there a . . .

ADAM SCHEFFLER

Ode to Zamboni Machines

There was a whole other section to the poem
here which I deleted, or zambonied over,
that had to do with bitterness, which
I for once in my life thought the better of—
believe me, there is a lot of my life for which I'd like
to employ a fleet of specialized zambonis,
a botox zamboni for removing wrinkles,
a nursemaid zamboni for when I lie sleepless treading
the iron escalator of my thoughts, a sunshine zamboni
to polish each day vigorously like a stray tongue-cleans
his bowl into a dog dish halo, but most of all
a zamboni for my knee-jerk stupidity,
for the stupid aggrieved remarks I made last night,
and the ones I will no doubt make today:
I wish I could be more like snails, the shining
zambonis of the soil, spinning mucousy, abalone
roads behind them before they're murdered
by persnickety gardeners who have a deep
knowledge of both flowers and poison, but yet
also have a patience I do not, in my constant
rushing and worrying and ugly conversational
blundering, that is not unlike the deep, quiet
patience that Frank Zamboni dreamed of after
his family left overheated Vespa-smoggy Italy
for overheated freeway-smoggy Los Angeles,
as he decided to dedicate his whole life to ice
and coolness, first making ice blocks to sell,
and then when compressor-based refrigeration
made this obsolete, devoting 9 years to his dream
of an eponymous ice resurfacer, which he stuck
with, as his son Richard claimed, for the very
reason that "everyone told him he was crazy,"
which is honestly how I have reacted every single time

someone has told me their idea for an invention,
and is another of the beautiful facts laid out in Frank's
Wikipedia page like pies lined up for no reason in
an open store window, or in a town of bakers
who have just up and left for no reason, except for
perhaps being raptured into a pie-makers' heaven
as a reward for devoting their whole lives to
making sugary confections instead of apps or weapons
or moving money around, which is the kind of thing
if God did more often in the Bible, instead
of arranging the harvesting of 200 Philistine
foreskins, I could really get behind Him,
but perhaps it's not too late to swap that foreskin
story out, to Zamboni-over the whole affair,
the way Frank never stopped trying to make improvements,
and died only after experimenting on astroturf, & working
on another ice-related invention (to remove ice from
the corners of rinks), for there's no such thing as one's
life's work being finished to oneself, but only to
others, who want you to die as soon as you've completed it.

ROY WHITE

Mind the Gap

There's a three-day test at the Oval.
They've turned around the down
escalators to ferry up
drifting crowds from the tube. The man
in the cage directs me to
a little door, an iron staircase
spiraling into the dark, where once
men with pocket watches
and ladies with their ankles hidden
carried their film of fine coal dust
back underground.

Underground, having minded the gap,
we hang from straps as the car luges
from side to side, then stops in mid-
tunnel; now we wait, our bodies
drooping in this muggy limbo
like slumbering bats.
The blind talk of a way out,
wrote Brecht.

Brecht wrote that the companion
who sits facing us, at last,
is Nothing. When it's time
to leave London, I get lost
and nearly miss the bus. The driver
mocks me in German, and the man
in the front row laughs, the one
who calls sheep "wool-pigs." Still, I know
this is not a dream. In a dream
they would make me drive the bus.

The Only Hill

There is pain in all the furniture, in the end,
contagious pain, but it's the chairs,
the chairs that bear the most. Every torque
makes a gap that never quite closes,
each nail or screw tears and scrapes
a small wound every time
it strains to hold the whole together.
The chair knows the score, knows that downhill
is the only hill, but its hands are tied.
Free radicals, splinters, swarms
of T-cells, frayed upholstery: always someone
winds up on their ass amid the kindling,
stared at by everyone.

There are a few Vicodin left,
rattling in the plastic bottle. I
am trying to make them last.
Before I can pass through, I must take off
my shoes, must leave my bag
unattended, must stand on one leg
and explain Scripture. On the other side
we will be sorted incomprehensibly,
the rich with the disabled, babies
with soldiers. On the other side,
the chairs will be indestructible,
the long sought-after bathroom
a blinding labyrinth.

ELLEN SAMUELS

After the Procedure

I didn't know I could
be broken in places
that were already

broken, blood-
tunnels weaving through
old bruise. When

that doctor put his
hands on me, he was not
prepared, I was

not prepared
for how loud my voice
could sound. And the

wrack of bone
against bone. The syringe-
screw. The counting. All

these alphabets
I didn't know
could be un-learned

and written again, in
an afternoon. And
could I be the same

person today,
harvesting mint's bitter
with bare

hands, chewing
wood sorrel's lemon-
sweet buds? I don't

know how
to know myself
anymore, how

even to see
my own skin's
ground. I forgot

to look in the mirror
for days. Still
in the garden, I find

myself, untangling
devil's thorn from
among the lilacs, handling

each needled stem
back to the root. And
the angled knife,

the shovel, boiling
water from the stove. This
is how you bury it

so it doesn't come
back. All
afternoon, this long,

tired work, the sun
an eye overhead, a lens,
white-hot.

JOSEPHINE BLAIR

fossil

I woke up already losing. Dreamt about eating
all night. Wrung out my scales to test the willpower
of my spine. Left babies
in the bathwater. Found new skin
on the floorboards. Screamed at cold coffee and dug trenches
under the sink.
If I starve myself enough I will fit
into the piping. I will cycle through weather
the way I am used to. Separate my tongue
from your body. I will gather
like honeybees in the combs of your eyes. Splatter
on concrete, a steering wheel, a woman's palm.
Fall soft.
You will drink me and not know
the difference.

DAN LEACH

Wasp Queen

I.

CONVENTION SAYS I SHOULD KILL you. By convention I mean my wife, the artist, who had plans to repurpose the vintage steel trash can inside of which you've built a nest the size of a small child. By convention I also mean my four-year-old daughter, who has been afraid to play outside since the day she bumped the trash can, prompting your drones to emerge and sting her on her face, and across her stomach, and even in the tiny pockets of flesh behind her knees. Twenty-six hits? Some might call that excessive.

II.

WHEN I invite people to think about you, everyone's an expert. *Burn them*, says my dad. *Wait until night, when they are sleeping, then douse the nest in gasoline and chuck a match inside.* My brother submits a different method: *Let's duct-tape the lid on. We'll dump it in the country and make it someone else's problem.* An old man at the hardware store tries to sell me something he calls a bug bomb. The old man says, *The best thing about the bomb is that it kills the bitch.* I say, *The bitch?* He apologizes. *The queen*, he says. *It's guaranteed to kill the queen.*

III.

EVERYONE who hears about you requests a picture, and everyone who receives a picture feels two sequential feelings. First, they are impressed by the size of your colony. Second, they are curious and sometimes excited about the possibilities for destruction. My friend from Chicago sends me an article that argues for professional involvement, an article that reveals how each spring you lay approximately fifty-thousand eggs then train up legions of soldier-children to protect the nest. My friend from Seattle tells me, *Whatever you decide on, film it. That kind of shit goes viral.* I thank all my friends for their enthusiastic support in imagining all the ways you might die.

IV.

I share the viable tactics with my wife. She hates any plan that would damage the trash can. The artistic project she envisions requires a clean, history-free object. No burn marks, no stains. On this she is clear—there must be no you, but also no sign of me removing you. With help from a young man at the hardware store, she secures a poisonous spray that promises to achieve this end. *It's simple,* says my wife. *Spray this at night and in the morning they'll be dead.* I ask, *The queen too?* My wife nods. *The queen too.* When I mention the article that asks if creatures such as bees and crabs could be said to have sentience, my wife falls silent for a moment then says, *How would you feel about lasagna tonight?*

V.

Which more or less brings us here, to this moonless spring night, where I stand in our backyard wearing three layers of clothing and gripping two cans of poisonous spray. Here where I stare down into the trash can and try to see you, or your family, or at least some part of what you've built. What I see, though, is nothing. So dark is the night that the trash can resembles the black throat of a bottomless well. I have to aim the poison not at you but at where I believe you are. I have to imagine you there. I aim but don't yet squeeze the nozzle. I hesitate. Listen—there is so much I want to tell you.

Translation Folio

ENDŌ SHŪSAKU

Translator's Introduction

Miho Nonaka

ENDŌ SHŪSAKU (1923-1996) WAS a leading author of postwar Japan, who received several nominations for the Nobel Prize for literature. Shortly after his birth, his family moved to then-Japan-occupied Manchuria. When he was ten years old, following his parents' divorce, he returned to Japan with his violinist mother, who raised him as a Catholic. To an English-reading audience, Endō is best known for his novels such as *Deep River* and *Silence*; the latter was adapted into a film by Martin Scorsese in 2016. In his major fiction, Endō explored spiritual and moral dilemmas from the unique perspective of being both Japanese and Catholic, which earned him the moniker, "the Japanese Graham Greene." In particular, he was concerned with the difficulties of reconciling his "Western" faith with his native culture and sensibility. While his "serious" work received the most recognition, Endō was also famous for his humorist writing, mischievous persona, and Kiza, Japan's largest amateur theatrical company he founded and directed.

The essay "Hara Tamiki" is Endō's homage to his close friend and mentor figure, Hara Tamiki (1905-1951), eighteen years his senior. Though Hara dabbled in Dadaism and Marxism in his early years, in his essence, he was a lyric poet more in kinship with the likes of Rilke. It is ironic then that Hara became most celebrated for "Summer Flowers," a survivor's account of the atomic bombing of Hiroshima in terrifying detail. After the loss of his beloved wife, Sadae (a sister of the literary critic, Sasaki Kiichi) to pulmonary tuberculosis, Hara had left Tokyo and moved in with his older brother at the family home in Hiroshima, where he experienced the bombing. "Summer Flowers" was based on the notes Hara scribbled down as he was escaping from the devastation of his native city. While struggling with extreme hunger and symptoms of radiation sickness, he tried to put into words the atrocity he witnessed "calmly, with as much detachment as possible."

At that time in Japan under the American occupation, all major publications were subject to the GHQ censors who were especially sensitive to the descriptions of the atomic bombings as direct criticism of the United States. Hara was forced to alter the title of his piece (its original title was "Atomic Bomb") and make several cuts in his manuscript. "Summer Flowers" was published in the June 1947 issue of *Mita Bungaku*, a non-commercial literary journal associated with Keiō University, where Hara had studied English literature and written his undergraduate thesis on Wordsworth.

Endō first met Hara at one of the meetings for the members of *Mita Bungaku*, a year after the publication of "Summer Flowers." Hara had returned to Tokyo from Hiroshima; Endō had just completed his study of French literature at Keiō University and was starting a career as a literary critic. In 1950, Endō left Japan to study French literature in Lyon. He was one of the first Japanese students to travel to Europe after World War II. Hara was to take his own life in the following year while Endō was still in France. Just before his death, Hara had heard the news that President Truman was considering the use of nuclear weapons in the Korean War. Though technically a suicide, Hara's death has been attributed to the repercussions of his trauma of experiencing the nuclear annihilation of Hiroshima.

Because part of Endō's goal here is to record the people and realities of Japan's literary scene that was trying to recover from the fresh wounds of the war, he makes the point of writing down quite a few names of authors and publishers which, I hope, won't be too repetitive or confusing to readers.

Endō's essay provides a rare and important glimpse into Hara Tamiki, not just as a tragic victim and a famous author of atomic bomb literature, but also as a man of great affection and endearing awkwardness. In his final years, what sustained Hara was a small circle of devoted friends and his need to give voice to the countless voiceless dead of Hiroshima through the expression of lament. In "Requiem," he wrote:

So, am I all finished then? Nothing left inside me? No more need to spin, to exist? No. . . . I have something. I do. I still have grief left. I do. I do. I have a lament. I do. I have a myriad of laments. A single lament links to a myriad of laments. A myriad of laments reverberate with a single lament. My own sound rings in my ears. I sound. I echo. Lament and I link. I connect. I connect with a myriad. . . . I must endure. Endure silence. Endure illusion. Endure the depths of life. Endure and endure and endure enduring. Endure a single lament. Endure a myriad of laments. Oh lament, pierce me through. Pierce me who has no more place to return. Pierce me in my abandoned world.

Hara Tamiki

ACCORDING TO AN OLD JOURNAL of mine, I first met the members of *Mita Bunga-ku* in the middle of June in 1948. I had recently graduated from Keiō University. One drizzly afternoon, accompanied by Yoshida, an old friend from school, I went to visit Maruoka Akira, who took up his temporary residence at Nōgaku-Shorin, a publishing house in Kanda. On its second floor, people had gathered to review *Mita Bungaku*. I recorded in my journal that the room—14-square-meters—was very dark because of the rain.

Next to Mr. Maruoka, who was dressed in a kimono, sat a man wearing a stylish pair of rimless glasses and a bow tie. With a downturned mouth, as if spitting out the food he chewed, the man was denouncing a fiction piece published in the previous month's issue of *Mita Bungaku*. His criticism was so harsh that Yoshida turned to a bloated-faced man and asked, "Who *is* that person?"

"The guy over there? He is Shibata Renzaburō. Is this your first time?"

The man with the pale, bloated face was kind enough to give us the names of those who had gathered at the meeting: Katsumoto Seiichirō, Watanabe Kieko, Suzuki Shigeo. He pointed to a man dressed in a black, banded-collar top, like a postal worker, who was watching wet trees in the rain outside the window, and identified him in a soft voice, "Mr. Hara Tamiki."

Perhaps noticing our look, the man in black turned his gaze on us. I tried to bow in his direction, but he kept staring at me in silence. I bowed again, but his eyes were still fixed on my face.

This was my first encounter with Hara Tamiki. The man with the bloated face was a playwright, Katō Michio. Mr. Katō, Mr. Hara, Yoshida Toshirō, who attended the *Mita Bungaku* meeting with me—each would commit suicide, and are all gone today.

MY EDITORIAL STAFF requested biographical fiction, but what I am about to write now is more a factual memoir than a piece of fiction. I will simply write down what I remember while flipping through my journal from those days.

As I mentioned before, the first time I met Hara-san was in June 1948. I do not know who he had been before then. I can't write about the person who fell for the Dadaist poet Tsuji Jun during his student years, nor the one who participated in the 1929 left-wing movement and the Japanese branch of International Red Aid.

According to the author's chronology, he lost his wife, Sadae, in September 1944; evacuated to his parents' home in Hiroshima in January 1945; experienced the atomic bombing on August sixth of the same year; moved to Tokyo in April 1946 and became involved in editing *Mita Bungaku* in October. In 1947 he published "Summer Flowers" in *Mita Bungaku*, for which he received the Minakami Takitarō Prize. My first encounter with Hara-san was after he published "Summer Flowers."

Nōgaku-Shorin, which became Maruoka Akira's temporary residence, had barely survived the war fires. The glass door opened to an ill-lit editorial office, and next to the space for taking off one's shoes, bound piles of the returned books stood high. In the back of the editorial room was where Mr. Maruoka's younger brother lived, and the Maruokas accommodated Hara-san with one of their rooms.

His single room appeared desolate, even to a young person like me. A shabby desk, a cheap book shelf, and a suitcase in the closet—that was all the author of "Summer Flowers" possessed in the world. He had only three pairs of clothes to wear all year round, summer and winter. I remember him wearing the black, banded-collar top while in his room and a tired jacket and flat hunting cap when we went out. Having lost his wife to an illness and everything else to the bombing in Hiroshima, Hara-san had neither home nor family.

In any case, I visited him at least once a week. Resting his cheeks in his hands, he gazed blankly at the sky above the walls outside the window. I don't like being alone myself, but I cannot stand someone else's loneliness. So I would keep up a chatter the whole time and make a racket in his room. Hara-san would only give me a puzzled look and sigh. But there were times when his clear eyes became lit with fear. I didn't really understand what made his eyes grow so fearful.

Early in the evening, he would put on the hunting cap and leave Nōgaku-Shorin. His slumped shoulders looked terribly lonely from the back. He was headed to an eatery that accepted government-rationed meal tickets. I followed him to his dinner destination once. He sat in the corner seat and ate soup with a meager portion of rice in a bowl.

"Hara-san, do you always eat here by yourself?"

"Yes."

On the way back, he walked with me in a stooped posture. When a street car heading to Jimbō-chō from Kudan passed us with a heavy, dull sound, it threw up sparks of fire that stopped Hara-san in his tracks with a sudden jerk. He turned his fearful eyes onto the street car.

"What happened, Hara-san?"

"Nothing." He shook his head.

He was born in Nobori-chō, Hiroshima in November of 1905. In middle school, he became interested in literature, and he started a coterie magazine with friends like Chō Kōta. In 1924, he entered Keiō University to study literature. He continued to compose poems and haiku. According to Yamamoto Kenkichi, one of his classmates at Keiō, he came up with a pen name for himself as a haiku poet: 杞憂 ("Kiyū"). It's a classic Chinese idiom, which alludes to needless anxiety about the heavens crumbling down, but later in Hiroshima, such fear would turn into a reality. Hara-san would witness the atomic bombing—a hellish sight where the heaven and the earth split and give way. At any rate, since he was a young boy, his eyes must have shown a kind of fearfulness I observed in him myself. Sasaki Kiichi writes that Hara-san had always been fearful of threats from the outside world, the way a small child is frightened of dark corners.

However, when the street car passed with sparks of fire on the track, he had remembered something very specific.

"You know, I . . ." he said to me after a while. "When I saw those sparks . . . I thought of the moment the atomic bomb dropped."

In those days, when I had just graduated from the university, Kanda was a stimulating city that fed my curiosity. It was one of the places frequented by the new post-war authors: Tokyo's version of Montparnasse. If younger writers like us wanted to meet the senior members of *Mita Bungaku*, we could visit Nōga-ku-Shorin, or go up the hill of Kudan and stop by a barracks of the old Imperial Guard Division. Inside the wooden barracks that looked like a burnt stable, two publishers, Kadokawa Shoten and Shisaku-sha were renting rooms that faced each other. Today, people have almost forgotten about Shisaku-sha, but it was the company that published a number of post-war critics and authors in the journals, *Shisaku* and *Kosei*, along with *Kindai Bungaku* (*Modern Literature*). From the corner of the room, I used to watch Katayama Shūzō, the president of Shisaku-sha, with a fedora and a cane between his knees, having a heated argument all day with Hotta Yoshie, who was still unknown, or with Shirai Kōji, who translated Sartre's *La Nausée*. One time, I was forced to sit on the chair by Mr. Katayama, who happened to find no one else to argue with that day. For four hours, he continued his talk about a topic that was utterly incomprehensible to me—"Dostoevsky and the density of existence." When I tried to sneak out, he yelled at me for being restless, and I found myself on the verge of tears.

It wasn't only the members of *Mita Bungaku* you could meet in Kanda. In the back of the publishing house, Fuzambō, there was a café bar called Rimbaud. In the evening, Haniya Yutaka or Sasaki Kiichi, the founder of *Modern Literature*, after finishing a literary discussion or a coterie magazine meeting, would show up there. Authors like Umezaki Haruo would be drinking with a gloomy face, and beside him, novelist Takeda Taijun would be asleep, using a cloth-wrapped bundle as a pillow.

Hara-san not only helped with editing *Mita Bungaku*, but by the recommendation of his brother-in-law, Sasaki Kiichi, he also became a member of *Modern*

Literature. As far as I know, he could finish only a short piece or two in a month, but when the deadline approached, he would work from morning till night. He was not a prolific writer. First, he would write his draft in large letters in a notebook. He would keep revising the notebook, and then, he would finally write a complete draft on the manuscript paper.

Some evenings, Maruoka Akira, who lived upstairs, would ask him, "Hara-kun, won't you go out for a drink?"

Mr. Maruoka wanted to cheer him up. It's as though I can still see the back of Hara-san, wearing his hunting cap, awkwardly following Mr. Maruoka in his casual kimono, and walking to a dingy pub called Ryūgū (the Dragon's Sea Palace) in Kudan.

Ryūgū was run by a middle-aged widow whose children were in elementary school. The price was very reasonable: a pot of stew and a bottle of shōchū would only cost a hundred yen. Fumi-chan, a fat woman of twenty-seven or eight, was helping the widow. We gave her the nickname, "Otohime-san" (Sea Princess). There were times Hara-san, who had lost his family, would show up even by himself. In the back of the room, he would drink saké in silence, and from time to time, start a conversation with the widow's sickly young daughter, Hatsuko. She was always wearing a bandage on her neck, and she was somehow very attached to him.

"Hara-san, take a look at the drawing I did at school."

"Yes, let me see."

Keeping his worn-out hunting cap on, he stared into the child's drawing for a long time. He didn't move his eyes even after she grew bored and went away. I felt pain watching the shadow of Hara-san on the wall of the dark room, who had lost his wife, home, and hometown. At the same time, I suddenly felt something like rage against all the things that had tortured him, someone so meek and innocent. When it came to the practical matters of life, he was as helpless as a small child. He was so shy that he could barely speak to a person he met for the first time; I have seen him at a loss even to buy a ticket for long-distance travel.

"I've heard that Hara-kun arrived in Tokyo on a jam-packed train all by himself right after the war ended," said Mr. Maruoka quietly, sipping his saké one evening at Ryūgū. "That must have been awfully difficult for someone like him."

Mr. Maruoka's words rang true to those of us who knew him. Enduring the horrific journey from Hiroshima to Tokyo on a mobbed train after the war, looking for a room to rent, and managing to find food—these things would be hard enough for us, but they must have been nearly impossible for Hara-san. If you read his short stories like "Childhood Painting" and "Death and Dream," you would understand how his elder sister protected him, and after he got married, his wife took over that protective role. There is a charming story that when Hara-san and his wife went to visit poet Satō Haruo for the first time, he simply bowed his head and stayed behind his wife. How painful it must have been for her to part with him! She was the elder sister of Sasaki Kiichi. Until the very end, she kept repeating to Hara-san that she simply could not die and leave him alone.

He always carried a photo of his wife in the wallet that contained his meal tickets.

"This is my mother," he suddenly said one night, showing me her photo after we returned from Ryūgū to his room at Nōgaku-Shorin. Inside a blurry, card-sized photo was a round-faced woman with a long hair, who was dressed in a classic kimono.

"Really? This is your mother."

Hara-san smiled for a moment, and then carefully put the photo of his dead wife back into his wallet. Though it was atypical of him, he was perhaps feeling playful enough to trick me, his junior. The woman in the photo must have been both wife and mother to him. "If I were to part from my wife by death, I would live just one more year," he once wrote, "to complete a handsome volume of elegies."

WHEN I REMEMBER Hara-san, what always comes to mind is his eyes. Sometimes, his eyes showed a flash of fear. When looking at wet green trees after a rain, resting his cheeks in his hands on the desk, his eyes seemed to have been pierced by grief. There were times when his face grew pale with saké, his gaze would become fixed on a single point in the air. Today, when I reread "Summer Flowers," about a living hell that appeared in Hiroshima, I remember his eyes. After he published it, it was followed by several other stories about the atomic bombing, but nothing comes close to "Summer Flowers," in which he neither cries out nor shakes his fist. He simply looks the atrocity in the face.

> After a while, two chicks started separately announcing the morning in a chicken coop next to the warehouse. Without enough practice, their voices were dissonant, which would amuse Jun'ichi and others at times, but right now, there was no one listening to the cries of chicks. Above the crape myrtle trees, a quiet sky appeared suffused with blazing sunlight. . . . They still had forty-some hours before the arrival of the atomic bomb in this town.

This restrained description ends "Prelude to Destruction," followed by "Summer Flowers," which reminds me of Hara-san's eyes fixed on the same point in the air while drinking saké at Ryūgū.

One day, Mr. Maruyama shared with me an anecdote. Hara-san was in dire financial straits; besides the fact that there weren't many literary journals that solicited his writing, he had used up the money that came from selling the land he once owned in his hometown. And so Mr. Maruoka made an arrangement for him to write for a women's interest magazine.

However, Hara-san simply said, "My manuscript is not something that should be published in such a magazine."

"That's how he turned me down," said Mr. Maruoka with a wry smile.

More than anyone, it was Mr. Maruoka who took great pains to care for Hara-san, who had arrived in Tokyo after the war. It could not have been easy to rent him a room and look after him in the chaotic postwar reality where everyone was impoverished.

In those days, besides Mr. Maruoka, there were also Ōkubo Fusao, who was an editorial staff member of *Gunzō*, Fujishima Udai, and Suzuki Shigeo, who offered help to Hara-san whenever possible. While Mr. Fujishima and Mr. Suzuki didn't have the financial means to support him, Mr. Ōkubo would lend him what little money he had out of his pocket. Hara-san had to rely on rationed meal tickets for dinner, but Mr. Ōkubo would invite him over for a homemade meal, cooking the fish he brought back from his hometown in Kishū. It was no small help that Mr. Ōkubo gave Hara-san the opportunity to publish his fiction in *Gunzō*, especially when *Modern Literature* and *Kosei* were caught up in a business slump, and he didn't know when he would receive their payment for his writing.

I must say, though, I still hold a personal grudge against Hara-san, stemming from an incident that took place in those days. One night, together with Mr. Ōkubo, he summoned me to Ryūgū, and they started criticizing how I dressed. I used to wear a green sweater back then, but they told me that not only was it in poor taste, but it was also a sign of my degenerate character.

It was one early evening in the summer of 1949. Negishi Shigeichi and I dragged Hara-san out and we were taking a walk along the road to Densha Street from Nōgaku-Shorin. All of a sudden, a flapping chicken appeared before us. A young lady was chasing after it with a cage.

"Would you like us to capture it?"

Negishi and I tackled with the chicken like rugby players, then brought the wriggling bird over to the lady. Frightened Hara-san only watched us from the corner of the fence.

"Do you wanna come over?" said Negishi. "We live very close by."

The lady smiled and nodded. She said she would stop by Hara-san's room in ten minutes.

He was clearly nervous. I told him he'd better clean his room and hide his laundry while Negishi and I went to buy snacks and shōchū. We went out on the main street still bright under the setting sun.

When we returned to Nōgaku-Shorin, Hara-san was struggling to clean his room with a broom. I had to take it away from him and do it over.

"Anyway, Hara-san, you are the master of this room, so you must talk to the lady," we said. "We'll play second fiddle; if you are the sashimi, we are its garnish."

"Don't be foolish!" Forty-four-year-old Hara-san was at a loss.

"Who cares if it's foolish or not?"

We had gone too far, I think, but we were curious to see how someone as timid as Hara-san would handle a conversation with a young lady. But she didn't show up. After a long wait, Negishi and I gave up and went home.

The next day, when I returned to his room, Hara-san had a serious expression on his face and spoke to me in a confidential tone: "Listen, last night, that lady came to visit me with sushi."

"What a surprise! What in the world did you talk about?"

"I didn't say anything. I just let her borrow my book."

"Uh-huh, your book. Why don't I go and visit her right now? I've already looked up where she lives. I'll go by myself," I said to tease him. When I stood up, he hastily put on his hunting cap.

"Why, Hara-san, are you coming along?"

"Well, yes. I will go with you."

With a stooped back and unsteady steps, he followed me to the lady's house. Her mother came out and informed us apologetically that Miss U had left the house to go to a public bath.

"Oh well, shall we go back?" I said.

To my great surprise, Hara-san suggested that we track Miss U to the bathhouse. I remembered that there was one near Ryūgū, so we decided to give it a try. Once there, he stood by the exit of the female side of the bathhouse. Embarrassed, I hid in the shadow of a nearby telegraph post. The women who had finished bathing came out with their washbowls and, as they were leaving, they would each turn back and give a questioning look to the man with a hunting cap who stood on one spot and peered into the exit. Hara-san showed no sign of giving up. In the end, Miss U didn't make an appearance.

Nevertheless, after that incident, she would occasionally visit Hara-san. Even though he wanted to, he was too shy to ask her out for tea. He finally sought Mr. Ōkubo's help. Hara-san sat face to face with Miss U in the tearoom in Kanda, but as usual, he couldn't say a word. Only Miss U spoke, and Mr. Ōkubo watched them impatiently.

After she left, he teased him. "Hara-san, if you won't say anything, I'll marry that lady. Is that alright with you?"

"You may," he said in a sad voice. "If that happens, though, I will come to visit your house everyday."

This is the lady who would add a gentle warmth to the desolate life Hara-san was to lead until his death. She appears in his fiction under the name of U-ko. He watched her from a distance; his affection towards her was more like that of a father or an older brother. I couldn't do much, but there is one event I am still glad that I was able to organize for him. Early in the spring of the following year, I invited Miss U to an outing with Hara-san by the Tama River. We met at the west exit of Shinjuku Station. She brought her cousin who was two years younger than she was. Hara-san wore a navy suit, his best clothes that had been sleeping in the bottom of his suitcase. He even put on a red tie.

It was a sunny day in early spring. I rowed the boat that carried Hara-san and the other ladies on the Tama River. He sat clumsily on one end of the boat and laughed. The water of the river was warm to the touch. We stopped by a teahouse on the bank; the ladies ate stewed *oden*, and Hara-san and I had beer.

"I am a lark," he suddenly said. "One day, I will turn into a lark and reach the sky," he said in a whisper. I don't know why he said such things. Had he already made up his mind about taking his own life then? Is that what he meant by reaching the sky? At the time, I merely thought he was joking.

AFTER MORE THAN a decade, Shirai Kōji introduced Miss U to Mr. Mukai Hiroo who had returned from Australia, and they got married. During their wedding reception, watching her happily smile and engage in conversation with those introduced by her husband, I remembered Hara-san's words and suddenly felt tears in my eyes. I felt as though Hara-san, who had become a lark in the sky, came back and was sitting in the corner of this room.

FOLLOWING THE OUTING, I was accepted to study in France as one of the first Japanese overseas students after the Second World War. Around the same time, Hara-san found a room he could rent in Kichijōji, and moved out of Nōgaku-Shorin. In those days, it was extremely difficult for the Japanese, the people marked by their nation's defeat in the war, to travel to Europe. Even to receive a visa would take a whole year. So, once I cleared all the hurdles, I was filled with pure excitement for France. Perhaps because of that, I failed to pay attention to how Hara-san had been doing at that time. A week before my departure, the senior members of *Mita Bungaku* and Sasaki Kiichi from *Modern Literature* gathered together to throw a farewell party for me. I was overjoyed.

Three days before I was to board the ship, I finally found the time to visit Hara-san in Kichijōji. On the way back, he walked with me to the station to see me off. It was a very long way from where he lived. Unlike that time we went out with Miss U, he was in a gloomy mood. I even wondered whether he was angry at something.

"What happened? You seem to be on edge. Have you been busy lately?" I asked. "What kind of work are you doing now?"

"I've been thinking about a certain thing."

Looking back now, I cannot remember whether he said a certain thing or a certain work, but I took it to be the latter for sure.

"What kind of work is it? Are you writing a long piece?"

"I can't tell you."

I was puzzled. Until then, Hara-san would always tell me something about his writing project. Under the hunting cap, his face somehow looked more exhausted than usual. It seemed pale, maybe a little swollen.

"It must be a long piece, then."

"I can't tell you . . . you will understand it . . . someday."

Once at the station, I waved goodbye. He nodded, suddenly turned around, and disappeared into the crowd.

Hara-san was probably giving me a hint. But more than the hint itself, I wonder about how he must have felt when his young friend was completely clueless as to what was weighing on his mind at the time. When I think of that, I can't help but hate who I was, how preoccupied I was with my own study abroad in France.

I had made a similar mistake once before, too—two days before Yoshida, who took me to my first *Mita Bungaku* meeting, would commit suicide. On that rainy day, he told me to meet him at a café in Shibuya. While he sipped coffee in silence, I, who had no idea, talked about our mutual friend N, who had been sick. Yoshida brought his coffee cup near his mouth and paused.

"I hope you'll live a long life." His voice was hoarse.

Even after we parted in rain, I couldn't grasp the meaning behind his words. Two days later, he took his life in the sea of Odawara.

With Hara-san, yet again, I failed to take the hint he gave me as he was leaving. If I could, I would have informed Mr. Maruoka, Mr. Sasaki, Mr. Ōkubo, or Suzuki Shigeo.

At half past five on June fourth, I embarked on the French ship called Marseilles at the Yokohama Port. It was a drizzly Sunday. When I arrived at the pier, my friends and members of *Mita Bungaku* had already gathered to greet me. Study abroad in France sounds luxurious, but my accommodation was what was called fourth class, in the luggage hold of the ship. It had only four portholes. When you stepped down nearly perpendicular stairs from the deck, you would see black soldiers wrapped in blankets in the dark corner. The air was saturated with body odor; I saw white tattoos on some of them. I learned that they were members of the French Foreign Legion in French Indochina, who had accompanied Japanese war criminals to Yokohama from Saigon.

"You better watch out," Shibata Renzaburō said to me, grunting. "They might eat you alive before the ship reaches Kōbe."

It was in fact a horrible place. As a porter carried my luggage, he said that he had been working for more than a decade since before the war, and yet he had never met anyone traveling to a foreign country in the hold of a ship like this.

Nevertheless, I was young and felt only excitement about the prospect of traveling. At six o'clock, a gong sounded, and I held onto the rail of the third-class deck. Next to the fat figure of Mr. Maruoka was Mr. Kojima from Kyōdō News. Suzuki Shigeo and Watanabe Kieko were waving at me. Hotta Yoshie stood there with his wife. Mr. Ōkubo unfortunately couldn't make it, but he had taken me out for a farewell sushi dinner the night before.

Hara-san stood a little distance from everyone else. I could see him wearing his hunting cap and gazing up in my direction for a long time while the ship gradually left the quay. I suddenly noticed a person on his left, who stood by himself, waving his hand. It was Katō Michio.

After Hara-san's death, when I read the manuscript he left, I was able to understand what was going through his mind as he watched my ship take off. What he saw there on the Marseilles was in fact not me, but himself taking leave of this world. Perhaps Mr. Katō, who would also later commit suicide, envisioned something similar at the same moment.

My voyage was not entirely comfortable. Being Japanese, I wasn't allowed to get off at any port; I was forced to stay inside the hold of the ship and endure its terrible heat. I was jeered at as a person of the yellow race. While the ship made a stop at the Port of Manila in the Philippines, people who still harbored hatred towards the Japanese came to search for me and other Japanese passengers. It was halfway through the voyage when I heard the news about the Korean War. In the middle of the night, I was leaning on the deck all by myself and watching the red glow of the Stromboli volcano when the ship received a radio message.

Though I was away from him, I could imagine what a shock this news must have been to Hara-san who was directly exposed to the atomic bombing. Mr. Maruoka wrote a novel called *A False Christ* with a character modeled after him. According to the story, he was constantly haunted by a sense that all his surroundings were about to collapse in a flash. What Hara-san would imagine from the sharp sound of jet aircraft flying towards North Korea was nothing less than Hiroshima's nuclear hell. I will not forget the spasm that shook his body when the street car from Kudan to Kanda sparked fire on the rail track.

I was assigned to study in a city called Lyon. It's an old, foggy city where Nagai Kafū once composed his *Diary of My Trip to the West*. I wrote to Hara-san every now and then, and he would write me back. His letters had a casual tone; it seemed that he was doing fine. I didn't even think about the possible meaning behind our conversations before my departure. I wrote him silly, frivolous letters.

One day, out of the blue, I received an airmail from him. I have included part of my journal from that day here:

March twenty-fourth. Cloudy. Hara-san's letter arrived in the morning. It read: "This is the last letter. What a good time we had last spring! Take care." He enclosed two poems, "Epitaph" and "Lament." My hands shook as I read. In the afternoon, an airmail from Mr. Ōkubo informed me of Hara-san's suicide. Outside, people are walking as usual in the city. A fine rain is falling. In the room next to mine, someone is playing piano badly. I don't understand a thing. I am writing this entry in a daze.

It says Hara-san's letter arrived in the morning. Mr. Ōkubo went through his belongings and the notes he had left to his friends, found one addressed to me, and forwarded it to me. In another letter I received in the afternoon, Mr. Ōkubo took the time to describe the manner of his death in detail.

"What a good time we had last spring!" must refer to the day Hara-san and I rowed the boat for Miss U and her cousin on the Tama River, ate stewed *oden*, and drank beer together. Staring at this sentence, I remembered his childlike smile when he sat down with Miss U on the edge of the boat I was rowing that spring day. His words, "I am a lark," came back to me.

Engraved in stone of the distant past
    Casting a shadow on the sand
It collapses between heaven and earth:
The phantom of a single flower

This is titled "Epitaph," one of the poems Hara-san wrote and enclosed in his letter to me. I couldn't be present at his death, nor place a single flower on his face, nor help carry his coffin with my hands. Eleven days after his death, in my room in Lyon, I learned that he had killed himself by lying down on the rail track about two-hundred fifty meters away from Kichijōji. Mr. Ōkubo's handwriting was unusually shaky, showing his shock and confusion. Reading it for the second time, the weight of the first line, "I must deliver sad news: Hara-san has died," hit me afresh.

In the evening of March thirteenth, Hara-san drank at a shōchū hall in Kichijōji, doodled on the back of an empty tobacco packet, and then started walking towards the rail track near midnight. Two women reported to have passed by someone whose appearance matched his during their walk. In *A False Christ*, Mr. Maruoka describes Shima, his protagonist, modeled after Hara-san near the end of his life:

> Both sides of the sloping road were covered in grass. On the right side, Shima saw a white puppy, as if asleep, lying on a quiet, sunny spot. . . . Shima paused. An inexpressible, peaceful silence seemed to emanate from the corpse of the puppy, gradually seeping out into the surrounding grass that had not yet reached its full height. Shima's body still reeked of death from the day of the atomic bombing and its hellish sight burnt on his eyes had not faded. But what a contrast there was between the death of this puppy and the vision of hell he witnessed! . . . Since then, five and a half years had passed. . . . Now he was to face the moment in which he would stake his life by burning himself up for one last time . . .

Hara-san's face was turned diagonally upward with a single streak of blood on his cheek. In his pocket he only had one ten-yen bill. During the night, Suzuki Shigeo and Shōji Soichi watched over his straw-mat-covered corpse. Eventually, Mr. Maruoka, Mr. Sasaki, Mr. Ōkubo, and Fujishima Udai heard the news and came running. In Hara-san's room in Kichijōji, they found over ten letters, but according to Mr. Maruoka, those were all "farewells from which emotions had been eliminated." The letters addressed to his relatives and to Mr. Ōkubo, one of his most trusted friends, were put in white envelopes. His letter asked Mr. Ōkubo to share his neckties among his friends, give his books to Suzuki Shigeo and his clothes to Fujishima Udai. According to Mr. Maruoka, the letter to Miss U read: "The time has finally come for me to turn into a lark and fly away. To come into contact with someone as pure as you in these desolate, final years of my life was a miracle. Please take care of yourself; may you live a life full of beauty and dignity."

On my third year of study abroad, I became ill and was forced to leave France. When I returned to Japan, it was a week before the second anniversary of Hara-san's death. I received an invitation to 花幻忌会 ("Kagenki-kai"), a gathering in his memory, and no matter how sick I was, I was determined to attend this event.

Poet Satō Haruo named it "Kagenki-kai" (the anniversary of the death of a phantom flower) after Hara-san's poem, "It collapses between heaven and earth: / The phantom of a single flower." I went to Levante, a beer restaurant in Yūraku-chō, to meet up with my friends and the senior members of *Mita Bungaku* I hadn't seen for a long time. I received Hara-san's red necktie from Mr. Ōkubo. When we went rowing with Miss U on the Tama River, he was wearing a red tie to look stylish. Was it the same tie? Even if it wasn't, I wanted to believe it was. The idea of the lark who had gone up in the sky wearing a red tie gave me some comfort.

"Why don't we make a point of wearing Hara-san's ties to attend Kagenki-kai from now on?" said someone. Nasu Kunio shook his head no. He said that the last time he wore his tie to go out for a drink, on the way back, he started walking as though his body were being pulled towards the rail track, perhaps because of the tie. It scared him. Everyone laughed.

The line-up of the people hadn't changed much since three years ago. In those days, the wounds of the war were all over Japan. No one had money, and if you wanted to drink, it would have to be inexpensive shōchū. While I was absent, however, the economic boom propelled by the Korean War had changed much of Tokyo, and the members of *Mita Bungaku*, who used to be able to only afford Ryūgū as their meeting place, were now ordering cheese and beer instead of shōchū. It was a strange sight to me. What was stranger, though, was that I would frequently be haunted by the feeling that Hara-san with his hunting cap was still sitting in silence in the corner of the room with us. Because of my illness, I couldn't drink alcohol. While sipping my juice, I kept thinking about him who wouldn't have said a single word at a gathering like this. I saw Yamamoto Kenkichi sitting on the other side.

Once, Hara-san, Mr. Yamamoto, and I took a walk in Kanda. Because of the war and other circumstances, the two had not seen each other for an entire decade. Yet even so, on that day, during the long walk and while eating chicken skewers at a street stall, the two reticent friends exchanged only the following words:

"Have you been alright all these years?"
"Yeah."
"You had a rough time of it, didn't you?"
"Rough, yes."

At the gathering, there were also literary critics and authors who recognized the value of Hara-san's literature: Itō Sei, Senuma Shigeki, Kusano Shimpei, and Umezaki Haruo. Seeing the faces of those who were present suddenly reminded me of a line from *Flames*, a short story collection Hara-san had self-published through Hakusui-sha in 1935: "Even though my work won't last, the memory of me will remain in the hearts of a few people . . ."

It made me want to visit those few who still carried his memory besides the members of our gathering. On a drizzly day, I got off the street car at Kanda to go and see Ryūgū. After three years, there were new buildings in Kanda; the café bar Rimbaud where the renowned postwar authors frequented had also been renovated and its owner had changed. Only Ryūgū stood at the same spot on the dirty, narrow backstreet, hanging a faded curtain at the entrance. The widow was overjoyed to see me and hurried me inside, but the woman who had helped her run the place, the one Hara-san had called Otohime-san, was gone. Hatsu-chan, the widow's daughter, whom Hara-san used to help with art projects and essays, was sick in bed.

I also searched for Miss U. She was working in the broadcasting office of the US occupation army next to Aoyama Gakuin University. When Hara-san hesitantly started forming a friendship with her, she was only seventeen or eighteen, but now she had turned into a fine, vibrant woman who smiled often.

It has been ten years since then. This year was the fourteenth anniversary of Kagenki-kai. At the beginning, many people came, but the number has decreased over time, and it feels a little emptier now. On March thirteenth, Tanida Shōhei contacts everyone and reserves a space for our gathering at Akita, a restaurant in Shinjuku. The tenth time we gathered, someone suggested that we stop meeting, having lost quite a few members. Poet Kusano Shimpei suddenly turned red and yelled in a loud voice, "Only those who want to come should come! I will keep coming forever."

I felt jealous of Hara-san. There aren't many authors whose friends would insist on gathering in their memory on each anniversary of their death.

I said softly, "After I die, I hope you will all gather like this on the anniversary of my death."

"Don't be silly; why would anyone bother to meet when someone like you died?" quipped the members in reply.

But this year's Kagenki-kai was not bad. It was a cold, rainy day. Mr. Umezaki, Mr. Kusano, and Haniya Yutaka, who had been showing up without fail, all fell sick and were absent this time, so the six of us, Maruoka Akira, Sasaki Kiichi, Ōkubo Fusao, Suzuki Shigeo, Tanida Shōhei, and I, drank and reminisced about Hara-san in the small corner room at Akita. We invited Miss U every year, but she had married and left Japan for Melbourne. We talked about her, and then, as usual, our conversation turned to the topic of Hara-san's monument in Hiroshima. Local children have been throwing stones at the monument inscribed with his "phantom flower" poem; the monument became battered and scratched, so much so that it is impossible to make out the words. Even the condition of the monument seems to symbolize Hara-san's life.

"At least for next year, can't we plan a grand meeting, including a public lecture?" someone said. I serve as an accountant for Hara-san's royalties, and I was a little concerned about our budget, but the members were all seriously enthusiastic about making a plan, and everyone's passion gradually won me over.

I only knew the last few years of his life. Hara-san in his final years was like a bird whose entire body was riddled with wounds yet still kept moving its wings, insisting on life. He wrote:

You had only yourself when you fled the atomic bomb. As you tried to rise in the midst of all that was falling over you, as your entire surroundings were turned into a whirlpool of human screams of death, and then, as you were fighting against a ceaseless hunger to survive, why was it that your life had to go on? What was it that commanded you to hold on to life?

From his delicate appearance, no one would have imagined such fierce words. And yet, these are the words that fueled Hara-san to live those last six years of his life.

translated from the Japanese by Miho Nonaka

MATTHEW VOLLMER

Burials

LESS THAN A MONTH PASSED between my mother and grandmother's deaths: my mother, at 74, died from complications related to Alzheimer's and Parkinson's, while my grandmother, who, after attempting to stand up from her wheelchair, fell, broke bones in her neck, and was taken to a local emergency room, where doctors claimed that, despite the fact that she was nearly 101, her vitals were better than 90% of the other patients there; even so, she died only days later in a hospice unit. I realized, as I typed this, that I didn't really know—not technically, at least—how either one of them had died. Like, I knew that my mother, for instance, had woken up on her last morning with a smile on her face and that when Tina, her hospice caretaker, had asked if she'd had a good night, my mother had responded with an emphatic "Yes!" In a few minutes, though, all the color had drained from her face and Tina led her back to bed, where my father held her hand until she breathed her last. Had her heart simply stopped beating? I texted my sister to see if she remembered. She didn't. Maybe, she said, mom had suffered a stroke. She couldn't imagine that she'd had a heart attack. I wondered if perhaps there'd been foul play. I typed "FOUL PLAY" in all caps. "Stop," my sister texted. I stopped. Still, it was strange to think about. How I didn't really know the official cause of my mother's death. I remembered, then, how "good" other people had said that she'd looked after she died—and she had. How her face retained such a peaceful expression. How my dad had slept in the same bed with her the night after she'd died and how weird I'd thought that had been at first—and then how beautiful. How, when it'd come time for to bury her, my sister and father and I had lifted the sheet where she'd been lying and used it like a hammock to carry her to the wooden coffin one of my father's friends had carved especially for her. How my father had taken the bouquet of flowers gathered by his grandchildren and a piece of foil-covered Dove chocolate and placed them in one of my mother's hands. I hadn't known, at the time, that objects buried with the dead were called "grave goods," or that the Etruscans used to engrave a word that meant "from a tomb" on objects they buried with the dead, to discourage grave robbery. I thought about how Buddhists who died in the Himalayas didn't have to worry about such things, because instead of in-ground internments, the Himalayan dead received so-called "sky burials." The dead were left on the sides of mountains, as a final act of generosity, to feed birds and other animals who might feast on the remains. In some cases, "sky burial masters" cut these bodies into sections, subsequently pounding different parts into paste using barley flour, tea, and yak's butter, joking and laughing all the while to give the impression that what they were doing was not unusual and to ensure the soul's safe passage to the afterlife; once vultures had stripped the bones of the deceased's flesh, the sky burial masters returned to grind up the remains for crows. I remembered seeing a depiction of a Cheyenne sky burial in the movie *Windtalker*, where an old warrior's body was wrapped in fur blankets and set atop a scaffold made of timber: such structures might have been initially conceived in lieu of burying during winter, when frozen ground would've discouraged digging, but also to prevent the dead body from being eaten by wolves. According to National Geographic's YouTube page, "On the Indonesian island of Sulawesi, the Torajan people believe that a person is not truly dead until water buffalo have been sacrificed at their funeral, serving as the vehicle to the afterlife. Until that time, the bodies may be kept at the family's home for weeks, months or years and are fed and cared for as if they were alive. Some Torajans continue their relationship with the dead through a ma'nene' ceremony, a type of 'second funeral' in which families bring out their ancestors every few years and change their clothes and clean their bodies and crypts." I texted my sister about the Torajan people, and she said that the idea of playing with a dead body was hard for her to think about. "So weird," she added, referring to our dead mother, "that the body she has inhabited for 73 years is there. Lying there. All the hard work those muscles did . . . but she isn't there." By "there," my sister meant the Vollmer family cemetery: a clearing in the woods about a hundred steps from the house our parents had built, and where our mother had been buried, mere feet from the graves of our paternal grandparents. "She might crawl back out tho," I said. By "she" I'd meant "mom." "Stop it!!!" my sister replied. "I think that's why they put rocks on papa's grave," I said, remembering the jagged, triangular stones that had been dumped on the place where my maternal grandfather been buried: three hours away, in Greenville, South Carolina, in the Gilbert family cemetery. "To keep him put," I added. It made a kind of sense to me. My grandfather, whose final resting place was located the far end of "the field," on the land where he'd grown up, had been the most stubbornly determined man I'd ever met; if anyone could defy the grave, I figured he'd be the one. As a toddler, my grandfather had lost three of his fingers when he'd rested a hand upon a chopping block, refusing to move it even as his six-year-old sister Effie proved true to her word by threatening to lower—and then lowering—the axe she'd been holding above her head. Because of this handicap, he'd grown up to become a scrappy boxer, strong and tenacious despite his size and the lack of a complete set of digits, the sort of hotheaded fighter other boys regretted tangling with, supposing the stories he'd told about himself had been true. Years later, he'd driven a cab in Washington, D.C., studying Chemistry textbooks at red lights while working his way through dental school. Eventually, he'd opened his own practice, built a house on the land where he'd been born. There, he, with his sweet and longsuffering wife, raised four kids, among whom he later divided the property. Both his sons, one a dentist and the other a stock broker, neither of whom had ever taken much of a liking to the other, and who had fought so brutally with each other as children that they often made my grandmother cry, built houses on this same property, each within sight of the other and both within sight of the house in which they'd been raised. My aunt Diana, an accomplished and celebrated interior decorator who'd married my mother's youngest brother, had designed the house where she lived with my uncle to resemble that of a French country estate, and had ordered materials from all over the world—floorboards from a factory in Georgia, a door with a stained glass window that had once belonged to a church in England—so that as soon as the house was finished, it would look as if it'd been standing there for a hundred years. Inside this house, there were exquisite drapes. There were dead animal heads on the walls. There were murky 19th-century landscapes with gilt frames. There was a library of books about the Civil War and a desk that stood upon an honest-to-God tangle of rhododendron branches. There were giant vases with ten-foot-long flowering tree limbs inside. And there were these unforgettable Victorian bird boxes: terrariums made of wood and glass that housed dioramas where stuffed birds were frozen forever in place. It was a house you could not walk into without thinking, *Wow*, and it was certainly a house that no one who'd known her could've walk into without thinking *This is so Diana*, which meant that visiting this house again to attend her wake felt like attending a party inside a wealthy person's very nice tomb. Diana had died unexpectedly on New Year's Eve, 2017, after a couple of policemen outside the Tipsy Taco noted her stumbling towards her car and said that she could either come down to the station and get booked or they could take her home. She'd chosen the latter but reportedly had not been happy about it, and after the police dropped her off, she turned right around and walked through the dark back to the Tipsy Taco to retrieve her car, but had fallen down as she was crossing East North Street and was subsequently hit by a car. She bled to death in the street. There was no one in our family more elegant—more refined—than Diana. She drove a Gucci-themed Fiat. She wore dangly earrings and shirts that shimmered and sparkly necklaces. She remembered to purchase Christmas presents for all the children in the family, and wrapped them in paper that looked as if it'd been made out of actual gold and silver. I don't know where Diana was finally lain to rest, but I know it wasn't the Gilbert family cemetery, where the remains of my youngest cousin, grandmother, and grandfather had been buried. "God's time," my father once said, "It's just perfect." This was on September 11, 2019: the day my mother had died. I was driving on I-81, headed toward their house. My father told me that, the night before, he'd prayed to God and said, "Lord, I'll take care of Sandra for as long as you need me to. For a day, a week, a month, a year. However long it takes." And then she'd died the next morning, 18 years—nearly to the minute—that the second plane hit the World Trade Center. Wow," I said. I didn't say, "Does it not strike you as ironic that you're saying 'God's time is perfect' eighteen years to the day that terrorists ran planes into the World Trade Center?" I didn't say, "Do you think the people who lost their fathers and mothers and sons and daughters and aunts and uncles and grandparents and cousins and friends on that day think that such an attack was somehow ordained by heaven?" I didn't say, "I don't believe that." As it turned out, I could think whatever thoughts I wanted to in the privacy of my skull. I didn't have to say everything I thought out loud. I knew that when my father used the phrase "God's time" that he meant God was in control, that He "had a plan," and that if one prayed that God's will be done and then whatever happened was, indeed, what God had willed. I had to admit: I didn't like thinking that God's plan was to kill my mother slowly over the course of ten years. I wasn't comfortable imagining God as a kind of giant overlord in the sky who pored over blueprints for human activity. When did God's time begin—and when did it end? Was mass extinction part of God's plan? Human trafficking? Child sexual abuse? If everything regarding my now deceased mother's life had actually been a part of God's so-called plan, were we supposed to think of the disease that slowly sucked the life out of her as . . . a *blessing*? In a way, I supposed, it could be read as such. It had certainly brought my parents closer: in her final year on earth, my mother seemed to long for my father's presence more than ever. And my father—a man who, for years, returned from work to be pampered with hot meals served by my mother, who also dutifully cleaned up whatever mess had been generated by the cooking and eating—had, over the past few years, taken up the tasks—breadmaking, applesauce canning, soup making, cleaning, bill-paying—that had once been such a central part of my mother's existence that everyone in the family had taken them for granted. And though I had feared my mother's disease would sour her otherwise cheerful disposition into a kind of foul, mean-tempered spirit, she never lost her ability to smile or laugh. Were these not the facts? Had not my last interaction with my mother, via FaceTime, been a joyful one? Had she not laughed at the faces I'd made? Perhaps her disease *had* been a kind of blessing. Or perhaps that was simply a story I was telling myself now, as I studied the numerals on her tombstone, her life reduced to a dash between them, an entire life shrunk to a horizontal line, reminiscent of a single person in repose.

PETER MISHLER

Struwwelpeter at Forty

And then he is struck.
And then he is laughing.
And then he is laughing
while struck. And then
he is struck for his laughing.
And then his saliva is leaking.
And then he's curled up
like a foundling, a flag
on the moon, in the snow
and soil, the small-but-
bad child with the pyre-
scented fragrance.
And then he is forty.
Look! There he is!
His hair, the same.
His nails, the same,
but worse as he rubs
the red hem of his costume
until it is warm,
until it is worn
to the color of rope
that was tied to the ankle
above the black boot,
the other end tied
to the plastic baggie of meat
and bread so long ago,
not a single gauzy
tartan-patterned genital shape
on the horizon encroaching
the place where he lies now
uncombed, unwashed,
untrimmed, unstitching,
re-stitching himself

in silence with silence's
sharp and effective tools.

Where Else But in Target

Where else
but in Target
am I at my best
and do my best thinking
and scratch my head
and surprise myself
to find the sticker
for very good ethics
and scratch again
to find the one
for very few toxins
and there on the floor
in the aisle of colognes
the afterbirth
of my very good thinking
I do not alert
a team leader
for clean-up
I return after close
to lick it in secret
I like to lick
my truths in secret
with only the laypersons
quietly stocking
what follows me there
my political life
my walking talking
gleaming-white
subway-tile backsplash
turned upright
a slim three-
dimensional tower
who walks and talks
and laps up its share
of afterbirth with me
I give him

the sticker
for very good ethics
the one
for very few toxins
my people
were screened
and cleared
for such things
they willingly bared
their legs
the patchy hair
the red and blue
vessels and veins
which I am told
were the inspiration
for the racing stripe
on the jogger pant
and in this way
contributed richly
to the early years
of athleisure
my people
were known
to cancel free trials
before the automatic
monthly withdrawal
when they stole
my people
were never questioned
by assets protection
they looked
above the stadium's eye
to watch the hellfires
cross in formation
and cheered
and now
when the multitudes
sees us in Target
they say to themselves
aw shucks they say

here he comes
the hardy industrious
truant here comes
his whitewashed fence
behind him
for we are an inspiration
to many
we pay our visit
to the aisle of décor
to claim our piece
of responsibly-sourced
inspirational
forest product
on unlacquered
particle board
on which is stenciled
a single word
the word is GATHER
a Protestant word
an ancient word
but is it not young
and refreshed
when centered above
our nontoxic daybed
the gathering place
where we do
our home licking
I lick my backsplash
it licks me back
beside the end table
I keep my glass jar
it contains the single
speck of myself
that has never
set foot in a Target
of course
I have taste
though I lap up
the floor
though my jeans

are distressed
this speck is pure
it is good no great
I keep it preserved

MIKE WHITE

Casket

Windows, windows,
and now tonight
a door.

And people
talking
of a second floor.

Rocks

We came to think
there is nothing
inside a snowball

but another
and another
snowball.

We had had
enough
of that life.

HEIDI SEABORN

In the Mirror

I fashion a body
out of the woman lying
on a blanket on a strip
of grass between street
and seawall. Her skin
tucked tight into a bikini
like the hospital corners
I fold. I fashion
a body out of my old
one—that wore a bikini
into the grocery store.
To stride without thought
down the gleaming
aisles, to move a body
through space unknowing
that it was a body in time.
I fashion my body
as a ghost, a secreted lover,
a cache of stolen paintings.
I blanket my body
in bedclothes, in the tall
meadow grass. Come look!
I've already disappeared.

D. S. WALDMAN

A Love Poem

Less the window
than the day, no longer
young, slipping

across it. Less
the silence
than its being riffled,

suddenly, by
what, though a treasure,
I turn from:

goosed together
and raucous,
two sparrows

aflutter,
mating by
the bougainvilleas.

Less the union.
More, always,
the ache toward it.

When I think
of time—that is,

the slow unraveling
of moments that
a life, in the end,

amounts to—it is
lately as a thread, long,
lengthening, as

from the frayed hem
of that darkest cloth,
the past—and I pull.

MATTHEW MINICUCCI

On Camping

For each person I've said *I love you* to, the lie
was always there but wasn't understood
until some later date.

Dormant, perhaps; some recessive gene that finally
finds a part in this stage production. Sudden context,
like reading the *Iliad* and realizing sure, there's anger,

but before that there's just a lot of camping.
And what strikes me most is the scepter of Apollo,
slowly slipping out of Chryses' hands as he loses

everything in the sounding sea; black ships.
Or how he, like any other father, invokes revenge
not as a single stroke, but a thousand bites.

Smintheus, the literal *mouse god*, or maybe
just some flea that won't leave
me. You need to understand

there's this particular tree, hemlock or poplar,
at this particular campsite where she told me
all of this; lectured through the long line of her lips

like ships parted and imparted. That *love* was a word
that could be pushed like pumice stone in glass of water:
light, and porous, and impossibly afloat.

OWEN McLEOD

My Abandoned Poems

Relapse Ballroom Some Common Misspellings Of Love A Brief Interview With Barbie's Parents Making Poseidon's Head Nutrition Facts I Know That My Redeemer Liveth Sort Of Recent Responses From The Sun Say It With Doves Based On Your Recent Listening The Last Fish On Earth Just Catching Up The Price Of Stardom Track Your Package Private Browsing Enabled These Changes While Difficult Are Necessary To Save The System Wichita 10:27 PM Awards Season A Tour Of The Local Monuments Press Here For Better Living By Bacon I Mean Me The Perfect Radius For All Your Abilities A Trip To The Museum Of Modern Poetic Objects The Amazing Results Are In This Will Do For You What It Did For Me Buddha In Lockdown Enjoy Your Issue Amazing Moment When Deer Sheds Its Antlers Potential Spam Your Rewards Are Waiting Love Space Store In A Cool Dry Place Reflections On The Last Supper Wallpaper I Saw In A Nashville Hotel Bathroom Please God Help Me This Poem Has No Value Until Purchased Asterisk

JULIE HANSON

My Best Death

I push off with my right foot sole.
Lily pads slide by.
The cross-board seat is hard and warm at first;
then these qualities are gone.

I call the poem *My Best Death*.
Fourteen years pass by
and that's still my shortest poem,
still unpublished.
Too late now! Someone else
has done it better, shorter, sooner:

the photograph to his obit
an empty pier,
foliage thick and nondescript on either side,
the traveled lake ahead.

Bios

SANDRA ALCOSSER's *A Fish to Feed All Hunger* (UVA, 1986) and *Except by Nature* (Graywolf, 1998) received highest honors from the National Poetry Series, Academy of American Poets, and AWP Award Series. Alcosser has received three National Endowment for the Arts fellowships and served as Montana's poet laureate. She directs San Diego State University's MFA program each fall and edits *Poetry Internaational*.

TYLER BARTON is the author of the story collection *Eternal Night at the Nature Museum* (Sarabande, 2021), and the flash chapbook *The Quiet Part Loud* (Split Lip, 2019). His stories have appeared in *The Iowa Review*, *Kenyon Review*, *Subtropics*, and elsewhere. He lives in Lancaster, Pennsylvania, where he leads free workshops for the elderly.

Poet, essayist, and translator DAN BEACHY-QUICK's most recent books include *Arrows* (Tupelo, 2020), a collection of poetry, and *Stone-Garland* (Milkweed, 2020), a translation of six poets from the ancient Greek lyric tradition. His work has been supported by the Monfort, Lannan, and Guggenheim Foundations, and he teaches at Colorado State University.

BRUCE BEASLEY is the author of eight poetry collections, most recently *All Soul Parts Returned* (BOA, 2017) and *Theophobia* (2012). His poems appear in *The Georgia Review*, *Kenyon Review*, *Poetry*, and elsewhere.

JOSEPHINE BLAIR is a 2019 Brooklyn Poets fellow whose work appears in *Epiphany Magazine*, *The Rumpus*, *Yes Poetry*, and elsewhere. She is a *Frontier Poetry* 2021 Emerging Poet's Prize finalist and lives in Tucson, Arizona.

DON BOGEN has authored five books of poetry, most recently *Immediate Song* (Milkweed, 2019). He was a Fulbright Scholar at the Seamus Heaney Centre of Queen's University, Belfast, in 2011. An emeritus professor at the University of Cincinnati, he serves as editor-at-large for *The Cincinnati Review*.

MARIANNE BORUCH's tenth poetry collection is *The Anti-Grief* (Copper Canyon, 2019). Her *Bestiary Dark*, due out in 2021, is based on her research as a Fulbright Scholar in Australia. Her prose includes three essay collections on poetry, and a memoir, *The Glimpse Traveler* (Indiana, 2011). A former Guggenheim and National Endowment for the Arts Fellow, Boruch is an emeritus professor at

Purdue University and continues to teach in the Graduate Program for Writers at Warren Wilson College.

JOHN YU BRANSCUM teaches Comparative Literature and Creative Writing at Indiana University of Pennsylvania. His collaborative translations have appeared in *The Cincinnati Review*, *3AM Magazine*, and *Strange Horizons: Samovar*, and are collected in *The Shadow Book of Ji Yun: The Chinese Classic of Weird True Tales, Horror Stories, and Occult Knowledge* and *Zhiguai: Chinese True Tales of the Paranormal and Glitches in the Matrix*.

CASSANDRA J. BRUNER, the 2019-2020 Jay C. and Ruth Halls Poetry Fellow, is a transfeminine poet and essayist. Their writing appears in *Black Warrior Review*, *Crazyhorse*, *New England Review*, and elsewhere. Her chapbook, *The Wishbone Dress*, won the 2019 Frost Place Competition.

LEIA DARWISH is a poet, editor, copywriter, and writing instructor based in Richmond, Virginia. Her poetry and nonfiction appear in *Diode*, *The Journal*, *PANK*, and elsewhere.

STEVEN ESPADA DAWSON is a writer from East Los Angeles and the son of a Mexican immigrant. His poems appear in *The Adroit Journal*, *Gulf Coast*, *Kenyon Review Online*, and the *Best New Poets 2020* anthology. A finalist for this year's Ruth Lilly Fellowship, he is a teaching artist at The Library Foundation in Austin.

Work by ALLISON deFREESE has appeared in *Crazyhorse*, *Indiana Review*, *Waxwing*, and elsewhere. Her book-length translations include María Negroni's *Elegy for Joseph Cornell* (Dalkey Archive, 2020), and Verónica González Arredondo's *I Am Not That Body* (Pub House, 2020).

Work by DANIELLE DeTIBERUS appears in *Academy of American Poets Poem-a-Day*, *The Missouri Review*, *Waxwing*, *Best American Poetry*, and elsewhere. Her manuscript, *Better the Girl Know Now*, was a finalist for Black Lawrence Press' 2018 Hudson Prize. She currently serves as the Program Chair for the Poetry Society of South Carolina and teaches creative writing at Charleston School of the Arts.

DANIELLE CADENA DEULEN teaches at Georgia State University in Atlanta. She is the author of a memoir, *The Riots* (UGA, 2013), and two poetry collections, most recently *Our Emotions Get Carried Away Beyond Us* (Barrow Street, 2015). She also hosts the literary podcast and radio show *Lit from the Basement*.

Among the most prolific and respected writers of postwar Japan, ENDŌ SHŪSAKU was born in 1923 and died in 1996. For more information, see page 243.

Award-winning poet, essayist, critic, and translator of contemporary Polish poetry PIOTR FLORCZYK's most recent work is a collection of poems based on Holocaust testimonies, entitled *From the Annals of Kraków* (Lynx House, 2020).

A founding editor of *Field*, STUART FRIEBERT (1931–2020) translated 16 books, most recently by Ute Von Funcke, Elisabeth Schmeidel, and Kuno Raeber. He also published 15 poetry collections, including *Decanting: Selected & New Poems, 1967–2017* (Lost Horse, 2017), and four books of prose, most recently *A Double Life: In Poetry and Translation* (Pinyon, 2019).

The recipient of a number of prestigious Latin American literary awards, including the National Ramón López Velarde Prize in Poetry and the Dolores Castro Prize in Poetry, VERÓNICA GONZÁLEZ ARREDONDO was born in Guanajuato, Mexico, in 1984. For more information, see page 55.

MARIANGELA GUALTIERI is an Italian poet and dramaturge of the famed Teatro Valdoca, which she co-founded in 1983. She has published more than a dozen books of poetry and theatrical works. For more information, see page 11.

MORGAN HAMILL is a disabled poet and a graduate student at Penn State, where she has been awarded a McCourtney Family Distinguished Graduate Fellowship. In 2019, she was a poetry semi-finalist in *Nimrod's* Francine Ringold Awards for Emerging Writers. Her poems appear in *The Cimarron Review* and *The Southern Review*.

JULIE HANSON's second collection, *The Audible and the Evident* (Ohio UP, 2020), won the Hollis Summers Poetry Prize. Her first collection, *Unbeknownst* (U of Iowa, 2011) won the Iowa Poetry Prize and was a finalist for Kate Tufts Discovery Award. Her poems appear in *Bat City Review*, *The Literary Review*, *Plume*, and elsewhere.

CHARLES O. HARTMAN has published seven books of poetry, including *New & Selected Poems* (Ahsahta Press 2008). His textbook *Verse: An Introduction to Prosody* came out from Wiley-Blackwell in 2015. In 2020 he edited, with Martha Collins, Pamela Alexander, and Matthew Krajniak, *Wendy Battin: On the Life and Work of an American Master.* He is Poet-in-Residence at Connecticut College and plays jazz guitar.

SEAN HILL, the author of two poetry collections, *Dangerous Goods* (Milkweed, 2014), and *Blood Ties & Brown Liquor* (UGA, 2008), has poems and essays in *New England Review*, *Poetry*, *Tin House*, and other journals, and in over a dozen anthologies including *Black Nature*. He directs the Minnesota Northwoods Writers Conference at Bemidji State University and will be Visiting Professor of Creative Writing at the University of Montana for 2020–2022.

Born and raised in eastern Washington and currently living in Texas, where he is a Michener Fellow at UT Austin, JACKSON HOLBERT's work has appeared in *Field*, *The Nation*, and *Poetry*. He has received fellowships from The Stadler Center for Poetry and The Michener Center for Writers, and has been a finalist for a Ruth Lilly and Dorothy Sargent Rosenberg Fellowship.

JESSICA JACOBS is the author of *Take Me with You, Wherever You're Going* (Four Way, 2019), winner of the Devil's Kitchen Reading Award. Her debut collection, *Pelvis with Distance* (White Pine, 2015), a biography-in-poems of Georgia O'Keeffe, won the New Mexico Book Award in Poetry. Chapbook Editor for *Beloit Poetry Journal*, she lives in Asheville, North Carolina, with her wife, the poet Nickole Brown, with whom she co-authored *Write It! 100 Poetry Prompts to Inspire* (Spruce/PenguinRandomHouse, 2020).

JERZY JARNIEWICZ is a Polish poet, translator, and critic who teaches at the University of Łódź. He edits *Literatura na Swiecie*. For more information, see page 211.

BRETT ELIZABETH JENKINS lives in Minneapolis. Her work appears in *Agni*, *Beloit Poetry Journal*, *Smartish Pace*, *The Sun*, and elsewhere.

JI YUN (1724–1805) was a writer, politician, and philosopher, during the Qing Dynasty. For more information, see page 83.

TROY JOLLIMORE is the author of four poetry collections, most recently *Earthly Delights* (Princeton, 2021), and three books of philosophy, most recently *On Loyalty* (Routledge, 2012). His debut poetry collection, *Tom Thomson in Purgatory* (Margie/Intuit House, 2005) won the National Book Critics Circle Award in Poetry. He teaches in the Philosophy Department at California State University, Chico.

ARIEL KATZ is a recent graduate of the Iowa Writers' Workshop. She's originally from North Carolina, and is at work on a novel. Her fiction is forthcoming in *Colorado Review*, and her critical essays and interviews have appeared on the *Ploughshares* Blog and at *Bookforum*.

RENÉE KAY is a queer poet in Brooklyn by way of Appalachia "and other beautiful, strange places." They serve as development manager at Brooklyn Poets and as an editor of *The Bridge*.

ASHLEY KEYSER is a queer poet based in Chicago who served with Peace Corps in Ukraine. Her work has appeared in *Pleiades*, *Quarterly West*, *Best New Poets*, and elsewhere.

Work by CINDY KING appears in *The Cincinnati Review*, *The Gettysburg Review*, *Prairie Schooner*, and elsewhere. Her book, *Zoonotic*, is forthcoming from Tinderbox Editions in late 2021. *Easy Street*, her chapbook, was published by Dancing Girl Press in 2020. She lives in St. George, Utah, where she teaches creative writing and is the faculty editor of *The Southern Quill*.

JASON KOO is the author of three poetry collections, most recently *More Than Mere Light* (Prelude, 2018). Coeditor of the *Brooklyn Poets Anthology* (Brooklyn Arts Press & Brooklyn Poets, 2017), he has published his work in the *American Scholar*, *The Missouri Review*, and *The Yale Review*, among other places, and won fellowships from the National Endowment for the Arts, Vermont Studio Center and New York State Writers Institute. Koo teaches at Quinnipiac University and is the founder and executive director of Brooklyn Poets.

Recent work by PETER KRUMBACH appears in *The Massachusetts Review*, *Salamander*, *Wigleaf*, and elsewhere.

Born in Asheville, North Carolina, GREY WOLFE LaJOIE is currently a Prison Arts and Education Fellow at the University of Alabama. Their work appears in *Mid-American Review*, *Puerto del Sol*, and *Salt Hill*, among other journals.

Living in the Lowcountry of South Carolina, DAN LEACH has published fiction and poetryin *The Greensboro Review*, *The New Madrid Review*, and *storySouth*. His debut collection, *Floods and Fires*, was released by University Press of North Georgia in 2017.

SHARA LESSLEY is the author of *The Explosive Expert's Wife* (U of Wisconsin, 2018) and *Two-Headed Nightingale* (New Issues, 2012), as well as co-editor of *The Poem's Country* (Pleiades, 2018), an anthology of essays. Her awards include an NEA Fellowship, *Birmingham Poetry Review*'s Collins Prize, and a Pushcart Prize. Her poems and essays appear in *The Gettysburg Review*, *Kenyon Review*, *The Nation*, and elsewhere. She lives in Dubai.

Recent poems by LISA LOW appear in *Bat City Review, Cream City Review, Redivider*, and elsewhere. Her nonfiction appears in *Gulf Coast* as the 2020 nonfiction prize winner. She is an assistant editor at *The Cincinnati Review*.

Recent work by MICHAEL MARK can be found in *Michigan Quarterly Review, The Southern Review*, and *The Poetry Foundation's American Life in Poetry*.

JOHN McCARTHY is the author of *Scared Violent Like Horses* (Milkweed, 2019), which won the Jake Adam York Prize. His work has appeared or is forthcoming in *32 Poems, Pleiades, TriQuarterly*, and *Best New Poets 2015*. He is the 2016 winner of *The Pinch* Literary Award in Poetry, and is an Associate Editor at *Rhino*.

OWEN McLEOD's debut collection, *Dream Kitchen* (UNT, 2019), won the Vassar Miller Prize. New poems appear in *Alaska Quarterly Review, New Ohio Review*, and *The Southern Review*. He teaches philosophy at Lafayette College in Easton, Pennsylvania.

Work by EMILIE MENZEL appears in *The Bennington Review, Black Warrior Review, The Offing*, and *Passages North*. Her manuscript *The Girl Who Became a Rabbit* was a recent finalist for Tupelo Press' Berkshire Prize. She curates *The Gretel* and is a librarian-in-training in North Carolina.

MATTHEW MINICUCCI's collection *Small Gods* (New Issues, 2017) won the Stafford/Hall Oregon Book Award in Poetry. His work appears in *Poetry, The Southern Review, Virginia Quarterly Review*, and elsewhere. He is the recipient of numerous fellowships and awards including the Stanley P. Young Fellowship in Poetry from the Bread Loaf Writers' Conference, a Writer-in-Residence fellowship from the James Merrill House, and the Poet-in Residence fellowship from Dartmouth College and the Frost House.

PETER MISHLER is the author of *Fludde* (Sarabande, 2018), which won the Kathryn A. Morton Prize. He lives in Kansas City.

South-Asian-American writer SRUTHI NARAYANAN won the 2020 Francine Ringold Award from *Nimrod* and has also been published in the *Mississippi Review*. She has received fellowships from Kundiman and the Anderson Center.

A bilingual poet from Tokyo, MIHO NONAKA is the author of *The Museum of Small Bones* (Ashland, 2020). Her poems and essays appear in various journals and anthologies, including *Kenyon Review, Ploughshares, Tin House,* and *Helen Burns Poetry Anthology: New Voices from the Academy of American Poets.* She teaches at Wheaton College.

JEANNE OBBARD received her bachelor's degree in feminist and gender studies from Bryn Mawr College, and is a project manager for oncology clinical trials. She was granted a Leeway Seedling Award for Emerging Artists in 2001, and her recent work can be found in *Construction, District Lit,* and *Vinyl,* among other publications. She is a poetry reader for *Drunk Monkeys,* where her pop culture writing also appears.

ALAN MICHAEL PARKER is the author of nine collections of poems and four novels, and the editor or co-editor of five scholarly works. His awards include two selections in *Best American Poetry,* the Fineline Prize, the Lunate 500 Prize, the North Carolina Book Award, three Pushcart Prizes, and three Randall Jarrell Poetry Prizes. He holds the Houchens Chair in English at Davidson College.

Essays by DUSTIN PARSONS appear in *Brevity, The Georgia Review, Pleiades,* and many other magazines. He is the author of *Exploded View: Essays on Fatherhood, with Diagrams* (UGA, 2018) and teaches at the University of Mississippi.

PAUL PERRY's most recent poetry books are *The Ghosts of Barnacullia* (2019) and *Gunpowder Valentine: New & Selected Poems* (Dedalus, 2014). His most recent novel is *The Garden* (New Island, 2021). Winner of the Hennessy Prize for Irish Literature, he teaches at University College Dublin.

EMILIA PHILLIPS is the author of four poetry collections, most recently *Embouchure* (U of Akron, 2021). They won a 2019 Pushcart Prize and a 2019–20 North Carolina Arts Council Fellowship and teach at the University of North Carolina, Greensboro.

RACHEL RICHARDSON's two poetry collections are *Hundred-Year Wave* (Carnegie Mellon, 2016) and *Copperhead* (2011). Her work appears in *Kenyon Review, New England Review, The New York Times,* and elsewhere. She serves as Poetry Advisor for the Bay Area Book Festival and co-directs the writing center Left Margin LIT.

STEPHANIE ROGERS' poems appear or are forthcoming in *New Ohio Review, Poetry Northwest,* and *Shenandoah,* among others. Her first collection of poems,

Plucking the Stinger, was published by Saturnalia Books in 2016, and her second collection, *Fat Girl Forms*, is forthcoming from Saturnalia in 2021. She grew up in Middletown, Ohio.

Poetry and creative nonfiction by ELLEN SAMUELS appear in *Brevity*, the *Journal of the American Medical Association*, *Mid-American Review*, and *Nimrod*. She is the author of a verse memoir, *Hypermobilities* (Operating System, 2021), and the recipient of two Lambda Literary Awards and a Pushcart nomination. She teaches at the University of Wisconsin-Madison.

CHRIS SANTIAGO is the author of *Tula* (Milkweed, 2017), which won the Lindquist & Venum Prize for Poetry. The recipient of fellowships from Kundiman and the Mellon Foundation/American Council of Learned Societies, he teaches at the University of St. Thomas in St. Paul, Minnesota.

ADAM SCHEFFLER grew up in California. His debut book of poems, *A Dog's Life*, was selected by Denise Duhamel as the winner of the 2016 Jacar Press Book Contest. Recent poems appear in *The Common*, *Academy of American Poets Poem-a-Day*, *The Yale Review*, and elsewhere. He teaches in the Harvard College Writing Program.

Executive Editor of *The Adroit Journal*, HEIDI SEABORN is the author, recently, of *An Insomniac's Slumber Party with Marilyn Monroe* (PANK, 2021), winner of the PANK Poetry Prize; *Give a Girl Chaos* (Mastodon, 2019); and the chapbook *Bite Marks* (Comstock, 2021). Her work appears in *Beloit Poetry Journal*, *The Missouri Review*, *The Slowdown* with Tracy K. Smith, and elsewhere.

OLIVIA SEARS translates primarily Italian women poets, including Patrizia Cavalli, Maria d'Arezzo, Eva Taylor, and Patrizia Vicinelli. Her recent translations of Mariangela Gualtieri's poetry appear in *The Arkansas International* and *The Common*. Excerpts from Sears' forthcoming translation of *BÏF§ZF+18: Simultaneities and Lyrics Chemisms* (World Poetry, 2021) by Ardengo Soffici appear in *Hyperallergic*, *Kenyon Review*, and *Poetry International*. She is founder of the Center for the Art of Translation.

STEPHEN SEXTON's poetry collections are *Cheryl's Destinies* (Penguin UK, 2021), which was shortlisted for the Forward Prize for Best Collection, and *If All the World and Love Were Young* (2019), which won the Forward Prize for Best First Collection, the E. M. Forster Award, and the Rooney Prize for Irish Literature. He teaches at Queen's University Belfast.

MARTHA SILANO's latest collection is *Gravity Assist* (Saturnalia, 2019). Her poems appear in *The Cincinnati Review*, *DIAGRAM*, *North American Review*, and elsewhere. She teaches at Bellevue College and Hugo House in Seattle.

ADAM TAVEL is the author of four books of poetry, including the forthcoming *Sum Ledger* (Measure, 2021). His most recent collection, *Catafalque*, won the Richard Wilbur Award (U of Evansville, 2018).

TESS TAYLOR's most recent poetry collections are *Rift Zone* (Red Hen, 2020) and *Last West: Roadsongs for Dorothea Lang* (MOMA, 2020). The recipient of a Distinguished Fulbright Scholarship to the Seamus Heaney Centre at Queen's University Belfast, and a long-time poetry reviewer for NPR's *All Things Considered*, she teaches in the Low Residency MFA program at Ashland University.

A Staten Island native, NATALIE TOMBASCO serves as the Interviews Editor for *Southeast Review*. Her poems appear in *The Boiler*, *The Rumpus*, *Third Coast*, and elsewhere, and her new chapbook is *Collective Inventions* (Cutbank, 2021).

ALICE TURSKI grew up in Houston, Texas. A finalist for the Princemere Poetry Prize and shortlisted for the Pacific Spirit Poetry Prize, she has published poems in *The Greensboro Review*, *The Iowa Review*, *Verse Daily*, and elsewhere. She is currently a PhD candidate at the University of British Columbia.

CONNIE VOISINE's most recent full-length poetry collections are *The Bower* (U of Chicago, 2019) and *Calle Florista* (2015). The recipient of a 2021 Guggenheim Fellowship in Poetry, she teaches at New Mexico State University.

MATTHEW VOLLMER is the author of two short-story collections, most recently *Gateway to Paradise* (Persea, 2015), as well as two collections of essays, most recently *Permanent Exhibit* (BOA, 2018). He edited *A Book of Uncommon Prayer* (Outpost19, 2015) and co-edited *Fakes: An Anthology of Pseudo-Interviews, Faux-Lectures, Quasi-Letters, "Found" Texts, and Other Fraudulent Artifacts* (W. W. Norton, 2012). He teaches at Virginia Tech.

D. S. WALDMAN is a Marsh-Rebelo Scholar at San Diego State University. His work has most recently appeared or is forthcoming in *Colorado Review*, *The Gettysburg Review*, *The Georgia Review*, and *Poetry Northwest*.

MIKE WHITE's second collection, *Addendum to a Miracle* (Waywiser, 2017), was awarded the Anthony Hecht Poetry Prize. Other work appears in *Ploughshares*, *Poetry*, and *The Threepenny Review*. He lives in Salt Lake City and teaches at the University of Utah.

ROY WHITE is a blind person who lives in Saint Paul, Minnesota. His work appears in *BOAAT*, *Kenyon Review*, *Poetry*, and elsewhere.

Poems by STELLA WONG appear in *Colorado Review*, *Poetry Northwest*, and the *Los Angeles Review of Books*. She is the winner of the Two Sylvias Press Chapbook Prize for her chapbook *American Zero* (2019). Her debut full-length collection *Spooks* won the Saturnalia Editors Prize and is forthcoming in March 2022.

YI IZZY YU teaches Cross-Cultural Communication and Multilingual Composition at Indiana University of Pennsylvania. Her collaborative translations have appeared in *The Cincinnati Review*, *3AM Magazine*, and *Strange Horizons: Samovar*, and are collected in *The Shadow Book of Ji Yun: The Chinese Classic of Weird True Tales, Horror Stories, and Occult Knowledge* and *Zhiguai: Chinese True Tales of the Paranormal and Glitches in the Matrix*.

Short stories by JULIAN ZABALBEASCOA are published in *American Short Fiction*, *The Gettysburg Review*, and *Ploughshares*, among other journals. He teaches in the Honors College at the University of Massachusetts Lowell.

Required Reading

(issue 33)

(For each issue, we ask that our contributors recommend up to three recent titles. What follows is the list generated by the writers in issue 33.)

Aria Aber, *Hard Damage* (Cassandra J. Bruner)

Hanif Abdurraqib, *A Fortune for Your Disaster* (Stella Wong)

Andrea Abi-Karam & Kay Gabriel, Eds., *We Want It All: An Anthology of Radical Trans Poetics* (Peter Mishler)

Gil Adamson, *Ridgerunner* (Julian Zabalbeascoa)

Kelli Russell Agodon, *Dialogues with Rising Tides* (Martha Silano)

Kaveh Akbar, *Calling a Wolf a Wolf* (Brett Elizabeth Jenkins)

Heather Altfeld, *Post-Mortem* (Troy Jollimore)

Callum Angus, *A Natural History of Transition* (Emilie Menzel)

Jessica Anthony, *Enter the Aardvark* (Julian Zabalbeascoa)

Cameron Awkward-Rich, *Dispatch* (renée kay)

Geoffrey Babbitt, *Appendices Pulled from a Study on Light* (Charles O. Hartman)

Taneum Bambrick, *Vantage* (Grey Wolfe LaJoie)

Cynthia Barnett, *The Sound of the Sea: Seashells and the Fate of the Oceans* (Dustin Parsons)

Kay Ulanday Barrett, *More Than Organs* (Ellen Samuels)

Tracey Bashkoff, Ed., *Hilma af Klint: Paintings for the Future* (Adam Tavel)

Clare Beams, *The Illness Lesson* (Julian Zabalbeascoa)

Sandra Beasley, *Made to Explode* (Stephanie Rogers)

Joshua Bennett, *Being Property Once Myself: Blackness and the End of Man* (Alice Turski)

Reginald Dwayne Betts, *Felon* (Jason Koo)

Bruce Bond, *Frankenstein's Children* (Adam Tavel)

Summer Brennan, *High Heel* (Owen McLeod)

Susan Briante, *Defacing the Monument* (Steven Espada Dawson)

Octavia Butler; Damian Duffy & John E. Jennings, Ad. & Illus., *Kindred: A Graphic Novel Adaptation* (Alan Michael Parker)

Sumita Chakraborty, *Arrow* (Ashley Keyser)

Victoria Chang, *Dear Memory: Letters on Writing, Silence, & Grief* (Tyler Barton)

Victoria Chang, *Obit* (Steven Espada Dawson)

Leila Chatti, *Deluge* (D. S. Waldman)

Felicia Rose Chavez, *The Anti-Racist Writing Workshop: How to Decolonize the Creative Classroom* (Emilia Phillips)

Don Mee Choi, *DMZ Colony* (Cassandra J. Bruner)

Bora Chung, *Cursed Bunny*, trans. Anton Hur (John Yu Branscum & Yi Izzy Yu)

Heather Clark, *Red Comet: The Short Life and Blazing Art of Sylvia Plath* (Jeanne Obbard)

Emma Cline, *Daddy* (Natalie Tombasco)

Tressie McMillan Cottom, *Thick: And Other Essays* (Lisa Low)

Lisa Fay Coutley, *tether* (Danielle Deulen)

James Davis, *Club Q* (Mike White)

Meg Day & Niki Herd, Eds. *Laura Hershey: On the Life and Work of an American Master* (Ellen Samuels)

Decur, *When You Look Up*, trans. Chloe Garcia Roberts (Emilie Menzel)

Natalie Diaz, *Postcolonial Love Poem* (Sandra Alcosser)

Rob Doyle, *Threshold* (Dan Leach)

Lee Durkee, *The Last Taxi Driver* (Dan Leach)

Jenny Erpenbeck, *Go, Went, Gone*, trans. Susan Bernofsky (Allison DeFreese)

Jenny Erpenbeck, *The Old Child*, trans. Susan Bernofsky (Allison DeFreese)

Danielle Evans, *The Office of Historical Corrections* (Sean Hill)

Blas Falconer, *Forgive the Body This Failure* (Sandra Alcosser)

Katie Farris, *A Net to Catch My Body in Its Weaving* (Michael Mark)

Madeline ffitch, *Stay & Fight* (Tyler Barton)

Nikky Finney, *Love Child's Hotbed of Occasional Poetry: Poems & Artifacts* (Sean Hill)

Leontia Flynn, *Nina Simone Is Singing* (Stephen Sexton)

Diamond Forde, *Mother Body* (Josephine Blair)

Carrie Fountain, *The Life* (Heidi Seaborn)

Damon Galgut, *The Promise* (Paul Perry)

Forrest Gander, *Twice Alive* (Troy Jollimore)

Benjamin Garcia, *Thrown in the Throat* (Natalie Tombasco, Alice Turski)

Mary D. Garrard, *Artemisia Gentileschi and Feminism in Early Modern Europe* (Danielle DeTiberus)

Ross Gay, *Be Holding* (D. S. Waldman)

Ross Gay, *The Book of Delights* (Sruthi Narayanan)

Peter Gizzi, *Now It's Dark* (Dan Beachy-Quick)

Jorie Graham, *Runaway* (Bruce Beasley)

Vince Granata, *Everything Is Fine* (Shara Lessley)

torrin a. greathouse, *Wound from the Mouth of the Wound* (renée kay, Sruthi Narayanan)

Miguel M. Morales, Bruce Owens Grimm, & Tiff Joshua TJ Ferentini, Eds., *Fat & Queer: An Anthology of Queer and Trans Bodies and Lives* (Emilia Phillips)

Saskia Hamilton, Ed., *The Dolphin Letters, 1970–1979: Elizabeth Hardwick, Robert Lowell, and Their Circle* (Heidi Seaborn)

Edward Hirsch, Ed., *100 Poems to Break Your Heart* (Michael Mark)

Tony Hoagland, *The Underground Poetry Metro Transportation System for Souls: Essays on the Cultural Life of Poetry* (Julie Hanson)

Michael Hofmann, *One Lark, One Horse* (Piotr Florczyk)

Kevin Honold, *The Rock Cycle* (Connie Voisine)

Doris Iarovici, *Minus One* (Ariel Katz)

Kazuo Ishiguro, *Klara and the Sun* (Don Bogen)

Frank Jacobs, *Strange Maps: An Atlas of Cartographic Curiosities* (Alan Michael Parker)

Sarah Jaffe, *Work Won't Love You Back: How Devotion to Our Jobs Keeps Us Exploited, Exhausted, and Alone* (John McCarthy)

N. K. Jemisin, *The Fifth Season* (Morgan Hamill)

James D. Jenkins & Ryan Cagle, Eds., *The Valancourt Book of World Horror Stories* (John Yu Branscum & Yi Izzy Yu)

Taylor Johnson, *Inheritance* (John McCarthy)

Walter Johnson, *The Broken Heart of America: St. Louis and the Violent History of the United States* (Owen McLeod)

Ilya Kaminsky, *Deaf Republic* (Sandra Alcosser, Morgan Hamill)

Patrick Radden Keefe, *Empire of Pain: The Secret History of the Sackler Dynasty* (Roy White)

Brigit Pegeen Kelly, *Song* (Marianne Boruch)

David Keplinger, *The World to Come* (D. S. Waldman)

Mohamed Kheir, *Slipping*, trans. Robin Moger (Olivia Sears)

Michael Kleber-Diggs, *Worldly Things* (Sean Hill, John McCarthy)

Julia Koets, *The Rib Joint: A Memoir in Essays* (Danielle Deulen)

Keetje Kuipers, *All Its Charms* (Morgan Hamill)

Aviya Kushner, *Wolf Lamb Bomb* (Jessica Jacobs)

Laura Lee, *A History of Scars* (Emilia Phillips)

Dell Lemmon, *Are You Somebody I Should Know?* (Jason Koo)

Paige Lewis, *Space Struck* (renée kay, Peter Krumbach)

Tao Lin, *Leave Society* (Matthew Vollmer)

Matthew Lippman, *Mesmerizingly Sadly Beautiful* (Jessica Jacobs)

George Lipsitz, *The Possessive Investment in Whiteness: How White People Profit from Identity Politics* (Peter Mishler)

Ewa Lipska, *Dear Ms. Schubert*, trans. Robin Davidson & Ewa Elżbieta Nowakowska (Piotr Florczyk)

Liu Cixin, *To Hold Up the Sky*, trans. Adam Lanther (Jackson Hobert)

Patricia Lockwood, *No One Is Talking About This* (Ariel Katz, Rachel Richardson)

Mimi Lok, *Last of Her Name* (Lisa Low)

Mahmood Mamdani, *Neither Settler nor Native: The Making and Unmaking of Permanent Minorities* (Piotr Florczyk)

Kwoya Fagin Maples, *Mend* (Grey Wolfe LaJoie)

Michael Martone, Ed. *The Complete Writings of Art Smith, the Bird Boy of Fort Wayne* (Grey Wolfe LaJoie)

Daniel Mason, *The Winter Soldier* (Julian Zabalbeascoa)

Hisham Matar, *A Month in Siena* (Shara Lessley)

Cleopatra Mathis, *After the Body* (Rachel Richardson)

Shane McCrae, *The Gilded Auction Block* (Stella Wong)

Rachel Mennies, *The Naomi Letters* (Josephine Blair)

Philip Metres, *Shrapnel Maps* (Leia Darwish)

Wayne Miller, *We the Jury* (Piotr Florczyk, Julie Hanson, Michael Mark, Paul Perry)

David Moloney, *Barker House* (Julian Zabalbeascoa)

Guido Morselli, *Dissipatio HG: The Vanishing*, trans. Frederika Randall (Olivia Sears)

Valzhyna Mort, *Music for the Dead and Resurrected* (Olivia Sears)

Sayaka Murata, *Convenience Store Woman*, trans. Ginny Tapley Takemori (Miho Nonaka)

John Murillo, *Kontemporary Amerikan Poetry* (Heidi Seaborn)

Michelle Neely, *Against Sustainability: Reading Nineteenth-Century America in the Age of Climate Crisis* (Charles O. Hartman)

Nhu Xuan Nguyen, *A System of Satellites* (Cassandra J. Bruner)

Naomi Novik, *A Deadly Education* (Jeanne Obbard)

Sigrid Nunez, *What Are You Going Through* (Adam Scheffler)

D. Nurkse, *The Border Kingdom* (Peter Krumbach)

Cynthia Dewi Oka, *Fire Is Not a Country* (Connie Voisine)

Jill Osier, *The Solace Is Not the Lullaby* (Don Bogen)

Kathleen Ossip, *July* (Stephanie Rogers)

George Packer, *Last Best Hope: America in Crisis and Renewal* (Adam Scheffler)

Frank Paino, *Obscura* (Jessica Jacobs)

Craig Santos Perez, *Habitat Threshold* (Martha Silano)

Katie Peterson, *Life in a Field* (Tess Taylor)

Deesha Philyaw, *The Secret Lives of Church Ladies* (Dustin Parsons)

Sarah Pinsker, *Sooner or Later Everything Falls into the Sea* (Roy White)

Harold Pinter, *The Short Plays of Harold Pinter* (Peter Krumbach)

Maya C. Popa, *American Faith* (Matthew Minicucci)

Maggie Paxson, *The Plateau* (Tess Taylor)

D. A. Powell, *Atlas T* (Stella Wong)

Dmitri Prigov, *Soviet Texts*, trans. Simon Schuchat with Ainsley Morse (Troy Jollimore)

Olga Ravn, *The Employees: A Workplace Novel of the 22nd Century*, trans. Martin Aitken (Matthew Vollmer)

Paisley Rekdal, *Appropriate: A Provocation* (Stephen Sexton)

Paisley Rekdal, *Nightingale* (Roy White)

Joshua Rivkin, *Suitor* (Chris Santiago)

Elizabeth Lindsey Rogers, *The Tilt Torn Away from the Seasons* (Charles O. Hartman)

Kay Ryan, *Synthesizing Gravity* (Julie Hanson)

Brooke Sahni, *Before I Had the Word* (Connie Voisine)

Sanjena Sathian, *Gold Diggers* (Ariel Katz, Sruthi Narayanan)

Riad Sattouf, *The Arab of the Future 4: A Graphic Memoir of a Childhood in the Middle East, 1987–1992*, trans. Sam Taylor (Jackson Holbert)

Georges Schehadé, *Poetries*, trans. Austin Carder (Dan Beachy-Quick)

John Sellars, *Hellenistic Philosophy* (Owen McLeod)

Diane Seuss, *frank: sonnets* (Steven Espada Dawson, Emilie Menzel, Adam Tavel)

Natalie Shapero, *Popular Longing* (Natalie Tombasco)

Lee Sharkey, *I Will Not Name It Except to Say* (Charles O. Hartman)

Gina Siciliano, *I Know What I Am: The Life and Times of Artemisia Gentileschi*
(Danielle DeTiberus)

Kevin Simmonds, *The Monster I Am Today: Leontyne Price and a Life in Verse*
(Don Bogen)

Jake Skeets, *Eyes Bottle Dark with a Mouthful of Flowers* (Bruce Beasley)

Cody Smith, *Gulf* (Dan Leach)

Danez Smith, *Don't Call Us Dead* (Brett Elizabeth Jenkins)

Zadie Smith, *Intimations: Six Essays* (Adam Scheffler)

Zadie Smith, *Grand Union* (Cindy King)

Pamela Sneed, *Funeral Diva* (Peter Mishler)

Maria Stepanova, *In Memory of Memory*, trans. Sasha Dugdale
(Dan Beachy-Quick)

Pete Stevens, *Tomorrow Music* (Tyler Barton)

Douglas Stuart, *Shuggie Bain* (Cindy King)

Adrienne Su, *Peach State* (Martha Silano)

Mary Szybist, *Incarnadine* (Marianne Boruch)

Lisa Taddeo, *Three Women* (Danielle Deulen)

Anne Theroux, *The Year of the End: A Memoir of Marriage, Truth, and Fiction*
(Paul Perry)

Adrian Tomine, *The Loneliness of the Long Distance Cartoonist* (Jackson Holbert)

Natasha Trethewey, *Memorial Drive* (Shara Lessley)

Giuseppe Ungaretti, *Allegria*, trans. Geoffrey Brock (Olivia Sears)

Corinna Vallianatos, *The Beforeland* (Matthew Vollmer)

Sarah Vap, *Winter: Effulgences & Devotions* (Chris Santiago)

Ellen Bryant Voigt, *Kyrie* (Marianne Boruch)

G. C. Waldrep, *The Earliest Witnesses* (Bruce Beasley)

Jane Ward, *The Tragedy of Heterosexuality* (Jeanne Obbard)

Lyall Watson, *Heaven's Breath: A Natural History of the Wind* (2019 reprint)
(Tess Taylor)

Eliot Weinberger, *Angels & Saints* (Ashley Keyser)

Alice Wong, Ed. *Disability Visibility: Voices from the Twenty-First Century*
  (Ellen Samuels)

Mark Wunderlich, *God of Nothingness* (Matthew Minicucci)

Yi Lu, *Sea Summit*, trans. Fiona Sze-Lorrain (John Yu Branscum & Yi Izzy Yu)

Dean Young, *Solar Perplexus* (Cindy King)

Charles Yu, *Interior Chinatown* (Jason Koo, Alan Michael Parker, Alice Turski)

Jihyun Yun, *Some Are Always Hungry* (Josephine Blair)

Lillian Yvonne-Bertram, *Travesty Generator* (Matthew Minicucci)

Michelle Zauner, *Crying in H Mart* (Dustin Parsons)

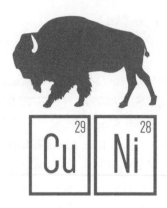

subscription rates

For regular folks:

one year (two issues)—$20
two years (four issues)—$35
five years (ten issues)—$60

For student folks:

one year (two issues)—$15
two years (four issues)—$25
five years (ten issues)—$50

For more information, visit: www.copper-nickel.org

To go directly to subscriptions
visit: coppernickel.submittable.com

To order back issues, email wayne.miller@ucdenver.edu